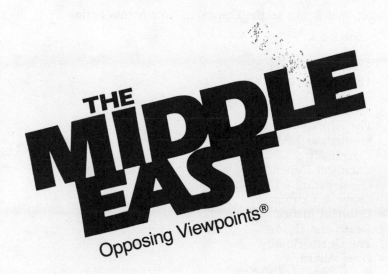

THE
MIDDLE
EAST
Opposing Viewpoints®

Other Books of Related Interest in the Opposing Viewpoints Series:

Additional Books in the Opposing Viewpoints Series:

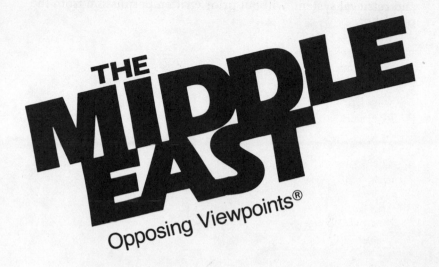

THE MIDDLE EAST

Opposing Viewpoints®

David L. Bender & Bruno Leone, *Series Editors*

Janelle Rohr, *Book Editor*

OPPOSING VIEWPOINTS SERIES ®

Greenhaven Press   577 Shoreview Park Road   St. Paul, Minnesota 55126

Library of Congress Cataloging-in-Publication Data

The Middle East : opposing viewpoints.

(Opposing viewpoints series)
Bibliography: p.
Includes index.
 1. Middle East—Politics and government—1945-
I. Rohr, Janelle, 1963-   . II. Series.
DS63.1.M5425 1988   956'.04   87-19789
ISBN 0-89908-428-1 (lib. bdg.)
ISBN 0-89908-403-6 (pbk.)

"Congress shall make no law...
abridging the freedom of speech,
or of the press."

First Amendment to the US Constitution

The basic foundation of our democracy is the first amendment guarantee of freedom of expression. The *Opposing Viewpoints Series* is dedicated to the concept of this basic freedom and the idea that it is more important to practice it than to enshrine it.

Contents

Why Consider Opposing Viewpoints?

"It is better to debate a question without settling it than to settle a question without debating it."

Joseph Joubert (1754-1824)

The Importance of Examining Opposing Viewpoints

The purpose of the Opposing Viewpoints books, and this book in particular, is to present balanced, and often difficult to find, opposing points of view on complex and sensitive issues.

Probably the best way to become informed is to analyze the positions of those who are regarded as experts and well studied on issues. It is important to consider every variety of opinion in an attempt to determine the truth. Opinions from the mainstream of society should be examined. But also important are opinions that are considered radical, reactionary, or minority as well as those stigmatized by some other uncomplimentary label. An important lesson of history is the eventual acceptance of many unpopular and even despised opinions. The ideas of Socrates, Jesus, and Galileo are good examples of this.

Readers will approach this book with their own opinions on the issues debated within it. However, to have a good grasp of one's own viewpoint, it is necessary to understand the arguments of those with whom one disagrees. It can be said that those who do not completely understand their adversary's point of view do not fully understand their own.

A persuasive case for considering opposing viewpoints has been presented by John Stuart Mill in his work *On Liberty*. When examining controversial issues it may be helpful to reflect on this suggestion:

> The only way in which a human being can make some approach to knowing the whole of a subject, is by hearing what can be said about it by persons of every variety of opinion, and studying all modes in which it can be looked at by every character of mind. No wise man ever acquired his wisdom in any mode but this.

Analyzing Sources of Information

The Opposing Viewpoints books include diverse materials taken from magazines, journals, books, and newspapers, as well as statements and position papers from a wide range of individuals, organizations and governments. This broad spectrum of sources helps to develop patterns of thinking which are open to the consideration of a variety of opinions.

Pitfalls To Avoid

A pitfall to avoid in considering opposing points of view is that of regarding one's own opinion as being common sense and the most rational stance and the point of view of others as being only opinion and naturally wrong. It may be that another's opinion is correct and one's own is in error.

Another pitfall to avoid is that of closing one's mind to the opinions of those with whom one disagrees. The best way to approach a dialogue is to make one's primary purpose that of understanding the mind and arguments of the other person and not that of enlightening him or her with one's own solutions. More can be learned by listening than speaking.

It is my hope that after reading this book the reader will have a deeper understanding of the issues debated and will appreciate the complexity of even seemingly simple issues on which good and honest people disagree. This awareness is particularly important in a democratic society such as ours where people enter into public debate to determine the common good. Those with whom one disagrees should not necessarily be regarded as enemies, but perhaps simply as people who suggest different paths to a common goal.

Developing Basic Reading and Thinking Skills

In this book carefully edited opposing viewpoints are purposely placed back to back to create a running debate; each viewpoint is preceded by a short quotation that best expresses the author's main argument. This format instantly plunges the reader into the midst of a controversial issue and greatly aids that reader in mastering the basic skill of recognizing an author's point of view.

A number of basic skills for critical thinking are practiced in the activities that appear throughout the books in the series. Some of the skills are:

Evaluating Sources of Information   The ability to choose from among alternative sources the most reliable and accurate source in relation to a given subject.

Separating Fact from Opinion   The ability to make the basic distinction between factual statements (those that can be demonstrated or verified empirically) and statements of opinion (those that are beliefs or attitudes that cannot be proved).

Identifying Stereotypes   The ability to identify oversimplified, exaggerated descriptions (favorable or unfavorable) about people and insulting statements about racial, religious or national groups, based upon misinformation or lack of information.

Recognizing Ethnocentrism   The ability to recognize attitudes or opinions that express the view that one's own race, culture, or group is inherently superior, or those attitudes that judge another culture or group in terms of one's own.

It is important to consider opposing viewpoints and equally important to be able to critically analyze those viewpoints. The activities in this book are designed to help the reader master these thinking skills. Statements are taken from the book's viewpoints and the reader is asked to analyze them. This technique aids the reader in developing skills that not only can be applied to the viewpoints in this book, but also to situations where opinionated spokespersons comment on controversial issues. Although the activities are helpful to the solitary reader, they are most useful when the reader can benefit from the interaction of group discussion.

Using this book and others in the series should help readers develop basic reading and thinking skills. These skills should improve the readers' ability to understand what they read. Readers should be better able to separate fact from opinion, substance from rhetoric and become better consumers of information in our media-centered culture.

This volume of the Opposing Viewpoints books does not advocate a particular point of view. Quite the contrary! The very nature of the book leaves it to the reader to formulate the opinions he or she finds most suitable. My purpose as publisher is to see that this is made possible by offering a wide range of viewpoints which are fairly presented.

David L. Bender
Publisher

Introduction

"Respect for the concrete detail of human experience, understanding that arises from viewing the Other compassionately, surely these are better goals than confrontation and hostility."

—Edward Said, *Covering Islam*, 1981

The region that witnessed the birth of three faiths—Judaism, Christianity, and Islam—has also suffered a long and bloody history of conflict, often centering on religion.

As early as 1095, Pope Urban II proclaimed that Christians should journey to the Holy Lands because "a race from the kingdom of the Persians, an accursed race, a race utterly alienated from God, has invaded the lands of those Christians and has depopulated them by the sword, pillage and fire." Urban's declaration led to the Crusades: Hundreds of Christian nobles and peasants went to the Holy Lands with the intent of capturing Jerusalem. The Crusades were ultimately an expression of medieval xenophobia—they victimized cultures alien to Christian Europeans. Some Crusaders stopped outside of European towns with large Jewish populations and slaughtered the inhabitants. Those Crusaders who reached the Holy Lands engaged in fierce battles that took the lives of many Muslims and Christians.

Paradoxically, while Europe's Crusaders were fighting the Muslims, its scholars were gaining from Muslims the knowledge that spurred the Renaissance. Muslim empires had preserved and expanded upon the works of Greek and Roman philosophers. About sixty years after Urban had proclaimed the Crusades, a Spanish scholar, Raymond of Toledo, founded Europe's first school of Oriental studies. Arabic works of philosophy, science, and mathematics were studied and translated at Raymond's school. A further irony is that the comprehensive analyses of ancient knowledge compiled by Muslim scholar Avicenna (Ibn Sina) were an invaluable source for Renaissance scholars.

This tortured relationship between Christians, Muslims, and Jews continues in the twentieth century, but its shape has been altered by modern ideologies. Nationalism in particular led to the creation of the Jewish state. For many Jews, Israel was the realization of a promise made to them by God—that after centuries of suffering they would return to their homeland. This new state awakened opposition among the Palestinian Arabs who had been living there and now felt their lands were threatened by the immigration of thousands of Jews. Palestinians have asserted their right to a state of their own and often have been supported by other Arab countries. The effects of this conflict continue to spread, notably in Lebanon, where Palestinian refugees, Israeli air raids, Syrian intervention, and rivalries among Lebanese ethnic groups have caused a civil war. Religion and nationalism have intensified twentieth-century conflicts.

Modernization and urbanization have been disruptive also. Oil has generated an enormous amount of wealth in some Middle Eastern countries. Governments use this money to modernize and develop their economies. Some Middle Eastern leaders emulate the Western model of development; many of them have been educated in the West. By using the Western model, modernization often introduces values that many Muslims feel are contradictory to Islamic teaching. It threatens traditional ways of life as many peasants move to cities where they hope there will be more jobs. The culmination of this process in Iran was a revolution that reasserted the importance of religious traditions. A debate continues over modernization—whether Iran needs it and whether it necessarily means emulating the West.

The Middle East: Opposing Viewpoints replaces Greenhaven's 1982 book of the same title. It contains entirely new viewpoints and introduces several new topics. The issues debated are: Why Is the Middle East a Conflict Area? How Has Islamic Fundamentalism Affected the Middle East? What Role Should the US Play in the Middle East? Are Palestinian Rights Being Ignored? and Is Peace Possible in the Middle East? On issues as heated and longstanding as those facing the Middle East today, this range of perspectives can provoke the questions that will help readers gain greater insight into the Middle East.

Why Is the Middle East a Conflict Area?

Chapter Preface

One of the first impressions a casual observer of the Middle East gets is that of a chaotic region frequently beset by kidnappings and bombings. This constant focus on spectacular, shocking events (like an American being shoved into a car and taken hostage in broad daylight) can obscure the day-to-day tragedy of those who live in the midst of civil war. Viewing the conflict in this latter context offers another perspective of events in the Middle East.

Consider the following economic facts about Lebanon's lengthy civil war: The average personal income of the Lebanese has dropped by sixty percent since 1982. Thirty-five percent of all Lebanese residents are unemployed. (By comparison, during the Great Depression in the US in the 1930s, unemployment stood at twenty-five percent.) Inflation—300 percent at the end of 1986—drastically reduces the value of the money the Lebanese do manage to earn. (Inflation in the US is 3.8 percent. In 1971, President Nixon declared a war on inflation, froze wages and prices, and cut federal spending, because the rate had gone over 4 percent.) While more Lebanese are unemployed and inflation is making their money worth less, the cost of living has increased about 250 percent over a period of two years. This limited example suggests how strongly war has affected one country's economy. There are other costs as well—in human lives, in psychological stress, and in governmental budgets.

The following chapter is a broad overview that offers several explanations for Middle Eastern conflicts. As you read, consider also the impact these conflicts have had on people's lives. This vantage point can give a broader picture of the Middle East.

"The U.S.-Israeli expansion, the alliance of imperialism and Zionism, and the neo-colonialist designs are the cause [of conflict in the Middle East]."

The US-Israeli Alliance Promotes Conflict

Dmitry Volsky

The following viewpoint is taken from an article published in *New Times*, a Soviet magazine. The magazine's associate editor, Dmitry Volsky, replies to a letter on the Middle East from a Soviet citizen. In his reply, Volsky criticizes the alliance between the United States and Israel. He argues that Israel is an expansionist country which makes war against its Arab neighbors to acquire more territory. Middle East conflict can be ended, he concludes, when US-Israeli imperialism is stopped.

As you read, consider the following questions:

1. What is the capitalist interpretation of the Arab-Israeli conflict, according to Volsky?
2. Why does the author believe it would be a mistake for individual Arab governments to make peace with Israel?
3. What approach does Volsky favor in bringing a just peace to the Middle East?

Dmitry Volsky, "Taking Up a Point," *New Times*, No. 35, August 1985.

Is it justified to speak of an "Arab-Israeli conflict"? After all, what is in question is open Israeli aggression, U.S.-Israeli expansion, a conspiracy of imperialist forces against freedom-loving peoples, neocolonialism, neofascism—anything but a conflict.

A.L. Rosenfeld, Nukus, U.S.S.R.

Associate editor Dmitry Volsky replies:

What you say about Israeli policy is more than justified. But this does not mean that there is no conflict in the Middle East. On the contrary. The U.S.-Israeli expansion, the alliance of imperialism and Zionism, and the neocolonialist designs are the cause rather than the effect. The effect is the conflict that has been going on for nearly 40 years now and is sometimes—let me repeat, sometimes—called the "Arab-Israeli conflict."

Defining "Arab-Israeli Conflict"

The term is used mostly to pinpoint the most explosive element in the overall conflict situation in the Middle East. There are also other elements, for instance, the Pentagon's striving to turn the Middle East region into its strategic springboard against the socialist community. Or the political collisions between Arab countries and also inside them. Israel unquestionably often provokes and fans such collisions. But equally clear is it that many of them stem from objective social causes that have no direct bearing on the Arab-Israeli conflict.

Political terminology cannot be apolitical. At times different meanings are attached to the one and the same concept and it is no doubt this that prompted your letter.

Bourgeois Interpretation

Take the interpretation given the Arab-Israeli conflict by bourgeois writers and politicians. In most cases they see in it an inevitable confrontation between the Arab peoples and the Israeli Jews. Though both are Semites, they are claimed to be imminently inimical to each other. The roots of this enmity are sought in the hoary past, "forgetting" that in those times the Middle East presented an altogether different picture both politically and ethnically. To conceal the historical fallacy of such excursions into the past, recourse is had to what could be called the "mythologization" of history and "mystification" of politics. The actual facts are adroitly made to fit into the pattern of, say, modernized racist theories or even Biblical prophecies. And at times the pattern of the "revelations of seers" of later years. For instance, the medieval French poet and physician Nostradamus, whose extremely nebulous verse is interpreted as a prediction of a global cataclysm beginning with war in the Middle East. Invoked too are modern astrologers, who, to believe the U.S. press, are frequent visitors at the White House. What conclusions are drawn from all this can be seen if only from the Washington Post observation . . . that in the preceding four years Ronald Reagan had said at least five times that in his opinion the "end of the world" could come in the lifetime of the present generation, and could specifically be precipitated in the Middle East.

An Anti-Historical Concept

But to return to the mundane affairs of today. The view that the Middle East conflict is of a purely national order caused by some sort of genetic "incompatibility" of the Arabs and the Israeli Jews is dangerous for other reasons as well. Paradoxical though it may sound, it is on this anti-historical concept that the separate deals Washington would want to substitute for a genuine Middle East settlement are pivoted. The argument goes roughly like this: since the peoples of the region are destined to be at loggerheads with each other, it is necessary to set the sights not on a comprehensive and just settlement supported by the broad masses but on exclusive agreements between Tel Aviv and various Arab governments prepared to reconcile themselves to the Israeli expansion. Only governments that represent the interests of the pro-Western privileged strata of Arab society can do so. And it is not by chance that all this goes on under U.S. patronage, just as it was under Carter's wing that Sadat and Begin concluded the Camp David agreements. The Israeli invasion of Lebanon, to which the impulse was given precisely by Camp David, clearly demonstrated that this dubious logic can only lead to a bloody impasse.

Recipe for Conflict

Israel's military preponderance in the Middle East and the undeniable lopsidedness of US policy vis-á-vis the Arab-Israeli conflict can lead only to the imposition of Israeli hegemony over the region, attained and maintained by coercion. This is the surest recipe for future conflict—rather than a menu for a durable peace.

Muhammad Hallaj, *The Christian Science Monitor*, March 26, 1985.

It is also obvious that only a just, comprehensive settlement can ensure lasting peace in the Middle East.

But to achieve such a settlement is by no means easy. If we consider this task in practical, not abstract, terms, it is essential to understand the real substance of the "Arab-Israeli conflict." And if our ideological opponents, without admitting it, go by class criteria in approaching the Middle East problem, we regard the class standpoint as the only correct one. At the risk of falling into oversimplification, I would formulate in brief my view of the Arab-Israeli conflict thus: it is a collision between the expansionist designs of the ruling bourgeoisie of Israel, which is closely connected with Western and above all American monopoly capital, and the interests of the Arab masses seeking to ensure the independence of their countries and their right to socio-economic progress. National enmity, though in the present situation extremely acute and tenacious, is of a derivative, secondary order. It is artificially whipped up by Tel Aviv by ingenious means. But what can be whipped up can also be stamped out. This is not easy to do, but sooner or later it can be done. Notwithstanding all the obstacles, this would help to establish a just peace in the Middle East. The events in Lebanon have provided conclusive proof that Tel Aviv's aggressive policy not only rebounds upon the true interests of the Israeli people, but also hastens the bankruptcy of the Zionist top crust.

"The Soviet Union relentlessly pursues the goal of global hegemony."

The Soviet-Syrian Alliance Promotes Conflict

International Security Council

Members of the International Security Council are government officials, military leaders, political scientists, economists, and diplomats from the US and allied countries who discuss issues related to international security. The following viewpoint is a statement from a conference the Council sponsored in Jerusalem in October 1986. In the statement, Council members agree that Soviet arms sales to Syria are destabilizing. Syrian terrorism promotes conflict, they believe, a fact that makes US support for Israel essential.

As you read, consider the following questions:

1. Why does the Council believe that Syria's alliance with the Soviets helps the Soviets gain influence in the Middle East?
2. How do the authors believe the US should respond to Soviet arms sales in the Middle East?
3. What relationship do the authors suggest the US should have with Israel to combat the threat presented by the Soviets and Syrians?

Global Affairs, "The Soviet-Syrian Alliance," Winter 1987. Reprinted with permission.

The Soviet Union relentlessly pursues the goal of global hegemony. Its arsenal embraces military weapons, conventional and nuclear, as well as the weapons of political, economic, diplomatic and psychological warfare—including terrorism. Increasingly, in pursuit of its global aim, the Soviet Union exploits and supports radical regimes and terrorism in every region, worldwide.

The Soviets' Strategic Designs

In the Middle East the Soviets now are focusing on particular opportunities to achieve strategic advantages in the area of the Persian Gulf, by securing a land bridge through Iran or Pakistan to the Indian Ocean and an enhanced ability to deny access to the region's oil resources.

Pivotal also to its overall strategic design is the Soviet-Syrian Alliance—which is fundamentally inimical to the security interests of the United States and Israel.

The scope and nature of the Soviet-Syrian Alliance, though obscure and even ambiguous, are central to the broader issues of regional peace and stability. The Soviet-Syrian Alliance was formalized in the Treaty of Friendship and Cooperation of October 1980, and was deepened by subsequent agreements between Syria and other Soviet Bloc countries. The increasing relevance of this system of alliances to the possibility of Syrian-Israeli hostilities is clear and ominous. The re-emergence of Syria as the predominant factor in Lebanon serves to exacerbate the threat of such conflict.

A Soviet Asset

Syria constitutes a significant Soviet strategic asset in the Middle East. Among other things, it provides Moscow with a political-military presence in the Mediterranean critical to reducing the vulnerability of its lines of communication from the Black Sea while increasing the vulnerability of NATO's southern flank.

For its part, Syria requires the support of the Soviet Union in pursuit of its own objective of a dominant role in the region between Turkey and Egypt and between the Mediterranean Sea and the Persian Gulf. Israel is the most formidable obstacle to the achievement of Syrian ambitions. Thus, Syria seeks superiority over Israel, what it calls "strategic parity."

Though there is much coincidence of interests between the Soviet Union and Syria, it is important to recognize that there are divergences as well. Thus, while both Moscow and Damascus seek the elimination of the United States presence and influence in the Middle East, the Soviets have little interest in Syrian goals which might result in a lessening of dependency. This is reflected in the character of the Soviet commitment to Syria. The Soviet Union

22

currently limits its commitment to the security of Syria itself. It is unlikely, moreover, that it would allow a decisive Syrian defeat in any foreseeable military conflict with Israel. It is expected that the character of Soviet military support will follow generally established patterns of intervention by Soviet naval, air and air defense units. However, the possibility of the introduction of Soviet ground and airborne forces cannot be excluded, in line with growing Soviet power-projection capabilities.

Aircraft and Missiles

Of particular concern is the significant change in the nature of the enhancements now being introduced by Moscow into the Syrian arsenal. The anticipated delivery of MiG-29 aircraft and SS-23 missiles crosses a qualitative threshold that will destabilize the prevailing military balance and increase the probability of a surprise attack on Israel. While it is doubtful that such an outcome is desired by the Soviet Union, its provision of these weapons systems to Syria reflects a degree of risk-taking that the United States can neither dismiss nor fail to counteract. These armaments, while considered merely as tactical weapons in the great power context, are indeed strategic weapons in the regional context and therefore fundamentally destabilizing.

Unbelievable Amounts of Arms

The Soviet Union's role is in encouraging the radical Arab countries. The amount of arms that the Soviet Union has shipped into Syria is really unbelievable. Syria gets quantitatively and qualitatively better armament, better military hardware, than any one of the communist countries in Europe. Whenever a new weapon is shipped out of the limits of the Soviet Union, it first ships to Syria then to Libya and only then to the so-called Socialist Soviet Republics. Unfortunately, the Soviet Union continues to play a negative role when it comes to the peace prospects, an unfortunate role in encouraging Arab countries that they are the source of helping terrorism in the region.

Yitzhak Rabin, speech at the Heritage Foundation, September 11, 1986.

Of further concern to the entire Free World is the complacency with which chemical weapons have been accepted as an instrument of conventional warfare, as evidenced by their use in Afghanistan and in the Iran-Iraq war. This trend must not continue to go unchallenged. Proliferation of this capability to radical states such as Syria reflects an ominous development.

It is now clear that Syria plays a major role in regional and international terrorism, directly and through surrogates, frequently

23

in cooperation and coordination with the Soviet Union and other radical states. Having taken a stand on principle against states sponsoring terrorism, the United States, in coordination with its allies, should apply the appropriate political, economic and such other measures as may be required to compel Syria to adhere to acceptable norms of state behavior.

Recommendations

1) Given the pattern of obstructionism and destabilization long engaged in by both parties to the Soviet-Syrian Alliance, any suggestion for including the Soviet Union in an international conference addressing peace in the Middle East should be treated with extreme caution.

2) The process of U.S.-Israel strategic cooperation should be intensified to improve response time during periods of crisis. Greater reciprocity in strategic and technological collaboration and exchange of intelligence should be effected through existing bilateral arrangements.

3) The United States should implement a coherent, consistent, forceful and principled policy regarding states sponsoring, supporting and controlling terrorism.

4) The United States should take all necessary measures to offset enhanced Syrian military capabilities. In light of the anticipated Soviet delivery of SS-23's and MiG-29's, which fundamentally alter the strategic balance in the region, the U.S. should reaffirm President Reagan's guarantee to maintain Israel's "qualitative edge."

5) Recognizing that U.S. allies in both the Middle East and Western Europe contribute to Syria's strength and its ability to engage in actions inimical to U.S. interests by financial and economic support and through military sales, the U.S. should apply diplomatic, political and economic measures to stop such practices.

6) Given the strategic realities brought about by the Soviet-Syrian Alliance, the U.S. must recognize the importance of Israel's freedom of action in responding to imminent threats.

"The years of bloodshed, massacres, and vendettas . . . between Muslims and Christians . . . will make it difficult to arrive at a consensus."

Ethnic Rivalries Caused Lebanon's Civil War

John P. Entelis

Since 1975 Lebanon has been in a state of bloody civil war which has cost the lives of thousands of its inhabitants. In the following viewpoint John P. Entelis traces the history of Lebanon's current political system. He believes that the causes of the civil war are found in Lebanon's inability to establish a national identity, a problem that he maintains has plagued the country since its inception. Entelis argues that an end to the civil war is impossible without a national consensus on what Lebanon should be. He is a political science professor and co-director of the Middle East Studies Program at Fordham University.

As you read, consider the following questions:

1. What does the author mean by the term "confessionalism"? How does he believe it has contributed to Lebanon's instability?
2. Why did Lebanon's underclass identify with the Palestinians in the early 1970s, according to Entelis?

Published by permission of Transaction, Inc., from "Ethnic and Religious Diversity in Lebanon," by John P. Entelis, SOCIETY, vol. 22, no. 3, March/April 1985. Copyright © 1985 by Transaction, Inc.

In 1860 a major conflict broke out between the two major groups living in the Mount Lebanon area, namely the Maronites and the Druse, and it resulted in a massacre of thousands of Maronites at the hands of the Druse. Like many massacres and outrages throughout history, the memory tended to be carried forward from one generation to another. . . .

Following that 1860 massacre, outside forces, specifically the Europeans, came in to establish a political arrangement in which these different minorities could live side by side without at the same time forcing them to concede the primacy of their own ethnic identity. An outside governor was brought in to rule over Mount Lebanon, and this system became the precursor of what was to be known as *confessionalism*, or the system of political and administrative organization based on the distribution of the various religious groups in the state. . . .

Distributing Political Power

On the national level, a kind of distribution of political and administrative functions evolved, and this was essentially formalized as a consequence of the 1932 census taken by the French to determine the actual proportionality of the groups within Lebanon. This was not a systematic official census as we understand the term. It was a fairly casual affair, but it is often cited simply because it was the only attempt in the modern period to conduct a census to determine the actual population and religious distribution in Lebanon. According to the 1932 census, it was determined that the Maronites were the largest ethnic group; that the Sunnis were the second largest; the Shiites the third; and that the Druse were probably the fourth. There were also several smaller groups: Greek Orthodox, Greek Catholic, Armenian Orthodox, Armenian Catholic, Protestants, Jews, etc., but the principal division was between Christians and Muslims; and that distribution was determined, based on the 1932 census, to be a six-to-five ratio of Christians to Muslims. All political and administrative seats in the state were subsequently determined by this six-to-five ratio. . . .

There was also what came to be known as a "gentleman's agreement," or National Pact. This consisted of what was virtually a handshake between the two leading communities, the Maronites and the Sunni Muslims, whereby it was agreed that the president of Lebanon would be a Maronite, the prime minister a Sunni Muslim, and the Speaker of the House a Shiite Muslim. This National Pact was neither a legal document nor a written statement, nor was it part of the Constitution. Nevertheless, it became the operating framework that established the nature of political arrangements in Lebanon based on the three leading religious communities.

Subsequently, elections were held, and these followed the

"Briefly, in the few seconds left, can you give a breakdown of all the warring factions in Lebanon and what their individual aims are?"

prevailing arrangement. Lebanon began to arrive at some kind of political consensus. It was a minimal consensus, even a negative consensus, based more on what all communities agreed Lebanon should *not* be as opposed to an agreement on what Lebanon *should* be. To the Muslims, it meant an agreement that Lebanon would not become a fully Western state. To the Christians, it gave the assurance that Lebanon would not become a totally Arab state. Each side's worst fears were put aside, but what was not determined was what Lebanon *should* be. . . .

The Palestinian Influx

The war of 1967 added another dimension to the slowly evolving cleavages in Lebanon. Now an atmosphere of revolution manifested itself, arriving with the new wave of Palestinian refugees streaming into Lebanon from the West Bank via Jordan, and particularly after the September 1970 elimination of the military terrorist group, Black September, by [Jordan's] King Hussein. In southern Lebanon the Palestine Liberation Organization (PLO) established its last bastion of operations against Israel. It found fertile ground amid the large mass of disaffected Palestinians who until this time had been politically and militarily innocuous. Now this revolutionary force came in, created a new sense of identity, and challenged the status quo of the Lebanese state itself. Added to it was a new indigenous Lebanese underclass, made up of Sunnis and Shiites, who were not benefiting from the economic prosperity of the upper classes. These groups found it useful to make common cause with the PLO and the disaffected Palestinians in their attacks against what they viewed as a small clique of Lebanese Christians and Muslims whose purpose was simply to maintain power over the other Lebanese and the Palestinians.

The serious question of Lebanese nationhood had been pushed further and further back, with no attempt to define in any clear sense of the word what it was to be a Lebanese national, or what it was to be a Lebanese. Increasingly there was a predominantly, but not exclusively, Muslim view which felt that Lebanon could not pretend to be part of the West, could not pretend to be liberal, and that it had to move much more toward the Arab world. Other groups—mainly Christian—felt that their only salvation was the opening to the West. In the 1970s the relationships of the various groups in Lebanon began to change. The Christians had a lower birthrate, and although no census was taken, it was evident to all observers that by the early 1970s there were more Muslims in Lebanon than there were Christians. Today the largest indigenous Lebanese group is that of the Shiites, who constitute possibly 1,500,000 people; the second largest group is that of the Sunnis, while the Maronites are in third place. Yet the political arrangements of Lebanon are still based on the assumption of a six-to-five ratio of Christians to Muslims.

Christian Fear

The more militant members of the Christian community in Lebanon, who were determined to maintain Lebanon's Christian ties, found the new situation more and more frightening. This was especially the case among the largest Christian political organization, and especially for the *Phalanges*, an organization founded in 1936 by a young pharmacist, Pierre Gemayel. . . .

In April of 1975 a busload of Palestinians returning from the Bekaa after burying one of the fighters was attacked by *Kata'eb* [Christian] forces as it passed through a Maronite village in Mount Lebanon. Everyone on the bus was slaughtered. This date is often cited as the moment when the civil war began.

The civil war represents the outburst of many elements rather

28

than a single act on the part of one side or the other. It is important to understand this, because if we do, we can understand much of the discontinuity and the disaggregation that we are witnessing in Lebanon today—why one group attacks another today, and tomorrow the two are friends, and the next day one of the two joins an enemy of its friend of the previous day. The explanation lies in the fact that the various socioeconomic, political, and religious forces did not evolve in a collectivist fashion as a means of promoting a particular movement or ideology, but from a combination of parochial, primordial, confessional entities. The present chaotic situation is, in brief, the consequence of Lebanese history beginning in the 1860s together with the interactions of the more current socioeconomic and regional forces.

Fragile Nationality

[Lebanon] is a geographical area marked by tragedy and death, defined by an artificial boundary that contains a bizarre agglomeration of feuding factions far more possessed by tribal loyalties—by family, religion, and ethnic survival—than by any sense of nationality. The concept of Lebanon as a nation is much too fragile to bear the weight of its bloody history.

George W. Ball, *Error and Betrayal in Lebanon*, 1984.

Lebanon is located in this environment, unable to escape all the regional and international forces imposing themselves on the country, and beset by complex internal problems. It was natural for all the various ethnic, religious, and national groups that began to play a part in this struggle to look for outside benefactors. They had done this in the past. The French have traditionally been the benefactors of the Maronites. The Egyptians were the benefactors of the Sunnis during the Nasserite period. Today, [Iranian leader Ayatollah] Khumayni is the benefactor of certain Shiite groups in the Bekaa Valley, and Israel has been the benefactor of the late Major Haddad and the Maronite forces in the south. . . .

Repeating the Past

The Lebanese groups and individuals who attempted to reassemble in Geneva in early 1983, and in Lebanon, are essentially the same as those who were part and parcel of the "gentleman's agreement" in 1943. Pierre Gemayel was there, almost eighty years of age; Camille Chamoun, who had attempted to amend the Constitution in 1958; Rashid Karami, the feudal lord of the Muslims in the north; Sa'ab Salam, the eighty-year-old Muslim chieftain of the Beirut Sunnis; Walid Jumblat, the son of Kamal Jumblat who was assassinated by the Syrians in 1976. The same feudal, con-

29

fessional leadership that had worked out this elite system of arrangements in which they cut up the Lebanese pie to their own advantage was again manifesting itself, either in the person of the individuals themselves or through their sons. Amin Gemayel is another of Pierre Gemayel's sons, the older brother of Bashir, who was assassinated shortly after his election as president. Amin Gemayel is a moderate and a lawyer with political leanings, and it is instructive that he also was in Geneva.

The Need for a Consensus

If all these factors can be disengaged, a piece-by-piece solution can be arrived at to settle the Lebanese problem. My own feeling is that the solution must begin with an identification of what the Lebanese dilemma is; that is, with an attempt on the part of the Lebanese themselves to agree upon what they would like a reconstituted Lebanon to be. If the groups cannot live together in a single entity, a Swiss system of cantons may be arranged. It is up to the Lebanese themselves to decide what kind of political and social arrangement they feel they can live with. My suspicion is that given the years of bloodshed, massacres, and vendettas that have occurred, not only between Muslims and Christians but among the Maronites themselves, the residue of hatred, given the long history of bloodshed, will make it difficult to arrive at a consensus. In the absence of a Lebanese consensus, everything else is almost beside the point: whether Israel is in or out of Lebanon; whether Syria is in or out; whether the United States is in or out. The presence of these factors involves United States, Israeli, and Syrian foreign policy issues, but they have nothing to do with Lebanon. For these powers, Lebanon is no more than a factor in their foreign policy calculations.

I must conclude on a pessimistic note. Those who can remember Lebanon as it once was knew the country as a delightful place. This explains why many Europeans and Americans made their home in Lebanon. It explains why they were willing—like Malcolm Kerr, the head of the American University of Beirut—to return with the expectation that Lebanon could possibly become again what it once was. Unfortunately, what Lebanon will be like in the future was, I think, in a sense presaged by Malcolm Kerr's assassination.

"Israel and Syria . . . have sowed the seeds
. . . for the dismantling of the Lebanese state."

Outside Intervention Caused Lebanon's Civil War

R.D. McLaurin

Part of the reason the civil war in Lebanon seems confusing to
the average person is because there are so many factions involved
in the dispute and each is supported by various foreign powers.
R.D. McLaurin, the author of the following viewpoint, believes
that attributing the civil war to Lebanon's ethnic divisions is inaccurate. He argues that the Lebanese war broke out because of
three external factors: the disruptive effects of change in Arab
countries, the increasing radicalism of the Palestinian movement,
and Syrian and Israeli interference in Lebanon. McLaurin is a consultant and political analyst who has written several books on the
Middle East.

As you read, consider the following questions:

1. Why does McLaurin disagree with people who argue that
   Lebanon's problems are caused by its historical lack of an
   identity?
2. What examples does the author cite to support his belief
   that the existence of many minorities does not explain
   Lebanon's civil war?

R.D. McLaurin, "Peace in Lebanon," from MIDDLE EAST PEACE PLANS, edited by
Willard A. Beling, © Willard A. Beling, 1986, and reprinted by permission of St. Martin's
Press Inc.

Lebanon is *not* a new country or society, and the much maligned Lebanese 'identity' has real roots in history and culture. . . .

We dwell on the history and identity of Lebanon for a reason. Those who aver that Lebanon's violence derives from its inauthenticity, from its lack of history or identity are mistaken, just as mistaken as those who assert that violence in Lebanon has been the rule not the exception. There is no country in the region save Egypt, Turkey and Iran that can point to a longer history as distinct political entities, none save Egypt to a history less marred by violence, and none at all to a longer cultural distinction.

But what of Lebanon's much analyzed divisions? Again, there is not a country in the Middle East, not one, without minorities, whether they be religious, ethnic, racial or tribal. Syria has far deeper and more numerous divisions than Lebanon. We are not arguing that primordial loyalties of whatever provenance are unimportant, any more than we suggest that the shallow roots of the country's institutions or the arbitrariness of its borders are insignificant. Yet these factors are insufficient conflict explanations by themselves, as any American, living in a country of even more numerous minorities and far more arbitrary boundaries, should understand. By any of the means we have considered, or all, Lebanon matches up quite well against other regional states. If these be the criteria for authenticity, and if on their bases Lebanon be judged inauthentic, then surely only Egypt in the Middle East has any claim to authenticity.

Questionable Explanations for the Conflict

Our intent here is to suggest that some of the most widely accepted arguments about the causes of conflict in Lebanon are at least questionable and certainly inadequate. If their proponents honestly applied these so-called explanations to all the Middle East, then conflict in Lebanon should be judged the least likely, or put differently, almost all the Middle East should long before have been charred by internal conflagrations far more destructive than that of Lebanon. Manifestly, neither is the case. . . .

External change factors have played a seminal role in creating Lebanon's current predicament and constitute perhaps the most immediate and undeniable set of constraints at present. We shall consider three external variables—the Arab world, the Palestinians and the Israeli-Syrian conflict. . . .

The Arab World

The country's historic links to the West, its long-established cosmopolitan identity, its openness to ideas foreign to the Arab world—all these characteristics have set the Lebanese apart and have, periodically, inspired Arab distrust of the Lebanese. In candour, it must be said as well that the size and vigour of Lebanon's

Christian community has also created tension in an Arab world that is overwhelmingly Moslem. . . .

[Paul A.] Jureidini has cogently pointed out that the Arab world into which Lebanon was born was a very different Arab world from today's. There was no Israel; the Arab states were all Western-oriented; there was no superpower rivalry; no Arab state was powerful enough to really project force beyond its borders against another Arab state. The creation of the state of Israel added a new actor that had not accepted Lebanese neutrality. The emergence of anti-Western Arab governments and the ideological revolution of the 1950s and 1960s meant that Lebanon's social-economic philosophies and ties to the West were now questioned, and in fact constituted grounds to deny or disregard Lebanon's 'neutrality'. A growing Soviet role added external pressure. And a regional arms race in which Lebanon did not participate soon left Lebanon vulnerable to either neighbour's military pressure.

After 1958 Lebanon, trying to adapt to the new circumstances, moved somewhat further from the West and endeavoured to make its peace with the 'positive neutralists' of the Arab world. In the process, which lasted until 1975, Lebanon suffered political marginalization both in the Arab world and in the West, thereby losing its traditional friends; Lebanon never did secure the support of those the country courted, thereby retaining its antagonists; and Lebanon alienated Israel, thereby creating an enemy it could ill afford. The truth is, after 1948, Lebanon's neutrality was no

Reprinted by permission of Don Wright, *The Miami News.*

longer acceptable in the Arab world; and Lebanon's unique nature meant any attempt to exit the conflict with Israel would *not* be supported by Lebanon's fellow Arab governments. The Arab record on Lebanon is a sad one—replete with broken promises, double-dealing, and outright subversion, when it is not characterized principally by apathy.

The Palestinians

Perhaps the best example of the Arab world's ambivalence toward Lebanon is the experience with the Palestinians who have themselves known Arab betrayal on more than a few occasions.

No Arab country welcomed the Palestinians more graciously or fully than Lebanon in 1948, when 150,000 Palestinian refugees poured into the country. A measure of Lebanon's relative peace and its comfort with the National Pact is that the inherent threat to the sectarian balance was perceived to be secondary to the need to welcome the refugees, despite the fact that the vast majority of refugees were Moslem.

During the period between the first and second Arab-Israeli wars, the large Palestinian refugee populations in Lebanon lived side by side with the Lebanese without incident. It was in the aftermath of the second war (the 1956 Suez War), however, that various Arab governments, especially Egypt and Syria, began to use the Palestinian problem and the Palestinians as an arm of their own foreign policies. From the inception of this phenomenon, Lebanon was victimized by Palestinians acting on behalf of non-Palestinian foreign interests.

The manipulation of Palestinians by Arab governments was only a part of the picture. In the 1960s a number of Palestinian groups moved toward ideological extremism both in the sense of the political spectrum and in the sense of apotheosizing the Palestinian problem. The moderate states—primarily Jordan and Lebanon—in which Palestinians were living, were beset by two distinct challenges: Palestinians who insisted that revolution in the Arab world was the first and necessary precondition to the realization of Arab and Palestinian objectives, and those who openly subordinated all Arab and 'regional' (i.e. national) interests to the interests of the Palestinian movement. . . .

Syrian co-operation with and attacks on the PLO in Lebanon alternated, and in 1983 Syria used its presence in Lebanon to support an 'internal' Fatah rebellion against the established leadership of Yasser Arafat. This initiative led to an 'internal' Palestinian war on Lebanese soil that cost the lives and property of many Lebanese. . . .

Palestinian raids led to the establishment of a local militia in the south under the command of the late Saad Haddad, to Israel's invasion of 1978, to Israeli support of the Haddad militia, and eventually to the Israeli invasion of 1982. . . .

Almost incredibly, few Palestinians are prepared to concede responsibility for a large part of what befell Lebanon. Leaving aside the 1975-6 fighting, and even the combat among Lebanese after that, the PLO exploitation of Lebanon has certainly been a principal factor in the violence in that country. . . .

Israel, Syria, and Lebanon

Borders are imaginary lines with real implications. Individual Israelis and Syrians have always had reservations about Lebanon's borders. In Syria many questioned the legitimacy of the Lebanese state as constituted in 1943 distinct from Syria. In Israel many questioned the legitimacy of the Lebanese state for other reasons. Both suffered Lebanese sovereignty, but grudgingly. When events allowed them to take actions that undermined this sovereignty, even if that was not the intent behind the specific actions, neither hesitated to do so. Both initially worked through Lebanese agents, both were pushed into military intervention, both used their occupations to create new political facts, and both have long since abandoned any pretence or intention of respecting Lebanese sovereignty.

Imported War

Senseless suffering and pain spills through the streets of Lebanon every day. Car bomb explosions strike innocent and unsuspecting people crowded together in areas of service or business. . . . The West assumes that the Lebanese are responsible for the reported atrocities. The press continues to cite a "civil war," a kind of in-house dispute that is tragic but something that the Lebanese can control as soon as they decide they have had enough. This simple explanation is grossly inaccurate. . . .

[The Lebanese people] are left homeless in their own homeland, as regional neighbors wage their wars or enlarge their land holdings or ideological territory. They are unable to defend themselves but bear the brunt of world criticism while imported outrages make headlines as "The Latest from Lebanon."

John A. Esseff, *Social Education*, April/May 1987.

History has shown that under a given set of circumstances Israel can dominate most of Lebanon, but not all. Given Israel's clear-cut military superiority over Syria, these circumstances involve Israeli public opinion and peace on the Egyptian front more than any other factor. Israeli opinion does not now permit such an extensive Israeli empire in Lebanon, and is unlikely to permit it for the foreseeable future.

History has shown that under a given set of circumstances, such as those prevailing today, Syria can dominate most of Lebanon, but not all. While Israel is more powerful, there are Lebanese and Israeli constraints on the extent of Israeli control, constraints that do not apply to Syria. However, Israel's military predominance precludes the extension of Syrian control to the southernmost part of Lebanon—or to any part Israel is willing to fight to keep away from Syria. . . .

The Seeds of Destruction

By the latter half of the 1970s, the eastern and northern border had little meaning to Syria, the southern no more to Israel. Both crossed Lebanese frontiers at will to carry out military, economic, and political actions. By the 1980s, after a succession of demands and pronouncements by the two antagonists, each indirectly 'recognized' the special security interests of the other in Lebanon, and both took pains to express, directly or through mouthpieces, their recognition of each other's needs. Note the implications. Israel not only crosses Lebanon's borders at will but concedes to Syria the same right; Syria acts on a parallel course. The frequency and magnitude of the disregard of Lebanese sovereignty have long since inured the international community, which tolerates and indeed anticipates continued disregard, to future violations. The Lebanese themselves, irrespective of their yearning for the return of Lebanese government authority, must look to Israel and Syria to meet their daily needs. For years, Lebanese of the Bequa'a have been forced to turn to Syria to respond to those needs; Lebanese of the south, to Israel. . . .

Both Israel and Syria, then, have sowed the seeds for even greater derogation of Lebanese sovereignty in the future, indeed, for the dismantling of the Lebanese state.

"Down deep, Iran still seems determined to spread its version of pure Islam."

Iran Threatens Middle Eastern Stability

Gerald F. Seib

When the Islamic government of Iran came to power in 1979, its leaders pledged to spread revolutionary Islam throughout the Middle East. Unlike most Middle Easterners who are Sunni Muslims, most Iranians are Shi'ite Muslims. Most Middle Eastern countries, including Lebanon, Kuwait, and Saudi Arabia, have a Shi'ite minority. Western observers have speculated that Iran could promote turmoil in other Middle Eastern countries by appealing to these minorities. In the following viewpoint Journalist Gerald F. Seib argues that Iran would like to become the superpower in the Middle East. Toward that end, it supports religious militants in other countries. Seib covers the Middle East for *The Wall Street Journal*.

As you read, consider the following questions:

1. What point does Seib make by reporting his conversation with a young Iranian in the state security service?
2. How does Seib believe the war with Iraq has affected the power structure in Iran's government?
3. In what way does Iran threaten Israel, according to the author?

A bearded young Iranian working in Tehran's state security service was explaining in passionate tones why Iran is a power to be reckoned with.

Iran's brand of pure Islam is attracting followers all over the world, he asserted. To which countries, a visitor asked, is Iranian-style Islamic rule most likely to spread?

"Kuwait first," the Iranian answered without hesitation. "Then Egypt. And after that, Saudi Arabia."

That exchange, which took place during a visit to Iran, illuminates an important question that has gone almost undiscussed in the flood of verbiage about the Reagan administration's secret arms sales to Iran. Is Iran, eight years after its own Islamic revolution, an expansionist power bent on seeing its version of Islamic government spread around the Middle East? Or has it narrowed its sights and resigned itself to living within the existing constellation of Islamic states?

Determined To Spread Islam

The answer is that, down deep, Iran still seems determined to spread its version of pure Islam. True, Iran's rhetoric has softened, and its protracted war with Iraq may leave Iranians with little appetite for expanding their power through brute force. Also, Iran's hamstrung economy is illustrating the need for cooperating with the outside world.

But plenty of Iranians still believe in the power, and the inevitable spread, of the Islamic ideas they espouse. The war with Iraq has prevented the kind of mellowing out and shift in attention to internal affairs that normally would follow a revolution like Iran's. Instead, the war has allowed hard-liners to keep a stronger grip on power than they might have otherwise.

Mushrooming Influence in Lebanon

So, for example, the tentacles of Iranian influence are spreading daily among the Shiite Moslems of Lebanon, where new posters of Ayatollah Ruhollah Khomeini are being put up daily. Some Lebanese think Iran's influence there will mushroom overnight if Iranian troops should score a knockout blow in the war against Iraq.

Almost without notice, Iran also is redefining the fight against Israel as a struggle between Islam and Israel rather than one between simply Arabs and Israel. That change, which transforms the struggle into a religious rather than a nationalistic one, has potentially profound implications that few in Israel seem ready to address.

And though Iran doesn't threaten the kingdoms and sheikdoms of the Persian Gulf as bluntly as it once did, it has used intimidation and strong-arm tactics to influence their oil policies—

The Middle East

Forbes in The Christian Science Monitor © 1982 TCSPS

indicating that even if Iran isn't forcing changes in the Gulf, it at least insists on influence. Iranians are members of the Shiite minority sect of Islam, but many think they also can inspire members of the majority Sunni.

All this doesn't mean there isn't an opening for American influence in Iran. There is. Some leaders, particularly powerful Parliament Speaker Ali Akbar Hashemi Rafsanjani, clearly are flirting with America. They are self-confident enough now to deal with the "great Satan," and seem to want at least some kind of relationship with the U.S. to acquire arms and to serve as a counterweight to the Soviet colossus on Iran's northern border.

The U.S. is wise to explore such openings, if only in hopes of countering some of the illogical anti-Americanism that pops up all over Iran now. Recently, for instance, a wailing crowd of mourners was carrying a casket through the streets of downtown Tehran. The casket contained the body of a man killed when Iraqi airplanes bombed an Iranian city. The Iraqi air force that killed the man uses, to a large degree, Soviet-trained pilots flying Soviet jets that drop Soviet bombs. So what was the crowd chanting as it mourned this air-raid victim? "Death to America," of course.

Iran Has Not Mellowed

But while probing for openings, the U.S. shouldn't delude itself into believing that Iran is a country that has somehow gone mellow or begun pulling in its horns. Nowhere is this clearer than at the front in the war against Iraq.

There, young Iranian volunteers—men dressed in ragged khaki uniforms and blue tennis shoes and armed with little more than red headbands carrying Islamic slogans—still show up in droves to fight for Islam. Amid the gnarled Iraqi corpses and the piles of spent artillery shells, nobody believes Iran is fighting only for some kind of limited political victory against Iraq.

Reaching Al Quds

"Our final goal is to reach Karbala and Al Quds, which is a goal for all Moslems," says Ali Husseini, a burly commander of Iran's Revolutionary Guards. Karbala is a city deep inside Iraq that is a holy site for Shiite Moslems like those in Iran. Al Quds is the Islamic name for Jerusalem.

Iranian soldiers, in short, believe that once they have cut through Iraq and replaced the government there with a truly Islamic regime, they will join with other Moslem fighters from around the region to wrench the holy city of Jerusalem out of the hands of Israel.

Many of the fighters in this coming battle for Jerusalem will come from Lebanon, Iranians believe. For in Lebanon, more than anywhere else, the Iranian revolution is reaching out and winning real converts. Members of Iran's Revolutionary Guards, the paramilitary force formed to preserve the Iranian revolution, are stationed in eastern Lebanon, helping militias there. Iran's ideas are promoted by the Hezbollah, a militia inspired by Iran's revolutionary Islamic system—so much so, in fact, that Syrian troops occupying Lebanon have felt compelled in recent days to try to clamp down on the growing power of Hezbollah and to paint over some of those Khomeini posters.

Iranian officials regularly meet Lebanese politicians to give pep talks and instructions. Ayatollah Hussein Ali Montazeri, the man designated to be Iran's religious leader after the Ayatollah Khomeini dies, met a group recently in the Iranian holy city of Qum.

Islamic sects, he told them, "like the five fingers of a hand, should turn into a fist against Israel and the infidels of the East and West." He added: "Now that the Palestinians are homeless and driven from the homeland, those who have houses should shelter them. [We should] equip them against Israel so that all continue the struggle against Israel as an Islamic task."

Iranian Rhetoric

Some Iranian leaders, to be sure, are toning down the rhetorical broadsides aimed at their neighbors. Mr. Rafsanjani, for instance, tried to sound a moderate tone when a reporter asked him about Iran's frequent criticisms of its Islamic neighbors. "Some [Islamic] countries aren't practicing Islam completely," he said. But, he added, "we aren't going to impose the Islam we practice here on them by force. . . . The only thing we expect of Islamic governments is that they allow people to practice Islam and live the Islamic way of life freely."

And, of course, many average Iranians don't share their leaders' passion for Islam or their eagerness to fight "infidels." They would prefer for the government to concentrate on improving the tattered Iranian economy. Iran is running an estimated $5.4 billion annual balance-of-payments deficit, hard currency is so short that a dollar changed into local currency on the black market fetches 10 times the official exchange rate, and Tehran's skyline is crisscrossed with idle construction cranes looming over half-finished buildings.

Speculating About the Future

Still, even some nonreligious Iranians can't resist speculating about the possibility that their country may someday become the superpower of the Persian Gulf that its size, strategic position and natural resources suggest it could be. For instance, one non-religious businessman in Tehran who is openly contemptuous of the mullahs who run the country mused the other day about what might happen if Iran somehow wins the war against Iraq.

"Can you imagine the power these people will have if we have our own oil reserves and Iraq's, too?" he says with a glint in his eye. "Business could be great here again."

For Iranian leaders, who are more concerned with spiritual than business advances, the prospect of increased power and influence must be equally attractive.

"Iran lacks the motivation, and probably the ability, to attack a gulf Arab country."

The Iranian Threat Is Exaggerated

Shireen T. Hunter

Shireen T. Hunter is deputy director of the Middle East Project at Georgetown University's Center for Strategic and International Studies. In the following viewpoint she argues that Iran's threat to the rest of the Middle East has been grossly exaggerated. Iran lacks the military hardware and money needed to successfully promote revolutions, Hunter contends. Furthermore, she writes, the Persian Gulf nations that feel threatened by Iran have taken security measures to ensure their internal stability.

As you read, consider the following questions:

1. For what reasons does Hunter believe Iran is incapable of attacking other Persian Gulf countries?
2. What examples does Hunter cite to argue that other Arab countries have tried to subvert Iran?
3. Why is it unlikely that Shi'ites in other Middle Eastern countries will support Iran, according to the author?

Shireen T. Hunter, "After the Ayatollah." Reprinted with permission from FOREIGN POLICY 66 (Spring 1987). Copyright 1987 by the Carnegie Endowment for International Peace.

The general view of Iran's threat to Persian Gulf security has three aspects:

- Iran could attack Kuwait or Saudi Arabia to prevent them from aiding Iraq;
- Iran could subvert current gulf regimes and replace them with Islamic republics modeled after itself; or
- A victorious Iran could intimidate the Persian Gulf states into following its policy lines on issues of special importance to the United States, such as oil-pricing levels.

Iran may want to do all of the above. But is Iran able to do them? So far the answer has been no. If Iran had the power to follow any of these policies, it would have acted long ago, and military success over Iraq is unlikely to change matters appreciably.

No Retaliation

It is no secret that Saudi and Kuwaiti financial assistance has enabled Iraq to continue the war. Saudi Arabia also provides Iraq with intelligence information, and, according to Iran, in 1986 the Iraqi air force even used Kuwaiti and Saudi territory to refuel on its way to bomb Iran's Sirri Island. Yet except for one air attack on Kuwait in 1981 and an alleged intrusion into Saudi airspace in May 1984, Iran has not retaliated.

There are reasons for this relative inactivity. Iran does not have much of an operational air force and lacks any viable air defense system. Saudi Arabia, by contrast, has acquired a reasonable air defense capability, including access to U.S. airborne warning and control system (AWACS) aircraft.

The Iranian government also is aware that an attack on a Persian Gulf state could generate a Western response. During his visit to the Persian Gulf in April 1986, Vice President George Bush reaffirmed the U.S. commitment, saying, "We will not wait for an invitation to intervene." Great Britain has also indicated that it will intervene to keep the Strait of Hormuz open and to assist if Kuwait is attacked. The Iranian government takes these threats seriously.

Finally, Iran is aware of the damage that an attack on any Arab gulf state would cause to its relations with its Arab allies, such as Syria and Libya, and to its image among Arab populations. Despite intra-Arab divisions, no Arab country could condone an attack by Iran on another Arab state. Syria, for example, has made clear to Iran that an attack on an Arab state would jeopardize their friendly relations. Iran's conflict with Iraq is different, because Iraq invaded Iran first. Indeed, Iran has tried, directly and through Syria, to reassure the Persian Gulf states that it has no territorial or other designs on them. Iran, unlike Iraq, has also said that it is not after Iraq's territory. . . .

Except under desperate circumstances, therefore, Iran lacks the motivation, and probably the ability, to attack a gulf Arab country.

Iran engages in hostile propaganda against some Persian Gulf states, such as Bahrain, Kuwait, and Saudi Arabia, supports their opponents, and has been implicated in a number of subversive actions. But Americans overstate the effectiveness of this program. Admittedly, the Khomeini regime cannot claim total innocence from terrorist acts, but no Iranian has been caught committing a terrorist act, and as the balance of forces inside Iran shifts, so may the Iranian position on terrorism. For example, referring to the hijacking of a Pan American airplane in Karachi, Pakistan, and the bombing of a synagogue in Istanbul, Turkey, in September 1986, Mousavi said, "Attacking people in a plane or in a synagogue cannot be accepted by revolutionary and Muslim forces."

Seeking Better Relations

While the rhetoric of "Islamic revolution" continues, in both theory and practice Iran has subjugated the goal of exporting its ideology in favor of better relations with neighboring countries. In theory, foreign policy circles in Teheran have established a guideline requiring that the national interest be accorded the highest priority so as not to jeopardize the survival of the "Islamic citadel." In practice, Iran has begun to establish a dialogue with its neighbors in the Persian Gulf region and to distance itself from acts of terrorism.

R.K. Ramazani, *The New York Times*, December 4, 1986.

Iran lacks a massive network of saboteurs and has been unable to infiltrate military or security forces. On the contrary, gulf Arab security forces—some of which, like Bahrain, receive valuable help from Britain—have been quite successful in foiling subversion attempts and in identifying and expelling suspect elements. Nor, despite the common assumption, is all subversion in the Persian Gulf directed by Iran.

Meanwhile, Iran itself has a case to make against others. Iranian opposition forces receive financial assistance from Arab countries. The Iranian government also has alleged that Saudi Arabia was involved in a 1982 coup attempt blessed by Ayatollah Shariatmadari, then one of Iran's few grand ayatollahs, and planned by former Foreign Minister Sadiq Ghotbzadeh, who was executed that same year. . . .

Shiites in the Gulf

Ethnic, linguistic, and religious differences limit Iran's ability to influence gulf Arab societies. Despite Khomeini's efforts to eliminate nationalistic tendencies in Iran and to emphasize Islamic unity, the Iranians are suspect elsewhere in the gulf, a feeling not tempered by religious affinity. Moreover, many of the Persian

Gulf's Shiites of Iranian origin are well-to-do merchants and shopkeepers who have benefited from the existing gulf governments and who are opposed to revolutionary regimes. Thus despite fears that Khomeini controls the gulf's Shiite communities, ethnic divisions and rivalries are strong within them, narrowing his ability to arouse them against their governments.

Iran's influence with the broader Moslem fundamentalist movement in the Persian Gulf—and elsewhere in the Middle East—is even more limited. A large majority of the gulf's Sunni fundamentalists are both anti-Iranian and anti-Shiite. Many of them are also supported by gulf governments and cooperate with them, as in Kuwait. In each country, the movement's fate will be determined more by social, political, and economic realities than by the outcome of the Iran-Iraq war. Ironically, rival Arab governments support each other's fundamentalist movements, as Jordan has done with the Moslem Brotherhood in Syria, while criticizing Iran for its fundamentalism. A survey of Islamic groups in more than 15 countries has shown that Iranian intellectual or political influence over these movements—with the exception of those in Iran, Lebanon, and, to some extent, Bahrain and Kuwait—is either nonexistent or minimal.

After the War

Many argue that Iran need only defeat Iraq to achieve the rest of its goals. The danger of an Iranian victory as a result of its troops' higher morale exists and must be watched carefully. If the threat became imminent, the United States—preferably in concert with other Western powers—might have to intervene by means of aid to local countries, support for joint Arab military action, and, in an extreme case, direct air support. But this possibility should not be exaggerated even if Iran were to gain more Iraqi territory. At the moment, Iraq has more trained men under arms than Iran. And Iran's larger population is not easily translated into advantages on the battleground. Training competent soldiers takes time and money, and its human-wave tactics so far have proved unsuccessful and increasingly unpopular.

In addition, Iraq's superiority over Iran in military hardware is roughly 5 to 1. The U.S. shipment of arms to Iran has not dramatically altered this balance, as evinced by recent successful and, until the Iranian land offensive in January, largely unanswered Iraqi aerial raids. Overall, the Iraqi military's performance—especially by its air force—improved in 1986. In December 1986 the Iraqis successfully turned away Iranians. . . .

If Iran Won the War

But even if Iran were to win the war, its ability to establish an Islamic republic in Iraq or to control it would be limited. Iran's population is 90 per cent Shiite, while Iraq's is almost equally divided between Shiites and Sunnis. An Iranian-imposed Islamic government in Baghdad would be Shiite-dominated and unacceptable to the Sunnis. And ethnic differences should not be underestimated. The Iraqi Arabs, although Shiite, would not accept Persian overlordship.

The Iraqi clergy traditionally has been far less organized and political than that of Iran. Despite the momentum created by the Iranian revolution, a 1980 attempt by Iraq's Islamic opposition to unseat the ruling Baath party failed, resulting in the execution of Imam Mohammed Bakr Sadr, the opposition's leader. It has not been able to cause significant damage in Iraq, nor has it been able to subvert the soldiers, most of whom are Shiites.

Unlike Iran, whose military traditionally has been kept out of politics, Iraq's military—whose top and midlevel leadership is exclusively Sunni—has been involved in politics since General Abdul Karim Kassim's coup de'état in 1958. It is hard to conceive that the Iraqi military, even defeated in battle, would stand by and watch Iran and its clerical allies take over Iraq. Nor would the Baath party, having run Iraq for 20 years, be likely to abdicate authority. . . .

Mired in a Stalemate

The ideological rigidity of Iranian leaders and their lack of experience in international affairs has been exaggerated. Many have proved capable of pragmatism, and have learned much about the demands of international life. Mired in its seven-year stalemate with Iraq, Iran is militarily incapable of overrunning its Arab neighbors or of effectively penetrating and destabilizing Arab societies.

Shireen T. Hunter, *Los Angeles Times*, November 25, 1986.

In the Persian Gulf, Iran's ability to intimidate the Arabs also has been exaggerated. Gulf Arab states have not appeased Iran since the Islamic revolution, although some of them, such as the United Arab Emirates and Oman, have sought a modus vivendi. On the contrary, the gulf Arabs' response to a real or perceived Iranian threat has been to pull closer together, to become more vigilant, to retaliate by expelling Iranian nationals, to continue or to increase assistance to Iraq, and occasionally to use force to deter Iran.

This basic attitude has not been changed by Iran's military successes. For example, after the Iranian capture of the Iraqi port of Fao in 1986, the gulf Arab states did not each rush to make a separate deal with Iran. Rather, the Gulf Cooperation Council issued a stern resolution warning Iran that a military attack on any one of them would be considered an attack on all. Another indication was Kuwait's decision to host the Islamic Conference Organization despite strong Iranian opposition and warnings.

In sum, the prospect of an Iranian victory over Iraq has not galvanized the kind of response that would be expected if the threat were taken all that seriously in the gulf. No doubt, the United States must remain steadfast in its support for the Persian Gulf Arabs' security. But it also should remain skeptical of the easy conclusion that a possible Iranian advance should outweigh U.S. interests in keeping Iran whole, independent, and out of the Soviet embrace. . . .

U.S. policymakers must take a long-term, broad view of Iran— not just of the Iran-Iraq war. And they should be willing to see the complexities of the Iranian situation, rather than seeing Iran as the only source of troubles for the United States in the Persian Gulf and the rest of the Middle East.

a critical thinking activity

Distinguishing Between Fact and Opinion

This activity is designed to help develop the basic reading and thinking skill of distinguishing between fact and opinion. Consider the following statement: "A 1981 study shows that 11 percent of the Iranian people have no strong religious leanings." This is a factual statement because it could be proved. But the statement, "Iran's Islamic fundamentalism is the sole reason for the demise of the Iranian economy," is an opinion. What effect religion has on Iran's economy is a debatable issue on which many people would disagree.

When investigating controversial issues it is important that one be able to distinguish between statements of fact and statements of opinion. It is also important to recognize that not all statements of fact are true. They may appear to be true, but some are based on inaccurate or false information. For this activity, however, we are concerned with understanding the difference between those statements which appear to be factual and those which appear to be based primarily on opinion.

Most of the following statements are taken from the viewpoints in this chapter. Consider each statement carefully. *Mark O for any statement you believe is an opinion or interpretation of facts. Mark F for any statement you believe is a fact. Mark I for any statement you believe is impossible to judge.*

If you are doing this activity as a member of a class or group, compare your answers with those of other class or group members. Be able to defend your answers. You may discover that others come to different conclusions than you do. Listening to the reasons others present for their answers may give you valuable insights in distinguishing between fact and opinion.

> O = *opinion*
> F = *fact*
> I = *impossible to judge*

1. The Pentagon is striving to turn the Middle East region into its strategic springboard against the socialist community.

2. The Israeli Jews and the Arab peoples are of the same Semitic heritage.

3. The US-Israeli expansion and their neo-colonialist designs are the cause of the Arab-Israeli conflict rather than the effect.

4. The Soviet-Syrian Alliance was formalized in the Treaty of Friendship and Cooperation in October 1980.

5. Some of the most widely accepted arguments about the cause of conflict in Lebanon are at least questionable and certainly inadequate.

6. It must be said that the size and vigour of Lebanon's Christian community has also created tension in an Arab world that is overwhelmingly Moslem.

7. Increasingly, in pursuit of its global aim, the Soviet Union exploits and supports radical regimes and terrorism in every region, worldwide.

8. As a result of the Arab-Israeli war in 1948, 150,000 Palestinians became refugees in Lebanon.

9. Syria plays a major role in regional and international terrorism, directly and through surrogates, frequently in cooperation and coordination with the Soviet Union and other radical states.

10. Iran is still determined to spread its version of pure Islam.

11. Like many massacres and outrages throughout history, the memory of the 1860 Maronite massacre tended to be carried from one generation to another.

12. Some Iranians don't share the passion for Islam or an eagerness to fight "infidels."

13. The Lebanese people must attempt by themselves to agree upon what they would like a reconstituted Lebanon to be.

14. The US is wise to explore openings with Iran in the hope of countering anti-Americanism.

Periodical Bibliography

The following articles have been selected to supplement the diverse views expressed in this chapter.

Edward E. Azar and
Robert F. Haddad
"Lebanon: An Anomalous Conflict?" *Third World Quarterly*, October 1986.

Dale L. Bishop
"Marching Toward Peace?" *Christianity and Crisis*, June 11, 1984.

The Economist
"The Iranian Hand that Stirs the Lebanese Pot," September 27, 1986.

John A. Esseff
"Lebanon: A Pawn in the Middle East," *USA Today*, May 1987.

Muhammad Husayn
Fadlallah
"The Palestinians, The Shi'a, and South Lebanon," *Journal of Palestine Studies*, Winter 1987.

Yo'av Karny
"Byzantine Bedfellows," *The New Republic*, February 2, 1987.

Saeed Naqvi
"The US Was Right To Mend Fences with Iran," *The New York Times*, January 3, 1987.

James A. Phillips
"America's Security Stake in Israel," *Backgrounder*, July 7, 1986. Available from The Heritage Foundation, 214 Massachusetts Ave. NE, Washington, DC 20002.

R.K. Ramazani
"Iran: Burying the Hatchet," *Foreign Policy*, Fall 1985.

Gary Sick
"Iran's Quest for Superpower Status," *Foreign Affairs*, Spring 1987.

William E. Smith
"A Country's Slow Death," *Time*, April 29, 1985.

Judith Vidal-Hall
"The New Battle for Lebanon," *World Press Review*, June 1987.

Dmitry Volsky and
Pavel Davydov
"Energy and Dynamism," *New Times*, no. 8, February 1986.

Martha Wenger, Joe
Stork, and Dick
Anderson
"The Middle East: Living by the Sword," *Merip Middle East Report*, January/February 1987.

How Has Islamic Fundamentalism Affected the Middle East?

Chapter Preface

"Moralistic" conveys a judgmental attitude, of believing one's standards to be superior to those of others, of criticizing others on the basis of standards that may not be appropriate to them.
—Moorhead Kennedy, *The Ayatollah in the Cathedral*, 1986.

Moorhead Kennedy formulated his book *The Ayatollah in the Cathedral* while he was being held hostage in the US Embassy in Tehran from November 1979 to January 1981. Kennedy examined cultural attitudes that he believed had prevented the US from recognizing the turmoil leading to Iran's revolution.

In January 1978, President Jimmy Carter toasted Iran as an "island of stability." Carter's praise was based on views held by many American observers and diplomats who saw the Shah as a valuable ally in an unstable region. The Shah's modernization programs fit American views of progress. These programs raised the per capita income of Iranians to $2,000, the highest in the Third World. They doubled the urban population, reduced illiteracy, and doubled the size of the middle class. But many Iranians did not view their ruler the way the US did. Much of the population was still very poor. Infant mortality in urban slums and rural areas was still high. Urbanization for many people meant leaving a lifestyle to which they were accustomed and living in poverty in the city. For many, the Shah's changes were alienating and foreign. Kennedy writes, "Many Iranians, disoriented, forced to think in new and strange ways, . . . sought above all for a renewed sense of their own identity."

One year after Carter's effusive toast, Iran's authoritarian government had been toppled and the Shah fled the country. Revolutionaries took over the government and Ayatollah Khomeini, a popular religious leader, returned from exile. As Khomeini became the leading influence in the government, it was difficult for Americans to understand how Iranians could prefer a theocratic government whose policies often seemed very harsh.

Egyptian journalist Mohammed Heikal suggests, "Just as we have to learn another man's language if we want to be able to talk to him, so we have to learn something about a people's history if we want to find any basis of understanding with them. . . . It is very easy to pass judgment on events, but much harder to sit down and attempt to understand how they happened." The wide variety of sources in this chapter can help readers gain a greater understanding of divergent perspectives in the Middle East.

"Islam . . . is the champion of all oppressed people."

Islam Has Liberated Iran

Ayatollah Ruhollah Khomeini

While Shah Reza Pahlavi ruled Iran [1941-1979], Ayatollah Ruhollah Khomeini was the leading religious figure opposing the government. For many years Khomeini had lived and taught in Qum, a religious center in Iran. He opposed the Shah's modernization and development programs because he believed they were secular programs that would corrupt society. He was exiled in 1964. Two weeks after the Shah fled in January 1979, Khomeini was welcomed back to Iran to be the spiritual leader of the country. In the following viewpoint Khomeini explains the measures the revolutionary government must take to be just and fair. He exhorts the people to make the sacrifices necessary to build the Islamic Republic.

As you read, consider the following questions:

1. Why was the Iranian revolution successful, according to Khomeini?
2. What was wrong with the training given to intellectuals at universities in Iran during the Shah's rule, according to the author?
3. Who does Khomeini believe is threatening the Islamic government?

Islam and Revolution: Writings and Declarations of Imam Khomeini, translated by Hamid Algar. Berkeley, CA: Mizan Press, 1981. Reprinted with permission.

God Almighty has willed—and all thanks are due to Him—that this noble nation be delivered from the oppression and crimes inflicted on it by a tyrannical government and from the domination of the oppressive powers, especially America, the global plunderer, and that the flag of Islamic justice wave over our beloved land. It is our duty to stand firm against the superpowers, as we are indeed able to do, on condition that the intellectuals stop following and imitating either the West or the East, and adhere instead to the straight path of Islam and the nation. We are at war with international communism no less than we are struggling against the global plunderers of the West, headed by America, Zionism, and Israel.

Dear friends! Be fully aware that the danger represented by the communist powers is not less than that of America; the danger that America poses is so great that if you commit the smallest oversight, you will be destroyed. Both superpowers are intent on destroying the oppressed nations of the world, and it is our duty to defend those nations.

Champion of the Oppressed

We must strive to export our Revolution throughout the world, and must abandon all idea of not doing so, for not only does Islam refuse to recognize any difference between Muslim countries, it is the champion of all oppressed people. Moreover, all the powers are intent on destroying us, and if we remain surrounded in a closed circle, we shall certainly be defeated. We must make plain our stance toward the powers and the superpowers and demonstrate to them that despite the arduous problems that burden us, our attitude to the world is dictated by our beliefs.

Beloved youths, it is in you that I place my hopes. With the Qur'an in one hand and a gun in the other, defend your dignity and honor so well that your adversaries will be unable even to think of conspiring against you. At the same time, be so compassionate toward your friends that you will not hesitate to sacrifice everything you possess for their sake. Know well that the world today belongs to the oppressed, and sooner or later they will triumph. They will inherit the earth and build the government of God. . . .

The Will of God

The noble people should be aware that all our victories have been attained by the will of God Almighty, as manifested in the transformation that has occurred throughout the country, together with the spirit of belief and Islamic commitment and cooperation that motivate the overwhelming majority of our people.

The basis of our victory has been our orientation to God Almighty and our unity of purpose. But if we forget this secret of our success, deviate from the sacred ordinances of Islam, and embark on the path of division and disagreement, it is to be feared that God Almighty will withdraw His grace from us and the path will be open again for the tyrants to drag our people back into slavery by means of their satanic tricks and stratagems. Then the pure blood that has been spilled for the sake of independence and freedom, and the sufferings endured by old and young alike, would be in vain; the fate of our Islamic land would remain for all eternity what it was under the tyrannical regime of the Shah; and those who were defeated by our Islamic Revolution would treat us in the same way that they treat all the oppressed people of the world. . . .

The Power of the People

What is certain is that the Islamic movement in Iran has released the power of the people of Iran as no other 'ideology' or nationalist emotion could have done. The Islamic Revolution is far from over; in some ways it is just beginning. The work of levelling the social order has barely begun. But, already, Islamic Iran has set another record: the record of survival against the combined counter-revolutionary efforts of the two super-imperialists and their regional and local clients.

Kalim Siddiqui, *Issues in the Islamic Movement*, 1983.

I see that satanic counterrevolutionary conspiracies, aiming at promoting the interests of the East and the West, are on the rise; it is the God-given human and national duty of both the government and the people to frustrate those conspiracies with all the powers at their command. I wish to draw particular attention to several points.

1. This is the year in which security must return to Iran so that our noble people can pursue their lives in utter tranquillity. I declare once again my complete support for the honorable Iranian army. I stress that the army of the Islamic Republic must fully observe military discipline and regulations. It is the duty of the President of the Republic, whom I have appointed Commander-in-Chief of the Armed Forces, to admonish severely all those, irrespective of rank, who foment disorder in the army, incite strikes, neglect their duties, ignore military discipline and regulations, or disobey military commands. If they are proven to have committed any of these offenses, they should be immediately expelled from the army and prosecuted. . . .

2. I declare once again my support for the Corps of Revolutionary Guards. I wish to impress upon them and their commanders that the slightest laxity in the fulfillment of their duties

is a punishable offense. If they act (God forbid) in such a way as to disturb the order of the Corps, they will immediately be expelled, and what I have said concerning the army applies equally to them. Revolutionary sons of mine, take heed that your conduct toward each other be inspired by affection and Islamic ethics.

3. The police and gendarmerie must also observe discipline. I have been informed that a remarkable laziness prevails in the police stations. The past record of the police is not good; they should therefore do their utmost to establish harmonious relations with the people, maintaining order throughout the country and regarding themselves as an integral part of society. A basic reorganization of the gendarmerie and police is envisaged for the future. In the meantime, the security forces must regard themselves as being at the service of Islam and the Muslims. . . .

4. The Revolutionary Courts throughout Iran must be a model of the implementation of God's laws. They must try not to deviate in the slightest from the ordinances of God Almighty; observing the utmost caution, they must display revolutionary patience in fulfilling the judicial tasks entrusted to them. The Courts do not have the right to maintain their own armed forces, and they must act in accordance with the Constitution. An Islamic judicial system will gradually assume the responsibilities now fulfilled by the Revolutionary Courts, and in the meantime, judges must do their best to prevent all irregularities. If any judge (God forbid) deviates from the commands of God, he will immediately be exposed to the people and punished.

Vigilance Against Counterrevolutionaries

5. It is the duty of the government to provide the workers and laborers with all they need for productive labor. For their part, the workers should be aware that strikes and slowdowns not only tend to strengthen the superpowers in their hostility to the Revolution, but also tend to transform into despair the hopes now placed in us by the oppressed of the world, who have risen in revolt in both Muslim and non-Muslim countries. As soon as the people learn that a strike is taking place at a factory in their town, they should proceed there immediately and investigate, identifying and exposing to the people all counterrevolutionary forces. There is no reason for the noble people of Iran to pay wages to a handful of godless individuals.

Beloved laborers, know that those who create a new disturbance every day in some corner of the country, whose only logic is that of armed force, are your determined enemies and wish to divert you from the course of the Revolution. They are potential dictators who will not even grant anyone the opportunity to breathe if they ever attain power. Oppose them in all areas, denounce them to the people as your number-one enemies, and expose the ties that bind them to the aggressive East and the criminal West. It is the duty of the government to punish severely anyone who participates in their disruptive activities.

6. I do not know why the government has failed to proceed with its suspended plans for promoting the welfare of the people. It must immediately implement existing plans and adopt new ones in order to remedy the economic situation in our country.

7. Everyone must obey governmental authorities in government offices, and stern action is to be taken against those who fail to do so. Anyone who wishes to create a disturbance in any government office must immediately be expelled and denounced to the people. I am amazed at the failure of the government to appreciate the power of the people. The people are able to settle their accounts with counterrevolutionaries themselves and to disgrace them.

Following Islamic Law

8. Confiscation of the property of miscreants by unauthorized individuals or courts lacking the proper competence is to be severely condemned. All confiscations must take place in accordance with the *shari'a* [Islamic law] and after a warrant has been obtained from a prosecutor or judge. No one has the right to intervene in these matters, and anyone who does so will be severely punished.

Islam Ends Exploitation

In an Islamic economy exploitation will cease; the product of the worker's labour shall belong to himself; the situation of class exploitation will be ended; all the relations of capitalism and exploitation will be destroyed and Islamic regulations will govern over production, exchange and market. Economic production will be put back into the right order.

Ayatollah Ali Montazeri, quoted in *The State and Revolution in Iran* by Hossein Bashiriyeh, 1984.

---

9. Land must be distributed according to the criteria of the *shari'a*, and only the competent courts have the right to sequester land after due investigation. No one else has the right to encroach on anyone's land or orchards. Unauthorized persons in general have no right to intervene in these affairs. They may place at the disposal of the competent authorities, however, any information they may have concerning the land, orchards, or buildings belonging to persons associated with the old regime who usurped the property of the people. Anyone who acts in defiance of Islamic and legal criteria will be subject to severe prosecution.

10. The Housing Foundation and the Mustazafan Foundation must each submit a report balance sheet of their activity as soon as possible to acquaint the people with their revolutionary operations. The Housing Foundation must show how much it has accomplished, and the Mustazafan Foundation must provide a list of the movable and immovable property it has acquired throughout the country from persons associated with the Shah's regime, particularly from the Shah and his vile family and hangers-on, and account for what it has done with this property. Is it true that the Mustazafan Foundation has fallen into the hands of the wrong persons? If so, it must be purged, and it is religiously forbidden not to purge it. These two foundations must explain precisely why they have not been able to act more swiftly. If anyone has committed any offense in the name of the Mustazafan Foundation, it is the duty of the courts throughout Iran to take swift measures against him.

Universities for Islamic Training

11. A fundamental revolution must take place in all the universities across the country, so that professors with links to the East or West may be purged, and the university may provide a healthy atmosphere for cultivation of the Islamic sciences. The evil form of instruction imposed by the previous regime must be stopped, because all the miseries of society during the reign of that father and that son were ultimately caused by such evil instruction. If a proper method of education had been followed in the universities, we would never have had a class of university-educated intellectuals choose to engage in factionalism and dispute, in total isolation from the people and at a time of intense crisis for the country; they overlooked the sufferings of the people so completely that it was as if they were living abroad. All of our backwardness has been due to the failure of most university-educated intellectuals to acquire correct knowledge of Iranian Islamic society, and unfortunately, this is still the case. Most of the blows our society has sustained have been inflicted on it precisely by these university-educated intellectuals, who, with their inflated notions of themselves, speak in a manner only their fellow so-called intellectuals can understand; if the people at large cannot understand them, too bad! Because the people do not even exist in the eyes of these intellectuals; only they themselves exist. The evil form of instruction practiced in the universities during the time of the Shah educated intellectuals in such a way that they paid no regard to the oppressed and exploited people, and unfortunately, they still fail to do so.

Committed, responsible intellectuals! Abandon your factionalism and separation and show some concern for the people, for the salvation of this heroic population that has offered so many martyrs. Rid yourselves of the "isms" of the East and the West; stand on your own feet and stop relying on foreigners. The students of the religious sciences as well as the university students must take care that their studies are entirely based on Islamic foundations. They must abandon the slogans of deviant groups and replace all incorrect forms of thought with the true Islam that we cherish. Let both groups of students be aware that Islam is an autonomous, rich school of thought that has no need of borrowings from any other school. Furthermore, let everyone be aware that to adopt a syncretic ideology is a great act of treason toward Islam and the Muslims, the bitter fruits of which will become apparent in the years ahead. Unfortunately, we see that because of a failure to understand certain aspects of Islam correctly and precisely, these aspects have been mixed with elements taken from Marxism, so that a melange has come into being that is totally incompatible with the progressive laws of Islam.

Beloved students, do not follow the wrong path of university intellectuals who have no commitment to the people! Do not separate yourself from the people!

Bastion of Colonialism

With the spread of colonial culture and westernised education, there sprung up a class of "intellectuals" among the aristocratic and rich classes with strong political and ideological affiliations with the West and ideas imported from the West. Bred in the debilitating atmosphere of the rich households, alienated from their own culture and traditions, secluded and separated from the bulk of Iranian masses who were Moslems, born and reared in nearness to political circles disposed to intrigue and conspiracy of royal courts in which the foreign elements actively participated . . . all these factors and numerous others helped in the creation of a class of intelligentsia in Iran which was the bastion of Eastern and Western colonialism in the country.

Islamic Propagation Organization, *Confessions of the Central Cadre of the Tudeh Party*, 1983.

---

12. Another matter is that of the press and the mass communications media. Once again, I request the press throughout the country to collaborate, to write freely whatever they wish, but not to engage in conspiracies. I have said repeatedly that the press must be independent and free, but unfortunately, I see some newspapers engaged on a course designed to serve the evil aims of the right and the left in Iran. In all countries, the press plays a fundamental role in creating an atmosphere that is either healthy or unhealthy. It is to be hoped that in Iran, the press will enter

the service of God and the people. . . .

13. These days, the agents and supporters of the Shah are unleashing a campaign against the beloved religious scholars who were among the most militant segments of society in both the time of the deposed Shah and that of his father: they staged numerous uprisings against the corrupt regime to expose its true nature, continuously led the just struggles of our noble people, and guided them to victory. When the religious scholars embarked on their determined struggle against the treacherous Shah in the years 1341 and 1342 [1962 and 1963], he labelled our committed and responsible religious leaders "Black Reaction," because the militant religious scholars, with their deep roots in the souls of the nation, represented the only serious danger to him and his monarchy. Now, too, in order to crush the religious leadership, which is the very foundation of the independence and freedom of our country, the agents of the Shah are putting the word "reaction" in the mouths of some of our young people who are unaware of the true situation.

My beloved, revolutionary children! Insulting and attempting to weaken the religious leadership strikes a blow against our freedom and independence and against Islam. It is an act of treason to imitate the treacherous Shah and apply the word "reaction" to this respectable class of our population that has always refused to submit to either East or West. . . .

United Against Satan

At the same time, I wish to draw the attention of the respected religious scholars throughout the country to the possibility that the devils hostile to our Revolution may be spreading malicious propaganda among them against our beloved youth, particularly the university students. They should realize that it is our common duty today to ensure that all segments of society—particularly the university students and the religious leaders, who together constitute the intellectual resources of our nation—unite against satanic and tyrannical forces, advance our Islamic movement in unison with each other, and guard our independence and freedom as jealously as they would their own lives. In the time of the tyrannical regime of the Shah, it was the plan of the world-plunderers and their agents to create a division between these two important classes. Unfortunately, they succeeded, and the country was ruined as a result. Now they wish to implement the same plan again, and the slightest lack of vigilance on our part will lead to the ruin of our country again. It is my hope that in the year that is now beginning, all classes of the nation, in particular these two respected classes, will be fully conscious of the stratagems and conspiracies that are directed against us and frustrate those evil plans with their unity of purpose.

"The revolutionary slogans of liberty, equality, independence and freedom from exploitation have been abandoned."

Islam Has Not Liberated Iran

Haleh Afshar

A diverse group of Iranians, including Marxists, Islamic leaders, intellectuals, feminists, and small business owners, worked together to overthrow the Shah. When the government collapsed in 1979, the religious leaders took control and built the new government. As the Islamic Republic cracked down on its former allies, many Iranians went into exile. Haleh Afshar argues in the following viewpoint that the Islamic government is oppressive. It has not redistributed wealth, she contends, and it has arrested and executed opponents. Afshar was a journalist and civil servant in the Ministry of Cooperative and Rural Development in Iran before the revolution. She is now a lecturer in Developmental Studies at the University of Bradford in Great Britain.

As you read, consider the following questions:

1. Why does the author believe that eliminating poverty would be against the interests of the religious establishment?
2. How has the government's efforts to reduce consumerism discriminated against women, according to Afshar?
3. If there is another revolution in Iran, what qualities does Afshar believe it should have?

The 1979 revolution in Iran was based on a widespread opposition to the Shah rather than on a chiliastic attempt to reach an Islamic Utopia. The loose alliance formed by reformists, Muslim radicals and Marxists used the Islamic medium to advocate their cause. The contradictory Islamic slogans bandied about during the revolution reflected the diversity of this uneasy alliance and its support amongst the merchants, the slum-dwellers and the urban middle and working classes. The revolution guaranteed to respect the sanctity of private property and provide a welfare state. In the event the Islamic government has failed to do either and as a result has lost much of its popular support. The absence of a coherent socio-economic policy, the continual power struggle and the substantial flight of capital have all contributed to the deterioration of the national economy and rapid underdevelopment in Iran. . . .

After four years of Islamic government in Iran the deep contradictions of Shiia ideology have remained unresolved. The revolution was to help the poor and yet remain within a theoretical framework that does not favour egalitarian measures nor provide any means for their implementation. Shiism is frequently seen as the religion of the oppressed, yet it does not oppose inequalities and does not provide for radical distribution of wealth. In fact the very influence and authority of the *ulama* [learned men of Islam] is in part based on their ability to extract *khoms* [tithes] and *zakat* [alms taxes on property] payment from the rich and give part of these to the poor. This process permits the religious establishment to maintain its patronage of the poor and retain their allegiance. Any radical measures which would result in the elimination of this process, either by eradicating poverty or by the state taking over taxation and welfare provisions, would in fact erode the most vital links between the religious establishment and its support base.

Power Struggles

The Islamic government has been unable to reconcile the traditionalists in the religious establishment to its theocratic rule. Despite the elimination of many influential ayatollahs, the power struggle continues between those who identify closely with the state and those who feel threatened and seek to retain their independence and their financial and spiritual control over their followers. There still remain a few religious leaders who continue to argue for a more extensive process of democratisation. It is this group which is regarded as one of the immediate threats by the state. The arrest of Ayatollah Shariatmadari has deprived them of their most eminent spokesman.

It is, however, by the alienation of one of the most important elements in its support, namely the merchants, that the theocratic

62

Jeff MacNelly. Reprinted by permission: Tribune Media Services.

government is most threatened. Without co-operation from the merchant classes the activities of the remainder of the private sector within the economy is gradually coming to a halt, and the government appears to have neither the ability nor the means to counteract the acute economic stagnation that the country is experiencing. The only solution offered, other than severe budgetary cuts and elimination of the few government-funded welfare services that existed, appears to be an attempt to secure socio-economic change through ideological propaganda. Iranians are asked to abandon their 'cultural habits of dependence' and realise that 'consumerism' is a Western value which has bound the nation firmly to its previous imperialist masters. Iranians are asked to break these bonds by acquiring the habit of 'Islamic austerity' and by accepting that 'saving is an Islamic revolutionary duty which mitigates against the Shah and the Western values of consumerism'. The new austerity includes the abandonment of 'false needs' such as washing machines, hoovers and rice-cookers which are classified as 'foreign products'. It is interesting to note in passing that all these items are those traditionally used by women in the home; electric shavers, cars and televisions, though similarly foreign-based, are not included in the list of false needs. As well, the exclusion of these products, which are assembled in Iran under licenses, would increase unemployment. The relation of dependence may appear easy to break, but as the Iranian theocracy has come to realise, the long-term results of expulsion of foreign capital has been a greater dependence on importing expensive foreign goods. In practice economic independence and political freedom require far greater experience and sophistication than that of the current regime.

War as an Excuse

It seems that the revolutionary slogans of liberty, equality, independence and freedom from exploitation, have been abandoned as unproductive and have been replaced by what appear to be rather severe monetarist policies which are unlikely to gain widespread popular support. It is arguable that the nationalist fervour whipped up by the war with Iraq is becoming the mainstay of the Islamic republic's survival and may explain the ardour of the government to continue the war despite Iraq's unilateral withdrawal in July 1982. The war not only legitimises the demands for austerity and self-denial, but also becomes a useful means of explaining away all economic failures. The war also provides employment of a kind for thousands of young men and keeps the potentially dangerous victorious army at a distance.

Judicial Reform

Attempts to purge all opposition, autocratic closure of the universities and many of the leading newspapers, total reorganisation of television and the radio and death sentences on 'un-Islamic' media personalities failed to forge the unity that the government sought of its people. Finally on 16 December 1982 Ayatollah Khomeini announced what appeared to be an end to police persecutions: the Eight Points Decree. Accordingly, the entire judicial and law enforcement system was to be reformed to ensure that people felt 'protected' rather than 'threatened' by the Islamic government.

The decree stipulated that 'Judges, the army police, militia and the committees must behave Islamically so that the people feel safe under the protection of the law of Islam and realise that Islamic justice does not dishonour and disappropriate them and protects their life honour and property'.

Summary arrests, execution and confiscation of assets were banned and the leader of the nation magnanimously granted Iranians the right to their own privacy, as well as the right to commit their own 'sins'. No one has the right to repeat other people's secrets.' Law-enforcement officers who inadvertently find 'instruments of debauchery or gambling or prostitutes or other things such as narcotics, must keep the knowledge to themselves'. 'They do not have the right to divulge this information' since doing so would 'violate the dignity of Muslims'.

Iran's Nightmare

I rub my eyes and think I am living through a nightmare or a frivolous comedy. I had to live to see the fundamentalists clamor for cutting off the hands of thieves, for stoning the adulterous and similar penalties which run counter to the spirit of our age! Can they really be serious in calling for a return to the glorious past while using the radio and other modern media which did not exist in that past and were created by the modern spirit?

Zaki Najib Mahmud, quoted in *Radical Islam: Medieval Theology and Modern Politics*, 1985.

The decree has been rapidly implemented and a number of high-ranking officials ranging from regional chiefs of the revolutionary guards *Spaheh Pasdaran* to Public Prosecutors were sacked. Many of the civil servants dismissed during the purges were allowed to appeal against their dismissals and, to speed up the process, theological students from Qum were incorporated into the judiciary. The Tehran Public Prosecutor explained to reporters that 'in the absence of a Faculty of Law, we have no choice other than employing religious scholars to achieve "judicial efficiency".' Nevertheless the government is yet to succeed in forging a new alliance with the mass of the urban poor, or in regaining the support of some of the capitalist classes to revitalise the productive sector, and it seems unlikely that the present regime would survive the war. The government is still relying on its powerful secret police and revolutionary guards, and the reign of terror seems considerably worse than that of the Pahlavis, without offering the small salve of consumerism that made many people more tolerant of the Shah than they would have otherwise been. It is difficult to believe that the Iranian people will continue accepting the total collapse of law and order and the current economic and socio-political disarray after the conclusion of the war with Iraq. However, one hopes that if there is another revolution it will be more than a rejection of a dictatorship and will have realistic and humane objectives and clearly formulated means of achieving them.

"Predictions of a rapid collapse due to internal conflict or economic crisis have not been fulfilled."

Islamic Fundamentalism Has Unified the Iranian People

Rudolph Chimelli

To many Westerners the Islamic Republic of Iran seems like a frightening place to live. The Iranian government has reportedly arrested and executed hundreds of people, has prescribed Islamic punishments for crimes, has issued decrees that women wear veils and not work outside the home, and has sent thousands of Iranian teenagers to fight in the bloody war against Iraq. Rudolph Chimelli, the Iran correspondent for the West German newspaper *Sueddeutsche Zeitung*, reports that these Western views do not reflect Iranian attitudes toward the government. The government's values correspond to the Islamic values of the Iranian masses, he argues, and for that reason the government will endure.

As you read, consider the following questions:

1. Why is martyrdom symbolically and culturally important to Iranians, according to the author?
2. What does Chimelli mean when he argues that the "national consciousness" of Iranians has changed? Why does he believe that is significant for the future of Iran?

Rudolph Chimelli, "Khomeini Digs In," *Sueddeutsche Zeitung*, February 22-23, 1986. Reprinted from the April 1986 issue of *World Press Review* by permission, 230 Park Ave., New York, NY 10169.

Very seldom, and only for brief periods, has righteousness ruled the world. These episodes of a Golden Age began in 622 with the flight of the prophet Mohammed from Mecca, his birthplace, to Medina, where he established an Islamic state. That era ended with his death.

The next began with the choice of his cousin and son-in-law, Ali, to be Caliph. It ended with his murder in Iraq. The latest began [in 1979] when a revolution destroyed the Shah of Iran's government and made the new Islamic Republic possible.

By the faith of Islam's Shiite sect—to which 90 per cent of Iran's 44 million people belong—everything in the intervening thirteen centuries was usurpation and error. No matter that this includes the blossoming of Islamic art and culture, science, and mysticism, and the vast empires of the Arab caliphs and Turkish sultans; only direct descendants of the Prophet, not elected caliphs, should lead the community of believers. To die in order to uphold this sacred principle is to share in the blood that Ali's son Hussein shed when martyred with seventy supporters in the Battle of Karbala in 680.

The Cult of Martyrdom

This enthusiasm for martyrdom was apparent during the 1979 Revolution and has been evident in Iran's war with Iraq. It explains the fountain of blood beside soldiers' graves at the huge Behesht-e-Zakra cemetery; the children who volunteer for the war, carrying keys to paradise as they charge into Iraqi shellfire (there are no sons of Westernized bourgeoisie among them); and the willingness to continue the fight despite heavy casualties: The nobler the goal, the more blood it demands from its supporters. The suicide terrorists who drive their car bombs into the enemy share the same emotion; they are fanatics of the cult of martyrdom.

The descendants of Mohammed who survived the massacre at Karbala were called *imams*—prayer leaders. Thus Khomeini allowed himself to be given the title *imam*, and the extremists who occupied the American Embassy described themselves as "students in the tradition of the *imam*." Conservative fundamentalist opponents of Khomeini within the Islamic Republic have bitterly contested his right to this title.

There also are social-reforming streams within Shiism as imperceptible as the Kanate, the underground channels that irrigate Iran's dry fields. They surface whenever marginal groups rise to fight for improvements. Rebellious farmers, Bedouins defending their predatory independence, the impoverished urban underclass—all these groups link themselves to the martyrs of Karbala. The question of how much social reform the Islamic Republic will carry out has been Khomeini's central domestic problem.

The political overthrow of the Shah was not followed by a social revolution. Only a few capitalists who owed their wealth to the

Shah had their holdings confiscated. Attempts at basic reform were defeated by the theological advisory council, which checks all laws to determine whether they are in accord with the teachings of Islam. The council vetoed a plan to nationalize foreign trade, and some properties were returned to their owners.

Since last fall young mullahs and intellectuals, most of them educated in American or British universities and somewhat Marxist in outlook, have been trying to change the direction in which Iran is moving. They gather the landless poor in urban slums and help them occupy unused land belonging to the rich. In North Teheran, among the rich villas at the foot of the Elburz Mountains, and in Shiraz, Isfahan, and other cities, thousands of squatters' huts have sprung up.

The Mustasafin, the barefoot troops of the revolution, gather at these sites before morning prayers. Then the revolutionary mullahs, surrounded by armed men, give out titles to the land. The procedure is illegal, but the activists know that it would be difficult to eject the new settlers.

The mentor of this movement is the Hojat-ul-Islam (teacher) Koeiniha, who organized the hostage operation at the American Embassy and later—to the Saudis' anger—sent Iranian pilgrims to demonstrate in Mecca, Islam's holy city. Koeiniha was recently named Iran's chief prosecutor. He was educated at Moscow's Patrice Lumumba University.

A Safety Valve

Iranian dissidents abroad seize on reports of complaining in Iran as evidence that the regime is about to collapse. In fact, its significance is precisely the opposite: Freedom to criticize is a safety valve, something that people consciously appreciate. Even the most unrevolutionary people say that it is one way in which life is better now than it was under the Shah.

Michael Field, *World Press Review*, May 1987.

Khomeini, seemingly interested in balancing the forces within the revolution against one another, apparently favors the radicals at the moment. The rich "who have spent their entire lives plundering society" are not the legitimate owners of their goods, he said recently. Prime Minister Musavi speaks of "opportunists" who have amassed "incredible wealth." Unfarmed land outside of the city now can be seized.

Musavi's reelection in October [1985] was not without opposition. The pragmatists both within and outside of Parliament wanted a head of state who is friendlier toward a market economy. They would have had their way had Khomeini not intervened in

Musavi's favor at the last moment.

Public debate over people, posts, laws, and political direction shows that the Islamic Republic, even after seven years, is not a dictatorship by European standards. The perfection that it should have attained certainly has eluded it. But predictions of a rapid collapse due to internal conflict or economic crisis have not been fulfilled.

The most critical forecast was that of Iraqi President Saddam Hussein. In September, 1980, he said that military pressure would cause Iran to fall like a house of cards. Instead, the Islamic Republic consolidated itself in the midst of the war.

The London Institute for Strategic Studies said that even if Iran did not seem able to win its war with Iraq militarily, it was winning the economic war. The institute observed that without any help, Iran has "been able to maintain reasonable growth."

Production is increasing at the Isfahan steel mill even though the Soviets have recalled their experts. The electrical system has a new national grid. Roads are being built, and construction is resuming in the cities. In some regions these developments are insufficient, but shortages are common occurrences in Third World countries.

The Islamic government has had its worst failure among those for whom it had the grandest plans—the farmers. The dreams of the urban unemployed returning to a newly green countryside have collapsed. The opposite has occurred. Modest public improvements in the villages have not prevented landless peasants from migrating to the cities.

Teheran, which had five million people at the time of the revolution, now has nine to 10 million—but it still lacks sewers and good public transportation. The government is silent about its basic reason for existence—to bring Islam into harmony with the demands of modern life. It has limited itself instead to imposing Islamic penal codes and rules of behavior.

The status quo continues: technicians work, businessmen deal, officials accept bribes, thieves steal, and the poor are miserable. The war is blamed for everything. The people's misery is perhaps slightly less than in other Arab countries. The mosques have created a welfare system that distributes food and other benefits, and that system fosters a client relationship to those who dole out the benefits.

Friday Sermons

Simple loyalty, religious sentiments, intellectual conviction, and sheer opportunism are blended confusingly. Alongside the terror of revolutionary courts, ruthless secret police, and a deliberate policy of destroying all competing sources of influence and power, the government has created a new means of control: Friday sermons.

No longer primarily a vehicle for spreading the faith, the sermons have become a system for issuing political directives. They are broadcast on television, published in the press, and analyzed by foreign embassies. They are written by a committee in Qom, a religious center, and sent across the country via telex. . . .

No Serious Opposition

"I think the revolution is broadly popular here," said a Western diplomat who has traveled widely throughout the country. . . .

"There is very little serious opposition to the regime," noted one diplomat. "Everyone blabs openly, (and) there is criticism of the government and ministers by name. It's a good safety valve."

Charles P. Wallace, *Los Angeles Times*, March 11, 1986.

Except in its early days, the Islamic Republic has not had good press. Iran does not conceal what Europeans and Americans regard as bloody excesses or crass denials of basic human rights. Other powers in the Middle East commit the same offenses, but they do so secretly and thus implicitly recognize Western attitudes.

Fundamentalism, seen through the veil of the blood of its martyrs and victims, seems horrifying. It seems destructive of culture when it bans classical Persian music. It seems to function as a time machine when, on Iran Air's international flights, the female passengers don their *chadors.*

A Change in Consciousness

What has changed decisively in the Islamic Republic is the national consciousness. The images of the old Iran—Mehrabad Airport, the international hotels in North Teheran, gushing oil wells in the Gulf—no longer matter. The nine tenths of the population that these modernizations did not touch are no longer marginal figures ashamed of their values. This shift in consciousness occurred among the active supporters of the regime, among the indifferent masses, and among the educated elite.

Members of the elite maintain that a return to the old ways is unthinkable, and that come what may a considerable measure of Islamization will remain. Unless it is destroyed in the war with Iraq or by a long-term oil price slump, the new Iran has every chance of outlasting Mohammed's—perhaps by many years.

*"Totalitarian and isolated, the regime is
loathed by the people."*

Islamic Fundamentalism Has Not Unified the Iranian People

Hélène Kafi

Many people believe that the Islamic Republic of Iran would collapse were it not for the personal popularity of the Ayatollah Khomeini and for the war against Iraq, which has rallied popular support. Hélène Kafi, the author of the following viewpoint, is a free-
lance journalist who left Iran in 1978 to live in exile in France.
Under an assumed identity, she returned to Iran in 1986 and
reports that the regime is highly unpopular. Corruption is ram-
pant, she argues, and the poor bear the burden of the war with
Iraq. Kafi predicts that civil war will break out when Khomeini
dies.

As you read, consider the following questions:

1. What evidence does Kafi cite to illustrate the large gap
   between rich and poor in revolutionary Iran?
2. What examples of corruption does the author describe?
3. How has the war with Iraq affected Iranians, according to
   Kafi?

"We live in a perpetual phantasmagoria," Firouz says quietly. "Iran is a huge insane asylum, a series of macabre carnivals, a comedy of the absurd." Firouz is half-serious, half-joking.

For three years he has been working on a study of his fellow Iranians' attitudes toward the revolution. He has collected hundreds of popular jokes from the bazaar, witticisms exchanged among friends and wall slogans. They constitute a portrait of the neuroses of one of the world's most oppressed peoples and a profile of Persian humor—mostly black these days.

A bit dazed from the effects of home-brewed *arak*, a fiery liquor made from raisins, Firouz prepares his first opium pipe of the day, indispensable to helping him forget the "irrationality of existence." He refuses to conform to the rigid laws of Iran's mullahs, and he is not alone. In the face of terrible repression, people pretend to follow the anachronistic directives of the Islamic republic—but small subversive groups form clandestine networks that thumb their noses at the "divine laws."

Clandestine Networks

The walls have ears, but also mouths. Despite the omnipresent "people's militia," hastily scrawled slogans denounce the mullahs' regime. Special patrols equipped with paint buckets undo the work of the "counterrevolutionaries," who risk severe punishments if they are caught. Akbar, an unemployed 20-year-old, was sentenced to 15 years in prison for turning a picture of President Ali Khamenehei into that of a vampire.

Despite their tough approach, the authorities have been unable to dismantle the clandestine groups that organize the secret activities of thousands of people. The state apparatus of coercion, with its intelligence services, morals committees and special revolutionary guards, focuses on fighting armed counterrevolution and uncovering plots that weaken the regime at the heart of its leadership.

According to Firouz, "The important thing is to keep from playing politics." If one avoids that sometimes mortal sin, deviations from the Imam's line are possible—for a price. Corruption has always been an accepted part of Iranian life; militant Islam has not changed that. Bribes, payoffs and illicit trade reach into the highest circles.

To dramatize the regime's resistance to corruption and to keep revolutionary fever at a high pitch, the authorities periodically mount spectacular crackdowns. On occasions such as Moslem unity week, squads of revolutionary militia charge through the streets. There are arbitrary arrests, public executions, repeated identity checks and absurd spectacles of humiliation, often directed against women.

Economic destabilization has kept pace with political oppression. The gap between the north of Teheran, with its chic neighborhoods, and the south, a huge open sewer of sordid shacks, has widened in the past seven years. North Teheran is lined with shops filled with foreign luxury items hidden from the view of passers-by. In a dozen opulent villas, clandestine activities, both commercial and cultural, continue.

An Iranian reports, "To enforce the Khomeini doctrine that regards beauty, sensuality and *joie de vivre* as sinful, morals squads have the right to pry into your intimate life. A marriage celebration has to be authorized by a neighborhood committee, which will require separate receptions for men and women. No music or dance is allowed, and certainly no alcohol. But if you do not want the ceremony to end up like a funeral, just grease the palms of a few militiamen and the party can begin."

Medieval Tortures

The existence of 120,000 political prisoners in Iran, representing a section of the nationwide resistance movement of the Iranian people, has now become a massive social problem for the paralysed regime of Khomeini. . . .

Furthermore, public protests and widespread disclosures about the unbounded medieval tortures inside the jails have continued to grow, bringing about condemnation of the Iranian rulers from all international organisations and assemblies advocating human rights. This has left the regime in isolation socially and politically on a global scale.

Iran Liberation, June 1, 1984.

We visit a superb home that also serves as a high-fashion boutique, an antique shop and a private club. Its clientele, formerly the ruling class, are now members of Iran's underground. The shop offers art objects, computers, videocassette recorders and other electronic products such as short-wave radios (which are forbidden in Iran). There is also an impressive array of printed matter.

A few artists, intellectuals and out-of-work professors meet there regularly. At the end of each meeting masses of new information and intelligence are fed into a computer, ready for distribution the next day.

"We have connections to the outside world through foreign embassies and friends in the West," explains the person in charge. "Our agents, who have infiltrated the various ministries, help us reconstruct events that are censored by the Iranian press. For example, last spring 11 bombs exploded in Teheran and its suburbs, but the media reported only two attacks."

Members of the club maintain that their activities are not

political, that they are working on a contemporary history of Iran. But the work they perform and the bribes they pay must cost dearly. Their financial "angel" is the sister of the late Ayatollah Godoussi, former prosecutor-general of the Islamic courts, who was killed in an attack in 1981. She reigns over the black market in electronic goods.

Bribing the Elite

The "club" provides many services: "Alcohol, drugs, girls, subversive literature—anything that is forbidden can be delivered to you at home," one member says. More important, the club has a list of confidential phone numbers that can help open doors at the highest levels.

The numbers are those of leading dignitaries in the regime, of top mullahs or of people like Ahmed Khomeini or Sadegh Tabatabai, the son and son-in-law of Ayatollah Khomeini, citizens above ideological suspicion who, club members say, are highly corrupt. Through their intervention one can obtain a passport and exit visa, the lease on a shop, even the liberation of a prisoner. All of this is expensive and payable in hard currency through a foreign bank. The cost of freeing a prisoner, for example, is $30,000 to $40,000.

The Iran of the privileged is not limited to the lavish home that serves as the "club." In the same chic suburb one finds bourgeois schools, aerobics classes and courses in painting and foreign languages.

The Poor Suffer

The great silent majority of Iranians continue to live amid great suffering. The war with Iraq is a constant presence. It has claimed more than a million lives and has left hundreds of thousands handicapped or homeless. It also has doubled the ranks of unemployed.

The Foundation of Martyrs, created in 1980 at the beginning of the war to aid the families of war victims, is now paralyzed by lack of funds and by increasing pressure from the government to serve as a propaganda vehicle. At its employment office long lines of women wait, mostly in vain. War widows are bluntly advised to marry a *janbaz*, a handicapped war veteran. Those who do so receive substantial state aid as "models of Moslem womanhood."

At the foundation's office of public assistance, a child is the object of a violent tug-of-war between its mother and grandmother. The older woman denounces her daughter-in-law as an adulteress and demands custody of the child. A somber mullah agrees, and the younger woman is sent to prison to be judged by a revolutionary tribunal.

Thus the poor suffer both from social injustice and from the terrifying application of Islamic justice. It is among the poor that women are stoned without trial, that small-time drug dealers are executed, that young delinquents are punished by an eye for an eye.

The Foundation of Martyrs

The Foundation of Martyrs is everywhere, involved in everything. Its stores burst with articles impossible to find elsewhere, and they are sold at ridiculously low prices. But not everyone has access to them. For example, only handicapped veterans suffering spinal injuries are allowed to buy refrigerators, vacuum cleaners or stoves.

Overthrowing the Revolution

Since the beginning of the Islamic revolution, some Iranians have fought against Khomeini constantly. More than 20,000 have been executed. More than 2 million have chosen exile. More than 100,000 are in prison. . . .

Overthrow is the Iranians' business, and they will manage to do it. There is a Persian proverb that says, "Mazangaran's wolf cannot be killed, except by Mazangaran's dog."

Amir Tahéri, *World Press Review*, May 1987.

The Foundation of the Underprivileged, which tries to improve the lives of the poorest, is the leading economic trust in the country. It oversees 200 industrial enterprises, 15,000 housing units, 50 mines, slaughterhouses and much more. Its budget is secret. Its director is appointed by the Ayatollah Khomeini and is accountable only to him.

The foundations' true activities, however, reportedly are the export of revolution. It provides financial support for several liberation movements, and it has helped organize terrorist training camps.

A Somber Revolution

Never has the face of Iran's revolution appeared so somber. Totalitarian and isolated, the regime is loathed by the people and vehemently criticized by both the internal opposition and some members of the Shiite clergy. "The Islamic republic," says a religious authority in Isfahan, "is a time bomb. When the Imam dies, Iran will see the hideous face of civil war." Has the countdown already begun?

"The Islamic movement must declare war on the influences of the political culture of the west in Muslim societies."

Muslims Must Avoid Western Influences

Kalim Siddiqui

Only 100 years after the religion of Islam was founded, it had spread across North Africa and into Spain. The Muslim empire had scholars such as Ibn Sina (Avicenna), al-Hasan Ibn al-Haytham (Alhazen), and Ibn Rushd (Averroes) whose knowledge and expertise were more advanced than that of medieval Europeans. By the nineteenth century, however, Europe had become much stronger and its dominating influence was felt in the Middle East and elsewhere. Since then, there has been an active debate over whether a society can become modern without undergoing a development process similar to Europe's and adopting Western attitudes. The author of the following viewpoint, Kalim Siddiqui, argues that Muslim society must remain Muslim and refuse to Westernize. Siddiqui is an author and the director of the Muslim Institute in London.

As you read, consider the following questions:

1. Why does the author believe that the philosophy and attitudes of Westerners are arrogant?
2. Who are the agents of the West in Islamic societies, according to Siddiqui?
3. To what factor does Siddiqui attribute the lack of popular support for post-colonial governments in the Middle East?

Kalim Siddiqui, "Struggle for the Supremacy of Islam—Some Critical Dimensions," in *Issues in the Islamic Movement*, edited by Kalim Siddiqui. London: The Open Press Limited, 1983. Reprinted with permission.

The environment of a religion is all other religions; the environment of a movement is all other movements; the environment of a civilization is all other civilizations . . . and so on. It is immediately clear that Islam is at once all three: religion, movement and civilization. When viewed in this context it is also clear that the history of Islam, in at least one of its dimensions, is a record of the Muslim *Ummah's* [community's] interactions with its non-Muslim and often, or nearly always, hostile environment. The *jahiliyyah* (primitive savagery and ignorance) of [Mecca] was the immediate environment of Islam. The *da'wah* [call] of Islam reclaims man from his *jahiliyyah* environment and makes him secure in a series of institutions, the highest and best form of these institutions being the Islamic State. The Islamic State represents the geographical area of the world that has been reclaimed from *jahiliyyah* and consolidated in Islam. Experience tells us that the environment does not retreat and go away. It leaves behind its traces, tries to creep back in and, in its own turn, reclaims Muslims and the areas of Islam for *jahiliyyah*. In Islam if any Muslim returns to a state of *jahiliyyah*, his punishment is very severe. Such is the deterrence with which Islam defends the human factor that is once part of itself. The persistence with which non-Islam tries to prevent Islam from spreading is all too familiar to Muslims. In this field Islam has rarely lost men in any great number in this way, with the possible exception of Spain.

Contest of Civilizations

The interaction of Islam as a movement, consolidated in a State, with other movements and un-Islamic States in its environment is another level of interaction. In the history of Islam this level of interaction began after the *hijrah* [flight] of the Prophet [Mohammed], upon whom be peace, to Medina. In time, this interaction turned into a contest between two civilizations, the civilization of Islam and the western civilization. At the present time we are almost exclusively concerned with the interaction of Islam as a civilization with its environment, the western civilization. . . .

Human Beasts

Allah . . . has created man physically weak in relation to most of his environment. He has also endowed man with faculties of mind and body that enable him to acquire control over all parts of his physical environment. But, in His Wisdom, He has not endowed man with the ability to discover for himself how best to arrange his relationships with other men and groups of men, from family to nation. A non-Muslim knows instinctively that he should procreate. He establishes temporary, permanent or semi-permanent relationships with the opposite sex. He sets up house

77

and family. He secures for spouse and children security in wider arrangements of clan, tribe, racial group, peer group, class, and ultimately nation and coalition of nations. He internalizes his experience into theories and combines these theories into 'knowledge,' now called 'science.' This is also otherwise known as the 'scientific method.' We know it as the secular development of man. The western civilization today is the epitome of man's secular development, though of course parts of it have gone through the Christian and Jewish religious experiences. Recent additions to the western civilization have 'enriched' it with such religious experiences as those of Hinduism and Buddhism. But, fundamentally, the west (which is no longer a geographical term, but a term used for a global 'civilization') has reduced all religious experience to the level of secular experience. Religion was merely a 'stage' in the secular development of man. According to the west, man is himself the repository of all wisdom. All the knowledge that man needs he either already has or is well on his way to acquiring. Man has no Creator, he is self-contained and sovereign unto himself. He owes nothing to anyone outside himself, he is not responsible for his behaviour to anyone or anything except to his own 'interests,' which he alone is capable of articulating and defending. Man's own good, as determined by himself, is the highest interest and responsibility of man. Man has no peer other than himself, and certainly no superior. He applies the same method, the empirical method, to all his needs of observation, explanation and prediction. He expects everyone, all men, to agree with him, otherwise they are 'backward' or worse. Such is the behaviour, such is the theory, such is the philosophy, such is the wisdom, and such indeed is the arrogance of man in the western civilization. What the western man does not know, or does not want to know, is that this secularism has become his religion; he is more fanatical with his secularism than any religious fanatic. On top of that, the secular man's behaviour is also free of any moral inhibitions, because his religion is free of notions of morality. The only morals known to the religion of science and secularism are those of convenience and short-term expedience. He is, in short, a human beast, and the modern world is a living testimony of beastly human behaviour at all levels.

Hostile Environment

Thus the whole of the religion of secularism is the environment of Islam and the Islamic movement. And because of the nature of secularism, the environment that confronts Islam is an intensely hostile one. It is probably true to say that Islam has always had to contend with a hostile environment. . . .

The victory of Islam was and must always be over its hostile environment. Within a few years of the Prophet's death, the

Islamic State he founded had extended its dominance to the shores of the Atlantic and the Pacific, and in the process the Muslims had also smashed the two superpowers of the time, the Byzantine and the Sassanid empires. From then until at least the eighteenth century Islam and the Islamic civilization remained the dominant civilization in the affairs of man. The west did not really succeed in finally dismantling the last political manifestation of the dominance of Islam until the defeat of the Uthmaniah State in the First World War and the abolition of the *khilafat* [caliphate] in 1924. Despite the tragedy of Spain (1610), according to A.J.P. Taylor, the celebrated English historian, the European civilization did not really get going until the twentieth century. In other words, the civilization of Islam did not finally lose its dominance within itself and in relation to the competing environmental civilization until the early part of this century.

Western Materialism

Humanity is every day more condemned to alienation, more drowned in this mad maelstrom of compulsive speed. Not only is there no longer leisure for growth in human values, moral greatness, and spiritual aptitudes, but this being plunged headlong in working to consume, consuming to work, this diving into lunatic competition for luxuries and diversions, has caused traditional moral values to decline and disappear as well. . . .

Democracy and Western liberalism—whatever sanctity may attach to them in the abstract—are in practice nothing but the free opportunity to display all the more strongly this spirit and to create all the more speedily and roughly an arena for the profit-hungry forces that have been assigned to transform man into an economic, consuming animal.

Ali Shari'ati, *Marxism and Other Western Fallacies*, 1980.

It is a particular characteristic of a hostile environment that it does not stop at the frontiers of the system it overcomes; a hostile environment goes on and penetrates the system. The hostile environment tries to absorb the system it overcomes into itself. If for some reason it cannot absorb, or realizes that it cannot absorb, the dominant environment tries to convert the system into a permanently subservient subsystem of itself. If one looks at the colonial period and the post-colonial experience of the traditionally Islamic societies, the point becomes clear. The western civilization has taken care to destroy all the traditional pillars of strength of the Islamic civilization.

The political, military, social, economic, cultural and educational structures and institutions that were the supports of the civilization of Islam have been either destroyed entirely or removed from the mainstream of life. In their place institutions developed in the west have been planted. It is not an accident that Muslims who are most westernized are most dominant in Muslim societies today. All institutions in Muslim societies are run by westernized Muslims. To put the point in its simplest form, the hostile environment has succeeded in creating its agents within the Islamic societies. . . .

A Source of Prosperity

Islam is the natural and popular choice of the Muslim masses, the principle of their identity and the root of their independence and integrity as a people. . . . Islamic movements alone can address the hearts of the Muslim masses, and only the revival of Islam in its primal strength as a comprehensive, liberating ideological force can free the Muslim masses from the colonial past and the neo-colonial present and reconstitute an independent Muslim world and Islamic civilization that can be, as it was in the past, a light and a source of prosperity and happiness for the rest of the world.

Umar F. Abd-Allah, *The Islamic Struggle in Syria*, 1983.

The fact of defeat and domination by an alien civilization was a new experience for Muslims. This was a situation they had not expected and were not prepared to face. Inevitably this new experience of weakness and domination by the environment caused a great deal of bewilderment in all parts of the *Ummah*. But the Muslim ruling classes, the landed aristocracies, and those whose livelihood was directly dependent upon the service of the State and political and military patronage, were most adversely affected. Their immediate reaction to defeat was to rationalize it, to reconcile with it, and to seek the service and patronage of the new rulers. The former rulers of Muslim States had ruled in their own interests; now their courtiers accepted foreign rule, also in their own interests. It is from this class of Muslim courtiers and sycophants that the new 'leadership' emerged; a leadership which persuaded Muslims to accept and internalize the culture and civilization of the new European rulers. It is this class that has thrown up men of the fame, calibre and notoriety of such men as Sir Syed Ahmad Khan, Mustafa Kemal, Reza Khan Pahlavi, Abd al-Aziz Ibn Saud, Gamal Abd al-Nassar, Abol Hasan Bani-Sadr and countless others. It is this class that has become ruler in its own right in the post-colonial nation-States. These rulers are today the instruments of the penetration that Islam's hostile environment has achieved and retains in the body of Islam. These rulers rule with political, economic and social structures created in the image of the colonial powers' structures, and they are still dependent for their survival on the environmental support systems provided by the dominant western civilization.

In its environmental dimension, therefore, the Islamic movement is bounded by a hostile civilization which has also acquired a foothold in the house of Islam itself. The power of this foothold of the alien civilization in the traditional areas of Islam has been clearly demonstrated in Iran. The ferocity of the late shah's regime against the Islamic movement was understandable and expected. But after the Islamic Revolution the westernized crust of the old order has stayed behind, and continues to fight a vigorous rearguard action to prevent the consolidation of the Islamic State. This counter-revolutionary campaign has been supported, supplied and orchestrated by the western civilization beyond the frontiers of Iran. There is no neat geographical line astride the Islamic movement and its environment. The interaction between the Islamic movement and the environment is also the struggle for supremacy within the house of Islam. This struggle is between the Muslim followers of the religion of secularism and the Islamic movement. In this sense the Islamic movement is unique; its hostile environment includes all the regimes and the ruling classes of modern nation-States in the Muslim world. The greatest success of the western civilization in its dealings with Islam is not scientific or technological; it is simply that there are now Muslims and Muslims' governments lined up against Islam. . . .

Muslim Masses Refuse Secularism

The overwhelming evidence would appear to suggest that Muslim societies have, by and large, not responded positively to modern political behaviour. The Muslim masses seem to resist modern political institutions, their style and content, and their leadership. As evidence, let us note that nowhere in the post-colonial Muslim world has the political system acquired a broad 'popular' base. In every post-colonial Muslim situation the political systems have become more and more authoritarian and dictatorial. In all these countries the Muslim masses have, if anything, moved in the direction opposite to the one desired by their governments and dominant political parties. In most countries, effective control and power have passed to a narrow-based elite, largely western in orientation and militarist in preferences. All the Muslim ruling classes that have emerged under the patronage of the colonial powers have one thing in common—their partial or total contempt for Islam and for the Muslim masses. It is hardly surprising, therefore, that the Muslim masses, too, have nothing but contempt for their post-colonial rulers, whose conduct is often worse than the conduct of the European colonialists had been.

All this is fairly obvious. Everyday observation also confirms that the Muslim masses do not accept the post-colonial political

81

systems as belonging to them or to their Islamic heritage. These political systems remain rootless, isolated impositions on traditionally Muslim societies. . . .

Not Even on Mars

Even if they [the imperialist countries] go to Mars, . . . they will not experience happiness, moral virtue, and spiritual exaltation. They will be unable to solve their social problems, because the solution of social problems and the relief of their own miseries require moral solutions, solutions based on faith. Attaining material power of wealth, the conquest of nature and space, all of this cannot cope with these problems. These things need Islamic faith, conviction, and morality to be completed, to be balanced and to serve humanity, rather than to endanger it. We possess this morality, this faith, and these laws.

Ayatollah Ruhollah Khomeini, quoted in *The Middle East Journal*, Spring 1987.

The Muslims have a political culture which is resistant to secular nationalist 'political processes' of the post-colonial period. This political culture has not responded even to the 'Islamic' political parties operating in the secular framework. This political culture of the Muslim masses is clearly opposed to the imported political culture of the secular post-colonial regimes and the westernized political elites of the nation-States. In Muslim societies today there exist two competing and mutually exclusive political cultures: these are the imported political culture of the ruling classes and the indigenous political culture of the Muslim masses.

Eradicating the West's Influence

This is an important dimension for the Islamic movement. The Islamic movement must now ensure that it does not become part of the western political culture of the post-colonial order. Instead, the Islamic movement must ensure that it belongs to and remains firmly rooted in the political culture of the Muslim masses. If this political culture of Islam has itself become contaminated by values and norms alien to Islam, then the Islamic movement must eradicate such influences. Whatever the situation, there can never be any reason or justification for participation in the imposed and oppressive political culture of the west which at present provides the rulers with their political theory and framework of government. The Islamic movement must declare war on the influences of the political culture of the west in Muslim societies.

"The chances for becoming modern without Westernization are about as good as conceiving children without sex."

Muslims Cannot Avoid Westernization

Daniel Pipes

Author Daniel Pipes is a lecturer in history at Harvard University. In the following viewpoint, an excerpt from his book *In the Path of God*, he argues that Muslims will have to accept Western influence if their countries are to become modern. Pipes believes that Islam can adapt and accept Westernization without losing its meaning and legitimacy. He contends that when the economic boom caused by the increase in oil prices subsides, Middle Easterners will need to devise new programs to encourage economic development. These programs will inevitably be based on Western development experiences, Pipes concludes.

As you read, consider the following questions:

1. Why does Pipes believe that modernization requires Westernization?
2. In the author's opinion, how will Islam eventually adapt to allow Westernization?
3. What does Pipes predict will happen to Iran after the Khomeini government collapses?

The decision to modernize ultimately comes down to a question of whether to adhere to the Shari'a [sacred law of Islam] and Islamicate patterns or to try out Western ways: fundamentalism, reformism, and secularism represent the principal responses. Which of the three the umma [Muslim community] adopts will determine, more than anything else, its success with modernization.

The Shari'a itself does not impede modernization so much as do attitudes toward the West; after two centuries of exposure, Muslims are still reluctant to acknowledge the West's power and cultural leadership. The result is what Naipaul terms the "Muslim disturbance," that is, admiration for what the West does mixed with resentment for the fact that it fares so well; a desire to imitate its results but an unwillingness to emulate its actions:

> The West, or the universal civilization it leads, is emotionally rejected. It undermines; it threatens. But at the same time it is needed, for its machines, goods, medicines, warplanes, the remittances from the emigrants, the hospitals that might have a cure for calcium deficiency, the universities that will provide master's degrees in mass media. All the rejection of the West is contained within the assumption that there will always exist out there a living, creative civilization, oddly neutral, open to all to appeal to. Rejection, therefore, is not absolute rejection. It is also, for the community as a whole, a way of ceasing to strive intellectually. It is to be parasitic; parasitism is one of the unacknowledged fruits of fundamentalism.

What holds truest of the fundamentalists holds true, in milder form, for the umma as a whole.

Two nearly parallel phenomena exist here: on one side, a religion that has strict requirements (the Shari'a) and a penumbra of cultural implications (the Islamicate way of life). On the other, a process of change (modernization) with its own penumbra of culture (the Western way of life). In theory, a Muslim faces few conflicts when he tries to reconcile the Shari'a with modernization, for they overlap only rarely—mostly in economics; with a few adjustments, he should be able to make the two compatible. The presence of so few areas of conflict between the Shari'a and modernization encourages some Muslims, the fundamentalists, to believe that they can become modern without Westernizing, that they can avoid most of those features of Western life that cause them such anguish.

An Illusory Belief

But this belief is illusory; if modernization is theoretically distinct from Westernization, the two are in fact inescapably intertwined. The chances for becoming modern without Westernization are about as good as conceiving children without sex. A Muslim intending to work as a jet pilot, for example, will not become adequately technicalized unless he is Westernized as well. Modernization is not some abstract principle but a very real force projected by teachers, administrators, investors, and writers from the Occident. The jet pilot's training has to be carried out in a Westernized environment either by Westerners or by Westernized persons. Also, Westernization is necessary because Muslims are influenced not only by the Shari'a but by the whole of Islamicate civilization. Even if the Shari'a rarely conflicts with modernization, Islamicate civilization differs from Western civilization on a wide array of issues.

Traditional Islam and Change

During what passed for the liberal age in the Arab-Muslim world, the liberals searched for the West's success and ended up importing its disembodied forms and pretensions, alienated from their habitat, and, when things really mattered, betraying their own principles. . . . Now the traditionalists insist that they have the proper remedy: Islam, the *turath*, the ways of the ancestors. They say nothing about what they intend to do with young men and women who have seen other ways and who do not wish to return to some imagined pure tradition. The discourse of the traditionalists is hopelessly simple in its assertion that the tradition lives and that there is an Islamic way of education, of income distribution, of government. It has yet to face up to the change that has swept the Muslim world.

Fouad Ajami, *The Arab Predicament*, 1981.

An outsider can easily see the faulty logic behind fundamentalism and reformism. Fundamentalism assumes that Muslims can modernize without Westernizing, leading to the contradictions Naipaul exposed; reformism holds that the two processes are compatible, leading to the falsehoods that so many scholars have noted. But secularism also fails, for even when Muslim leaders do dispense with the Shari'a itself, the Islamicate legacy persists. Formally giving up the idea of a caliph has hardly eased the predicament of Muslim governments vis-à-vis nationalism; nor has outlawing the veil (as the Iranian authorities did in 1936) achieved much more than heighten Muslim fears of social and sexual anarchy. Muslims are tied to the Islamicate legacy; even when they disavow the Shari'a and try to technicalize, Islamicate elements remain, holding them back from fully Westernizing.

Emotional Turmoil

The result is disarray and ambivalences. In the words of a Pakistani lawyer, "Our people emotionally reject the West. Materially, we may be dependent on the West." Equivocation of this sort paralyzes Muslims and prevents them from decisive action. Individuals and governments muddle along, rarely willing to devote themselves either to a secular program or a fundamentalist one. Reformism, with its hesitations, empty rhetoric, false promises, misrepresentations, sleights of hand, tortured logic, and flights of fancy, wins by default. It demands the fewest commitments and tolerates the most contradictions, offering a vacuous but optimistic middle ground for Muslims unable to decide on fundamentalist or secularist programs. Reformism does not satisfy, but the alternatives do not attract. Secularists and fundamentalists offer sharper, more persuasive programs, but few Muslims wish to experiment with them. Except in a few states, notably Turkey and Albania in one direction, Iran and Pakistan in the other, Muslim leaders have avoided committing themselves to clear-cut solutions. The result is cultural stagnancy and political volatility. . . .

To escape anomy, Muslims have but one choice, for modernization requires Westernization; the fundamentalist option is illusory, with most of its proposals "too unsophisticated to be of any value in solving the complex issues now facing the world." Islam does not offer an alternative way to modernize. So long as the umma insists on looking for solutions to current problems with patched-up versions of archaic programs, it will remain poor and weak. Secularism cannot be avoided. Modern science and technology require an absorption of the thought processes which accompany them; so too with political institutions. Because content must be emulated no less than form, the predominance of Western civilization must be acknowledged so as to be able to learn from it. European languages and Western educational institutions cannot be avoided, even if the latter do encourage freethinking and easy living. Only when Muslims explicitly accept the Western model will they be in a position to technicalize and then to develop. Secularism alone offers escape from the Muslim plight.

Adapting Religion

A comparison with the modern history of the Jews suggests that Islam is likely to witness a weakening of the law over time. Today's debate over the observance of the Shari'a corresponds roughly to the Jewish debate about a century ago; then as now, advocates of Westernization were gaining strength, just as adherents of the law held strong. The Jewish experience indicates that legalist forces, however strong, numerous, and well-organized, will fail, for they are defying the prevailing ethos of the age, antinomian Westernization. Too much occurring in life today undermines adhesion to the law; it is inconceivable that Muslims can withstand Westernization any more than Jews could.

If they accept Westernization, it is the opinion of some that the

86

essence of Islam will be lost and the religion forsaken; as M. Jamil
Hanifi sees it, abandoning the Shari'a means "an all-powerful Allah
without adequate guidance concerning his will, a holy book
without agreed upon interpretations, a religious emotion without
clear ethical and social consequences, and authority in the community without traditional legitimacy." H.A.R. Gibb sees it in even
starker terms: "To reject the Sharia *in principle* is . . . in some sense
apostasy. . . . With the maintenance of the Sharia is linked the sur-

vival or disappearance of Islam as an organized system." But this is overly rigid: religions, like all human institutions, survive through adaptation, and if Islam must discard the law and adopt faith and ethics, as Judaism did, it will do so. It can flourish too, for a Protestantized Islam will serve Muslims no less well than a legalized one; decline in the law need not impair the relations of men to God. This said, the efforts of those Muslims who do persevere in keeping the law deserve respect, for they are maintaining important traditions in the face of great challenge.

If Shari'a precepts often conflict with Western ways, so too do Jewish ones, at least in the private sphere, where the Halakha [Jewish sacred law] outdoes the Shari'a in the number and scope of its regulations. Even the Christian churches advocate precepts that differ from the customs of the modern West (such as the Catholic prohibition of divorce). All three religions discourage or prohibit taking interest on money, yet this does not hinder the free use of interest payments in the West and in Israel. In some ways, the sacred law has helped the Jews modernize; devotion to Talmudic studies is widely credited with giving Jews literacy and analytic skills which proved of great value outside the ghetto or shtetl.

The eventual adaptation of Jews to modern life makes it clear that attitude, not sacred law, is the key. Whereas most Jews accept Western ways and work hard to incorporate them or adjust to them, Muslims too often attempt to finesse Westernization and become modern without it.

The Oil Boom

To prosper again, the umma faces an inescapable set of demands: worldly success requires modernization; modernization requires Westernization; Westernization requires secularism; secularism must be preceded by a willingness to emulate the West; and this willingness will. gain acceptance only when Muslims are unalterably convinced that it is their only choice. Westernization is an unpleasant prospect which Muslims will not pursue unless all other efforts fail. Thus, were the Westernizers to flourish and the fundamentalists to fall behind, Westernization would look good and attract more Muslims. But is was precisely this that did not happen in the 1970s, when changes in the umma dramatically increased the power of fundamentalists and weakened that of the Westernizers. This was the worldwide phenomenon known as the Islamic revival.

To the extent that the Islamic revival is based on the oil boom, it is a mirage. Legalist and autonomist impulses strengthened and proliferated during the 1970s in large part because some activist Muslim regimes had huge amounts of discretionary revenues and others were able to exploit oil's disruptive effects to agitate for power; but neither of these can endure for long. . . .

As the financial circumstance of the sheikhdoms decline, Islamic hopes in many countries will suffer. The excitement of the early boom years will sour, signaling the end of an era. The confidence that played so large a role in leading Muslims to experiment with fundamentalist and autonomist solutions will be destroyed. . . .

Iran's Future

Iran's moral influence is fated to end as surely as the sheikhdom's financial power. Thirteen and a half centuries of Islamic history make it clear that the fundamentalist ambition to implement Shari'a precepts *in toto* must fail, and this is even more so in the modern era. The effort to wrench Iran back to a standard that no one has ever been able to live by is doomed; as the Khomeinist regime falls, non- or anti-Islamic forces seem likely to take its place. Having found the fundamentalists' vision impractical, harsh, and unstable, Iranians will probably reject any role for Islam in politics and return to a program which approximates that of the shah's (though in less ambitious form), to develop the country along Westernizing lines. No people's modern experience will have harmed Islam so much as the Iranians', whose experiment with theocratic government will surely be consigned to what Imam Khomeini calls the "refuse bin of history.". . .

A Freak Circumstance

In retrospect, the revival will appear as a curious aberration. Just as the power of a commodity price-setting organization (OPEC) defied long-term trends, so the concomitant resurgence of Islam was fortuitous and transient. Islam's revival was inappropriate because it resulted in such large part from freak circumstances, not Muslim achievements; the unearned nature of the oil wealth cannot be ignored. Buoyed by unexpected good fortune, Muslims allowed themselves to imagine that they had solved their basic problem, the inability to come to terms with the West. As the deluge of free wealth improved the umma's economic and political position without requiring it to deal with this problem, fundamentalists sounded increasingly convincing; it did appear that the umma could modernize without confronting its reluctance to Westernize. When some of the most primitive and observant Muslims flourished without effort, seemingly through strength of faith alone, false hopes were raised, giving many Muslims the unrealistic expectation that God's bounty might allow them to retreat into faith, to glorify their heritage, and to reject Western ways. Wilfred Cantwell Smith observes that "the new Islamic upsurge is a force not to solve problems but to intoxicate those who cannot abide the failure to solve them."

Recognizing Ethnocentrism

Ethnocentrism is the attitude or tendency of people to view their own race, religion, culture, group, or nation as superior to others, and to judge others on that basis. An American, whose custom is to eat with a fork or spoon, would be making an ethnocentric statement when saying, "The Chinese custom of eating with chopsticks is stupid."

Ethnocentrism has promoted much misunderstanding and conflict. It emphasizes cultural and religious differences and the notion that one's national institutions or group customs are superior.

Ethnocentrism limits people's ability to be objective and to learn from others. Education in the truest sense stresses the similarities of the human condition throughout the world and the basic equality and dignity of all people.

Most of the following statements are derived from the viewpoints in this chapter. Consider each statement carefully. *Mark E for any statement you think is ethnocentric. Mark N for any statement you think is not ethnocentric. Mark U if you are undecided about any statement.*

If you are doing this activity as a member of a class or group, compare your answers with those of other class or group members. Be able to defend your answers. You may discover that others will come to different conclusions. Listening to the reasons others present for their answers may give you valuable insights in recognizing ethnocentric statements.

E = *ethnocentric*
N = *not ethnocentric*
U = *undecided*

1. After two centuries of exposure, Muslims are still reluctant to acknowledge the West's superior power and cultural leadership.

2. There can never be any reason for Muslims to participate in the oppressive culture of the West.

3. One hopes that if there is another revolution in Iran, it will have humane and realistic objectives.

4. Islam is an autonomous, superior school of thought that has no need of borrowing from any other school.

5. The past record of the police is not good; they should therefore do their utmost to establish harmonious relations with the people.

6. The Shah's modernization did not improve the lives of the vast majority of Iran's population; it is no wonder that fundamentalism, which at least respects their Islamic values, seems a better option.

7. God allowed Iran's revolution against the Shah and America, the global plunderer, to succeed because Iran obeys God's will.

8. The items designated "false needs" by the fundamentalist government tend to be convenient, time-saving appliances used by women in the home; men's electric shavers are not considered "false needs."

9. Islamic art, culture, and science was for centuries among the most advanced in the world.

10. Secular man is a human beast because he has no morals.

11. It is among Iran's poor that women are stoned without trial and that young delinquents are punished by an eye for an eye.

12. Worldly success requires emulating the West; patched-up versions of archaic Islamic programs will not work.

13. Western man expects everyone to agree with him and his view of "progress," otherwise they are "backward" or worse.

14. Iran's experiment with backward, theocratic government will surely be consigned to the "refuse bin of history."

15. Intellectuals: rid yourselves of the "isms" of the East and the West; stand on your own feet and stop relying on foreigners.

Periodical Bibliography

The following articles have been selected to supplement the diverse views expressed in this chapter.

Abdullahi Ahmed An-Na'im — "The Reformation of Islam," *New Perspectives Quarterly*, Spring 1987. Available from The Institute for National Strategy, 11500 W. Olympic Blvd., Suite 302, Los Angeles, CA 90064.

John Barnes — "Looking Past Khomeini," *U.S. News & World Report*, October 20, 1986.

Fergus M. Bordewich — "Holy Terror," *The Atlantic*, April 1987.

Adeed Dawisha — "Power, Participation, and Legitimacy in the Arab World," *World Policy Journal*, Summer 1986.

Mansour Farhang — "Khomeini's New Order in Iran," *The Nation*, March 1, 1986.

Khosrow Fatemi — "3,000 Days of Ayatollah Khomeini," *The Wall Street Journal*, April 30, 1987.

Hirsh Goodman — "The Terrible Tide," *The New Republic*, March 24, 1986.

Fereydoun Hoveyda — "Iran After Khomeini," *Global Affairs*, Winter 1987. Available from International Security Council, 393 5th Ave., New York, NY 10016.

Ali Mohammadi and Annabelle Sreberny-Mohammadi — "Post-Revolutionary Iranian Exiles," *Third World Quarterly*, January 1987.

Afsaneh Najmabadi — "Iran's Turn to Islam: From Modernism to a Moral Order," *The Middle East Journal*, Spring 1987. Available from The Middle East Institute, 1761 N St. NW, Washington, DC 20036.

Carlo Rossella — "The Fundamentalist Threat to Egypt," *World Press Review*, November 1986.

Robin Wright — "Iran Looks Beyond Khomeini," *The Nation*, February 7, 1987.

Robin Wright — "Militant Islam Gains Ground," *The Nation*, May 23, 1987.

What Role Should the US Play in the Middle East?

Chapter Preface

Each year, when the president presents his foreign affairs budget to Congress, the strategic importance the US places on the Middle East is once again clear. In the Reagan administration's budget requests for 1988, $5.3 billion was requested for the US's two main allies in the Middle East, Israel and Egypt. Approximately $3.1 billion of that total was for military aid.

One reason for the long-term US interest in the Middle East is the vast oil reserves located there. The Persian Gulf alone has sixty percent of the proven oil reserves in the non-communist world. In explaining the administration's budget requests to the Senate, US Assistant Secretary for Near East and South Asian Affairs Richard W. Murphy said, "This oil will continue to be critical to the economic health of the West during the next decade and beyond."

US interests in the Middle East have led successive presidents to encourage negotiations that would establish a lasting peace. The results have been mixed. One of the biggest successes was the Camp David meeting in 1978 when President Jimmy Carter met with Egyptian President Anwar Sadat and Israeli Prime Minister Menachem Begin. The accords led to a peace treaty between Egypt and Israel, the first time in history that an Arab country and Israel had signed a peace treaty. Yet the treaty did not solve the Palestinian problem and did not please other Arab countries, who were angry that Sadat had acted independently. Since even this major breakthrough failed on some accounts, there is naturally a debate over how much influence the US can exert toward successful Middle Eastern peace negotiations.

The following chapter considers what issues should be preeminent in determining US policy toward the Middle East.

"The United States enjoys a predominant position in the area, particularly when it comes to the peace process."

US Influence Can Promote Middle East Peace

El Sayed Abdel Raouf El Reedy

In 1977, for the first time since the creation of the state of Israel, an Arab leader visited the Jewish state. Egypt's President Anwar Sadat went to Jerusalem to promote the peace negotiations supported by US President Jimmy Carter. In the following viewpoint El Sayed Abdel Raouf El Reedy points to the US role in improving Egyptian-Israeli relations as proof that the United States can work with moderate Arab regimes to solve the Arab-Israeli conflict and defuse the threat of extremist violence. A diplomat for the past thirty years, El Reedy is currently Egypt's ambassador to the United States.

As you read, consider the following questions:

1. How does the author justify his belief that the Arab-Israeli conflict is the key cause of conflict in the Middle East?
2. What signs of unity among moderate Arab countries does the author cite?
3. According to the author, what is the lesson of the Camp David peace treaty?

El Sayed Abdel Raouf El Reedy, "New Opportunities for Peace in the Middle East," *The Annals*, vol. 482, November 1985, pp. 12-18. Copyright © 1985 by the American Academy of Political and Social Science. Reprinted by permission of Sage Publications Inc.

It is no great source of satisfaction for a Middle Easterner, like me, to refer to this region as one of the most dangerous, if not the most dangerous, region of the present-day world. It is sufficient to glance at the daily headlines to realize what is going on in this part of the world: in Lebanon, on the West Bank, in the Gulf, in Afghanistan, and elsewhere. In these places there are active conflicts of all kinds. Many young men and women are both the victims and the instruments of these conflicts. So are many innocent civilians, regardless of their age or associations.

There can be no doubt that the United States is involved in the Middle East. It is, therefore, essential that American policymakers, diplomats, and political scientists understand both the causes and the current politics of the region in order to determine guidelines for an American approach to the region.

Revolutionary Changes

If we review the four decades from 1945 to 1985, which is by no means a long span of time in the history of nations, we would find that much has happened over these years. There was the establishment of the Arab League, the independence of Syria and Lebanon from France, and the first Arab-Israeli war in 1948. Old regimes disappeared, new revolutionary and military governments took over, and, on the heels of the Suez war, Arab nationalism rose to an even higher level. The Soviet Union entered the region through arms deals and its role in building the High Dam. There followed the unity between Egypt and Syria, the American-British expedition in Lebanon in 1958, the revolution in Yemen, the departure of the British from east of the Suez to the Persian Gulf, the collapse of Egyptian-Syrian unity, the triumph of the Algerian revolution, the reemergence of a Palestinian national movement, the War of Attrition, and the emergence of the Qaddafi phenomenon in the Arab world. Then came the 1967 war, the 1973 war, the dramatic rise in oil prices, the beginning of the Lebanese tragedy, the Egyptian peace initiative, and the Camp David accords and the Egyptian-Israeli peace treaty. The rest of the Arab world reacted to the Egyptian-Israeli agreements and attempted to isolate Egypt; they failed to create an Arab system without Egypt. Finally, we have Israel's invasion of Lebanon, the decline of oil prices, the failure of the Israeli campaign in Lebanon, and, most recently, the Jordanian-Palestinian agreement to join the peace process.

These events were never divorced from factors external to the Middle East. But I submit that the Arab-Israeli conflict has been a major, if not the central, factor in most of these events. Indeed, the Arab-Israeli conflict has been the most important single factor in the shaping of history in the Middle East during the past four decades. Had it not been for that conflict, we would have been able to see in that area a much more stable order, the orientation of which would have been liberal and rational. We would have been saved from much upheaval and destruction.

Camp David

Certainly there have been numerous attempts to find a peaceful solution to that conflict. These attempts never succeeded until 1977, when Egypt undertook a major historic initiative under the leadership of President Anwar el-Sadat that shattered all obstacles and resulted in the conclusion of the Camp David accords and the Egyptian-Israeli peace treaty of 1979.

An Even-Handed Mediator

The role of the United States is crucial. After his unsuccessful attempt in 1983 to resolve differences among Lebanon, Israel, and Syria, Ambassador and special negotiator Philip Habib remarked: "In all of the travels that I have made through the area I never found anybody who said to me, 'Go home, Yankee!' The response was 'Stay here, Yankee, but agree with me.'"

For many years, America's leaders were known and expected to exert a maximum influence in an objective, nonbiased way to achieve peace. In order to resume this vital role, the United States must be a trusted mediator, even-handed, consistent, unwavering, enthusiastic, a partner with both sides and not a judge of either. Although it is inevitable that at times there will be a tilt one way or the other, in the long run the role of honest broker can again be played by Washington.

Jimmy Carter, *The Blood of Abraham*, 1985.

The Camp David accords rested on the basic principle of exchanging peace for territory and aimed at the final resolution of the Arab-Israeli conflict, which entailed the solution of the Palestinian problem in all its aspects. The most complex area of the conflict pertained, naturally, to the West Bank and Gaza. The Camp David accords envisaged a solution that would lead to a transitional period in which the Palestinian people in those territories would elect a Palestinian self-governing authority that would exercise full autonomy over the territories pending negotiations that would determine the territories' final status. While the Camp David accords successfully led to the conclusion of the Egyptian-Israeli peace treaty, no agreement was reached on the Palestinian question, due to the narrow Israeli negotiating position on the definition of autonomy, despite three years of negotiations between Egypt and Israel.

This disappointment was soon followed by a series of unfavorable events in the area culminating in the Israeli invasion of Lebanon in June 1982. Aside from its disastrous consequences in Lebanon, the invasion resulted in the diversion of attention from the Palestinian question to the newly created problem in Lebanon. The years 1983 and 1984 were consumed in that exercise, and Egypt's endeavors to pursue its peace initiative had to be delayed until the emergence of a favorable climate. . . . We believe that such a climate is emerging and deserves a new round of activities that, by necessity, should involve the United States as the catalyst.

New Movement Toward Peace

I wish to refer to some of the encouraging signs of this new, favorable climate for peace. Let us begin with the recent elections in Israel, which led to the formation of a new government whose position on the peace process is obviously more flexible than that of the previous government. First, the present Israeli government does not reject one of the important peace proposals on the table, namely, President Reagan's peace initiative of 1 September 1982. Second, this government made the decision to withdraw its forces from Lebanon, thus bringing to an end a situation that has obstructed the pursuit of negotiations regarding the Palestinian question. We must make sure that this withdrawal is complete, genuine, and final.

A third development came from the United States. President Reagan's election to a second term of office by an impressive landslide has given him the authority to enable him to engage the United States in a bold policy for peace in the Middle East.

Arab Unity

Fourth, there have been developments on the Arab side. I refer, first, to the restoration of diplomatic relations between Egypt and Jordan, both with special responsibility to the West Bank and Gaza. Second was the restoration of relations between Egypt and the Palestine Liberation Organization (PLO), symbolized by the visit of Chairman Yasir Arafat to Egypt [in 1984] . . . . Then came the meeting of the Palestine National Council in Amman last November [1984] in which King Hussein of Jordan launched a peace initiative based on the underlying principle of exchanging peace for territory, an initiative that was not rejected by the PLO. The meeting of the Palestine National Council led to a series of negotiations between the Palestinian and Jordanian leadership, which culminated in the Palestinian-Jordanian agreement of 11 February 1985.

We believe that this agreement could be a watershed. Here we have at long last an Arab position in which the official, organized Palestinian leadership is formally committed to negotiate jointly with Jordan a settlement of the Palestinian question in all its aspects. The PLO also agreed that the right to self-determination, to which the Palestinian people, like any other people in the world, are entitled, is to be exercised in the form of establishing a confederate relationship with Jordan. No less important is the provision to form a Palestinian-Jordanian delegation as the interlocutor of the Arab side.

Sustaining the Momentum

Egypt viewed these positive developments in the region with a sense of appreciation and a sense of urgency. We felt that such developments, long awaited, deserved to be employed within a plan of action that would strengthen the rhythm of progress toward peace. We do not think that the momentum created should be allowed to fade away, nor that the Palestinian-Jordanian agreement should be allowed to constitute merely one more paper in a large pile of documents and missed opportunities on the shelf of the Palestinian question.

A Dangerous Back Burner

The problems of the Middle East are painful and difficult: that is clear. The United States has already borne tragic costs as a result of its involvement there. Yet the alternative—neglect—promises to return even more bitter dividends. The problems of the Middle East may have gotten too hot to handle on the front burner—and Washington did indeed get burned. Nevertheless, given the ingredients, a period on the back burner threatens to develop even more explosively.

Mazher A. Hameed, *The New York Times*, April 6, 1986.

It was for this reason that when President Hosni Mubarak came to the United States in April 1985 he urged the United States to make use of that newly emerging opportunity for peace, no matter how fragile it was. The glimmer of emerging hope should never be ignored. We fully realize the difficulties, the obstacles, the hardships, and the pains involved in the pursuit of the peace process. But we equally believe that the promise is worth the endeavor, particularly since the alternative to the pursuit of peace is even bleaker than what we see today in the Middle East and would certainly be more menacing for world peace.

In an endeavor to keep the momentum alive and to generate a sense of confidence and reassurance with the people who have long been victimized by that problem, namely, the Palestinian people, President Mubarak proposed as an initial step that the United States commence a dialogue with a Jordanian-Palestinian delegation. Such a dialogue would not be a substitute for negotiations nor would it be a form of prenegotiations. It would only be a confidence-building measure intended to break through the wall of isolation and mistrust behind which the Palestinians have been living for generations. We do feel that the United States has received this proposal with a measure of understanding and appreciation.

Choosing the Moderates

The choice between war and peace in the Middle East is all too evident. There are on the one hand the moderates, who are eager to find appropriate solutions to the conflicts that are causing so much suffering for the people concerned and that are condemning the countries involved in more arms spending rather than development. On the other hand, there are those who are all too eager to exploit existing problems to destabilize the area even more. In our view, a solution of the Israeli-Palestinian conflict would have monumental impact in achieving a final solution of the entire Arab-Israeli conflict and decisively steering the area toward a course of moderation and development.

I also believe that the parties in the conflict are today more prepared and willing to be engaged in a search for peace. The two parties most directly involved are the Palestinians and the Israelis. Obviously, the majority of the Palestinians wish to put an end to the occupation and, in association with Jordan, to be able to assume responsibility for their own affairs. They have explicitly committed themselves to that course, through the signing of the Palestinian-Jordanian agreement. I would say that the majority of the Israelis are also eager to have a settlement.

No Substitute for the US

In these circumstances, the United States cannot afford to sit back and let events, in a critical area such as the Middle East, merely take their course. On the contrary, the United States should intervene to shape events.

There is no substitute for the United States in this regard. For a variety of reasons, the United States enjoys a predominant position in the area, particularly when it comes to the peace process. No other country or group of countries enjoys such a position. I was a member of the Egyptian delegation at Camp David, and I would confidently say that had it not been for the active and persistent role of the United States, it would have been impossible for the parties to reach an agreement.

The Most Dangerous Region

Active participation by the United States in bringing about a peaceful settlement of the Arab-Israeli conflict would be a most significant contribution to world peace. No doubt, the Middle East, as is almost universally recognized, constitutes today the most dangerous region of the globe. The United States recognized this fact when it entered into bilateral talks with the Soviet Union on questions related to the Middle East. These talks are aimed at reducing the possibility of confrontation—planned or accidental—between the superpowers. For the situation in the Middle East carries with it the seeds of wider conflicts. One can think of various scenarios in which events could lead to superpower confrontations, which obviously would constitute serious threats to world peace.

A Worthwhile Investment

The most tangible fruit of the US's many labors for peace in the Middle East has been Camp David. Our total economic and military aid to Egypt in the 15 years (1962-77) preceding Camp David was $2.9 billion; our *annual* assistance level to Egypt is now almost that high.

Has the investment been worthwhile? Without a doubt. And we must recognize that any future assistance to other countries central to the peace process—Jordan being the prime example—will be worth the price, compared with the potential loss of priceless human life.

Charles H. Percy, *The Christian Science Monitor*, December 22, 1986.

I also believe that the United States would stand to benefit from an investment in peace in the Middle East. The United States has many stakes—political, strategic, economic, and others—in that critical region. Nothing could serve U.S. interests better than a peaceful solution of the Arab-Israeli conflict. Such an achievement would enhance the position of the moderates in the Middle East. It would vindicate them. It would prove that the policy of reason and moderation pays off. A failure to move on the peace front would tend to strengthen the rejectionists and extremists on both sides.

Seize the Opportunity

The Palestinians and Jordanians have gone a long way to meet the requirements for entering negotiations. It would, indeed, be a setback for the moderates if the present momentum is wasted and they are left out in the cold.

It has been said that the history of the Middle East is a history of missed opportunities. The blame has always fallen on the parties in the region. But this time the parties are prepared to engage in movement toward peace. It is up to the one great power, which is uniquely positioned to play the role of a catalyst. We do not believe that the United States can afford to let that opportunity slip away.

"In a region where the conflict is over God's religion and national identity, there is little the United States can do."

US Influence Cannot Promote Middle East Peace

Farid el-Khazen

In the following viewpoint, Farid el-Khazen examines the long-standing Arab-Israeli conflict and several new conflicts—the rise of religious fundamentalism, civil strife within Arab countries, terrorism, and the war between Iran and Iraq. He argues that the Middle East has become a low priority for the United States and believes there is nothing the United States can do to end conflicts caused by factors native to the Middle East. El-Khazen is a writer and a doctoral candidate at the Johns Hopkins University School of Advanced International Studies.

As you read, consider the following questions:

1. Why are most Arab countries currently uninterested in challenging Israel or actively supporting the Palestinians, according to the author?
2. Why does the author believe that the Arab goal of ending the Palestinian-Israeli dispute conflicts with Palestinian goal of a homeland?
3. What conclusions does the author draw from the Camp David peace negotiations?

Farid el-Khazen, "The Middle East in Strategic Retreat." Reprinted with permission from FOREIGN POLICY 64 (Fall 1986). Copyright 1986 by the Carnegie Endowment for International Peace.

Never before have Arabs and Israelis shared as much disillusionment with the existing order in Middle East politics as they do today. Consumed by regional conflicts or internal turmoil, both Israel and its Arab neighbors find that war is no longer an immediate option and that peace is not negotiable.

Slogans, Not Initiatives

Those peace initiatives still being proposed remain slogans for domestic public consumption. In fact, all parties are aware that no one can deliver the kind of peace that would meet the minimum requirements of the others. Jordan's King Hussein is too shrewd and experienced to put his trust in the empty promises of Yasir Arafat, chairman of the Palestine Liberation Organization (PLO), or in the governmental decisions of a deeply divided Israel.

The other Arab regimes are greatly removed from the Arab-Israeli scene. While Iraq is bogged down in a bloody war with its neighbor Iran, Saudi Arabia and other Persian Gulf countries are struggling to avoid being sucked into the same pit. Openly allied with Iran and clinging to a taut understanding with Israel, Alawite-ruled Syria would be the last Arab country to endanger its internal stability by launching a self-destructive assault against Israel. The recent reports of threats of war between the two countries for the most part reflect Israel's apprehension, not the true gravity of the situation. The Syrian-Jordanian rapprochement is at best a tactical move aimed at neutralizing Arafat.

Staving Off Iran

As for Egypt, it shares a major concern with most Arab countries aside from its own domestic unrest: containing Iranian ruler Ayatollah Ruhollah Khomeini's brand of Islamic expansionism. Egypt's military support for Iraq and political backing of those Arab countries at odds with Syria are dictated by the common interest of all the predominantly Sunni Arab states in shielding their populations from Iran's revolutionary fever. Ironically, Egypt's stature in inter-Arab politics stems partly from its position outside the Arab state system, at peace with Israel.

No War, No Peace

It is no wonder that Middle East politics are becoming increasingly perplexing. Today, although the struggle continues, no Arab regime is conducting military operations against Israel. Missing on the battlefront as well are the Palestinians, who, after the loss of Beirut, are capable only of undertaking occasional acts of counterproductive terrorism. As a result of this no-war, no-peace stalemate, the Arab-Israeli conflict is becoming internalized by the protagonists.

In the past, each Arab-Israeli war left some parties thirsting for revenge. The 1948 conflict leading to the creation of Israel

103

decimated Arab armies and marked the beginning of the Arab war against the Jewish state. Four other wars followed the Arab debacle of 1948. In each, at least one party was clearly on the offensive: Israel in the Suez campaign in 1956; both Israel and Egypt in the Six-Day War in 1967; Arab countries led by Egypt in the Yom Kippur War in 1973; and Israel in the Lebanon war in 1982.

The 1982 war was the first full-scale military confrontation between the two real adversaries—that is, the two claimants to the same land—Israel and the PLO. In a way, this war was to the PLO what the 1967 war was to the late Egyptian President Gamal Abdel Nasser. The devastating Palestinian defeat in 1982 knocked the PLO down from unprecedented heights of power, international recognition, and prestige. Two decades of political achievements, armed struggle, and luck crumbled almost overnight.

Pan-Arabism Is Dead

The 1982 war revealed many truths that had been veiled by the ideological politics and sectarian ways of the PLO's headquarters, Beirut. Arab reactions to the devastating war—the first to be fought in densely populated areas—once again demonstrated the obsolescence of pan-Arabism and of the belief in a common Arab destiny.

No Simple Issues

While the United States can play a helpful role, we cannot end either the Iran-Iraq war or the Arab-Israeli conflict if local forces remain intransigent. It is sheer folly to oversimplify these issues—and our failure to produce miracles in the Middle East need not be destructive of American interests.

Barry Rubin, *The New York Times*, August 29, 1984.

Arab regimes occasionally condemned Israel's expansionism, but mainly they sought to confine the damage to the Palestinians. These governments wanted no part in the defeat, since they, after all, were not Israel's targets. They had no interest in sharing in the humiliation of a PLO they never really liked and supported only reluctantly. These Arab attitudes are partly understandable. The Palestinians traditionally have shared only their setbacks with the Arabs; achievements and victories have been treated as exclusively Palestinian. . . .

A Political Wild Card

Yet the PLO's crisis does not make the prospects for peace any brighter. Nor does it make Israel any more at peace with itself. For after half a century of Arab-Israeli-Palestinian wars, the conflict has come full circle: Once again, enemy lines have been redrawn to match the original adversaries. Not only has the conflict been "de-Arabized," but also it has regained its pre-1948 setting and become a struggle between natives trying to preserve their land and others trying to occupy it; between Palestinians living under repressive occupation and a new breed of Zionists settling a land they claim to be theirs by history, religion, and force.

Contrary to the 1930s and 1940s, when the balance of forces between the two adversaries was not completely one-sided, the conflict now pits one party on the offensive against another—the Palestinians in the occupied territories—stripped of even the right of self-defense. The dismantling of the Palestinian state in Lebanon has rendered Israel's enemy impotent militarily and feeble politically, leaving Israeli society to grapple with its own problems and to try to settle its seemingly endless domestic controversies. . . .

By the late 1970s, when the Palestinians were solidly in possession of a state dominion in Lebanon, they found themselves facing an Israel freed from its other Arab conflicts and determined to deal with the problem on its northern border. To nobody's surprise, neither Beirut nor the Palestinians were judged worthy of Arab help. Both had become a heavy burden on Arab regimes: Beirut for having been the only refuge for Arab political exiles and thus the cause of Arab headaches, and the Palestinians for having implicated Arab regimes in a conflict they preferred to end, forget, or simply ignore. Arab regimes have supported and funded the PLO presence in Lebanon, only to regret having done so once the organization began to lay a claim to Arab leadership and resources.

More Pressing Priorities

Arab states clearly have many priorities more pressing than the liberation of Palestine—especially now that Egypt has found its way to peace with Israel; that Iraq and the Persian Gulf countries have become embroiled in a war against another enemy; and that the Palestinians themselves have become deeply divided, corrupt, and more bureaucratic than revolutionary. In the age of the supremacy of the nation-state, no Arab regime can take time out to fight the Zionists in Palestine.

Many Arab countries would like to see the Palestinian-Israeli conflict end, not so much because they have lost emotional and religious attachment to Palestine, but because they want to rid themselves of the Palestinian burden and defuse any potential Palestinian-related time bomb in their midst. Arab regimes have grown accustomed to accepting Israel's presence in the region. They have not grown to love Israel, but they realize that Israel is no longer an act of "Western imperialism" that can be reversed by war, diplomacy, or rhetoric.

Like the various Israeli generations who have come to look at the Arabs from different standpoints, some Arabs have also come to accept Israel to varying extents. Some have accepted Israel as a fact of life and are not greatly displeased to coexist with the Jewish state; others have accepted Israel, but only as an enemy that can no longer be defeated or annihilated.

The Middle East Trap

The United States has not been around to pull anyone's chestnuts out of the fire—or to inflame the passions of the purists. . . .

It's doubtful if the consequences of American activism would be . . . benign. The notion of our own indispensability is a trap. We should not walk into that trap when others set it for us. Certainly, at least, we should be able to avoid entrapping ourselves.

Fouad Ajami, *The New York Times*, April 14, 1985.

Today, many Arab countries are ready to entertain the idea of coexisting with Israel so long as they are not forced to express it publicly—and more important, so long as Israel does not shame them by exposing that desire. A certain code of silence should be observed between Arabs and Israelis, just as is the case among Arabs themselves.

The Palestinians cannot afford to remain silent about anything. But they have little room to maneuver and little chance to make their voices heard. They have also run out of luck, and a return to the pre-1982 golden age is impossible. . . .

Neither Peace nor War

In a region where the conflict is over God's religion and national identity, there is little the United States can do. And between the rights of natives and the visions of settlers, there is little hope of rendering justice that will be accepted. Only in September 1979, when then President Jimmy Carter, the late Egyptian President Anwar el-Sadat, and Begin went into seclusion for 13 consecutive days at Camp David, was the United States able to broker genuine peace between an Arab state and the Israelis. Peace was possible between Egypt and Israel mainly because three figures emerged at an opportune time: a missionary American president, a pragmatic Arab war hero, and a Jewish ideologue above hard-liners' suspicions. None of this can be recreated today.

It is unlikely that America will produce another president who, like Carter, could "keep faith" in Arab-Israeli peace talks. Just reading Carter's account of the hard work, dedication, patience,

106

and energy that went into the making of the Camp David accords may deter any successor from undertaking a similar mission.

But above all, peace was negotiable between Egypt and Israel. The possibility truly existed of a swap involving desert and wasteland virtually empty of people and devoid of great moving symbols. More important, the two countries recognized one another as legitimate adversaries. They dealt as two sovereign nation-states. In such a situation, the United States could play a neutral role between two equals.

Impasse Between PLO and Israel

No such role is possible between Palestinians and Israelis. Washington cannot deal with an entity—the PLO—it does not recognize. And if recognition were granted, America would still have to face Israel's opposition. Only if the PLO unequivocally recognized Israel's right to exist would the United States step in and sponsor new peace talks. But even then, the Palestinian-Israeli conflict would reach only the stage to which Sadat's 1977 visit to Jerusalem brought the Egyptian-Israeli conflict. From then on, the right leaders and the proper circumstances would be needed to recreate another Camp David.

Nothing on the horizon suggests that peace between Palestinians and Israelis is possible. As for Arafat, he now is nearing the age of retirement. He would not want to be remembered as the man who betrayed his people by recognizing Israel's right to exist. He would rather end his 30-year career as a national hero than sit at a negotiating table with people he has fought for so long. And even were Arafat to utter the magic words, there is no guarantee that post-1967 Israel could "think the unthinkable" and come to terms with its Palestinian problem. Nor is a civil war between Palestinians in the occupied territories and Israel likely, contrary to some recent arguments. After 20 years of "pacification" by Israeli troops, the West Bank Palestinians have not been left with the necessary leadership, weapons, or resolve.

The Jordan Option

There remains one unexplored dimension in the campaign for peace: the Jordan option. Leon Wieseltier of the *New Republic* has argued that this alternative can be pursued only if two changes occur. First, Hussein "must become a brave man," and second, "the Labor Party in Israel must recover its identity." Unfortunately, the situation is just the reverse: Israel needs brave leadership in the Labor party to break the prevailing deadlock, while the Hashemite monarch has yet to proclaim a definitive national identity and purpose for his kingdom. Both parties seek mutual support, but neither is capable of delivering the other from the hold of third parties that have come to symbolize bold leadership and to capture national symbols—the PLO for Hussein and the Israeli

Right for the Labor party.

Indeed, all parties to the conflict are hostage to one another in a great chain. The PLO is holding Hussein hostage to Arafat's machinations and empty promises; the king, in turn, is holding Israeli Prime Minister Shimon Peres hostage to his own insecurity and uncertain political future; and the Labor party is keeping Hussein's fate sealed by its inability to prevail over Likud and halt the rise of radicalism within Israeli society. Paradoxically, the Jewish state, too, has fallen prey to the demoralized and defeated outlook of Palestinians in the occupied territories. They, in turn, have become a political ball in the court of a divided and exhausted Palestinian leadership in exile—itself captive of the trappings of its former power and hardened by the reality of rejection and defeat. In such a zero-sum game, existing "conditions," as Meron Benvenisti, the former deputy mayor of Jerusalem, put it, "have no solutions. They are insoluble givens." And as such, they have little bearing on peace.

No Peacemaking Role

Why pursue negotiations that can only collapse into acrimony and even greater tension? The plain truth is that, as things now stand, there is no peacemaking role for the State Department to play in the Middle East. It should wait and watch and be patient. A peaceful settlement of the Arab-Israeli dispute has eluded American policy for almost four decades now. All the evidence suggests that no kind of turning point is at hand.

Irving Kristol, *The New York Times*, August 11, 1985.

Washington and the Middle Eastern parties share an insufficient determination to pursue peace, but this does not translate into a preference for war. In today's Arab-Israeli conflict, the threat of war has momentarily receded, but not because peace is any more attainable than at any time in the past. Instead, conflicts have been internalized and absorbed differently in each society and each political system. But as the dust settles from the Iran-Iraq sandstorm, the Arab-Israeli conflict may well recede in importance. An Iranian victory in particular would lengthen the long list of unresolved national questions facing the Arab world.

Superpower Priorities

In these conflicts, it becomes difficult to determine where superpower interests lie. Were it not for the renewed terrorism, the Middle East would preoccupy few U.S. policymakers. Indeed, with the neutralization of Iran and the declining strategic value of oil, the Middle East has become a lower priority on Washington's and

Moscow's foreign-policy agenda, as was made clear at the November 1985 summit in Geneva.

The old attractions and charm of the Middle East—exotic places and oil in the Arab world, the utopian vision of a successful democracy in Israel—have faded. When the outside world, including the United States, looks at the region now, it sees only hijackers, kidnappers, Khomeinis, Kahanes, and Qaddafis.

Several decades of incessant conflict in the Middle East have left many people frustrated, disillusioned, and simply bored. Commitments to local allies will continue to be honored, but more because of domestic pressures than out of a genuine conviction that vital strategic stakes are involved. Israel will always be in the "mind of America," but it will be a different Israel and a less mindful America. Likewise, moderate Arabs will remain on America's list of foreign allies, but less because of America's need for regional support than because Arabs, too, would like to be kept in mind.

Living with Chaos

The Middle East has become normalized. Like other Third World states, the Middle Eastern countries will have to live with border conflicts, internal chaos, and neglect by the outside world. And, like many other Third World regions, the Middle East will become a conglomeration of marginal states. The United States is no longer a power that needs to intervene in the Middle East either to end conflicts or to defend vital interests. Nor is it a power in retreat. Rather, it is a blasé power in an unstable, unrewarding, and incomprehensible Middle East—itself in strategic retreat.

"If the US is serious about making the difference, it may start by issuing a deadline of its own: Release our hostages fast or else."

The US Should Retaliate Against Middle East Violence

Dimitri K. Simes and Noel Koch

The authors of the following viewpoint believe that the United States must stop Middle East terrorists by strongly retaliating against them. In Part I Dimitri K. Simes, a senior associate at the Carnegie Endowment for International Peace, suggests a tougher policy toward members of the radical Hizbullah faction in Lebanon, a group that is believed to be holding American hostages. Noal Koch, the author of Part II, owns an international security firm and was formerly head of the Pentagon's counterterrorism program. He contends that the United States invites attack by failing to respond strongly to terrorism.

As you read, consider the following questions:

1. What would be the consequences of military action against Middle Eastern terrorists, according to Simes?
2. What does Simes mean when he contends that the US cannot be both "a model of morality" and "an effective superpower"?

Dimitri K. Simes, "Is the US Ruthless Enough?" *The Christian Science Monitor*, February 12, 1987. Reprinted with the author's permission. Noel Koch, "Music to Assad's Ears," *The Wall Street Journal*, October 31, 1986. Reprinted with the author's permission.

I

Does the United States possess the determination and ruthlessness necessary for a superpower? It would be nice if this country could protect its global interests without hurting a single innocent. But that is simply not in the cards. There is no international supergovernment to compel aggressors, terrorists, and perpetrators of other hostile acts to refrain from abusing America and Americans. Whatever virtues the Organization of United Nations may have, the power to enforce international law is not one of them.

Accordingly the US has three options: to reduce the scope of its involvement in the world; to communicate through both words and—most important—deeds that pushing the US around may be deadly; or to risk a great deal of damage to its prestige and the effectiveness of its foreign policy. It is unfortunately the third option that has been pursued by default by all administrations since the defeat in Vietnam. Few highly visible military actions such as the invasion of Grenada and the raid on Libya were directed against regimes so isolated and weak that they could be performed quickly and on the cheap. When confronted with more formidable opponents in Damascus and Tehran, US foreign policy was reduced to a pitiful mixture of bluffing in public and appeasement in private. No wonder hard-nosed rulers of Syria and Iran were not impressed.

Endless Humiliation

And so we stand today, grateful that the kidnappers of American professors in Lebanon, citing "repeated calls of the hostages themselves for a deferment of the deadline, mounting pleas by their families and national Lebanese bodies as well as the Indian government," have agreed to postpone the execution of their victims. Is there anything the US can do to put a stop to this endless humiliation? The answer depends upon the price we as a society are willing to pay for protecting our positions and dignity.

It is hard to be certain regarding the identities of the kidnappers. It is even harder to undertake a military mission against them without risking the lives of hostages and innocent Lebanese, including women and children. There would be nasty pictures the next day on TV. There would be angry demonstrations in Arab capitals. And there would be the possibility that the Soviet Union would exploit the situation to its advantage. If such costs are prohibitive, the US could, despite all its military hardware, expect to be treated as a hapless giant. That would not happen always, or everywhere. But there would inevitably be plenty of instances when the US became a target.

By that logic, of course, it was a mistake to drop atomic bombs on Hiroshima and Nagasaki, or, for that matter, to carpet-bomb

Dresden and other German cities. To be blunt: If protecting enemy civilians is the highest priority, military operations cannot be conducted. Conversely, if Americans do believe that enough is at stake in the fight against terrorism to justify hurting the innocents, the US has formidable instruments to project its will.

Release the Hostages or Else

I am not talking about a token retaliation against terrorist camps in the Bekaa Valley. To bomb them would be a cop-out for domestic consumption. The destruction of the camps resolves nothing. It would not frighten President Assad or Ayatollah Khomeini. And the supply of fanatics in the Middle East makes certain that dead terrorists would be quickly replaced.

Swift and Sure Retaliation

Catering to Arab terrorists' sense of ''justice'' will not end attacks. The antidote to international terrorism is not appeasement but, in Secretary of State George P. Shultz's words, ''The certainty that swift and sure measures will be taken against those who engage in it.''

Phil Baum and Raphael Danziger, *The New York Times*, November 1, 1984.

If the US is serious about making the difference, it may start by issuing a deadline of its own: Release our hostages fast or else. If they are not out in 24 hours—so go Hizbullah party installations all over Lebanon. If they are not out in 48 hours—so go fortified Syrian positions in the Bekaa Valley. If they are not out in 72 hours—so go the Iranian Navy, Air Force, and oil processing facilities. And let those on the receiving end guess what might come next. All these things and beyond are militarily perfectly feasible. The risk of a direct confrontation with the Soviet Union would be minimal. Moscow could be relied upon to launch a propaganda crusade, offer post facto assistance to those under a US attack, all the while carefully avoiding a military clash with another superpower.

A Choice Between Morality and Effectiveness

A brutal punishment of US enemies would not necessarily save those who are now hostages. And it would not instantly put an end to terrorist attacks against the US. On the contrary, initially a massive US operation would run the risk of triggering more of them. In the long run, however, terrorist groups cannot operate for long without support of governments. And governments—the Iranian and Syrian regimes are no exception—rarely take unnecessary chances if their very survival is clearly at stake. And the demonstration of US ruthlessness might encourage US friends, give a pause to US opponents, and, even by upping the ante, contribute to more moderate geopolitical conduct by the Soviets.

A brutal display of force is not a panacea. It is not a substitute for an understanding of local sensitivities, for a creative diplomacy, for patience, or—yes—for generosity. And blessed are the nations that can live happily and proudly without hurting a single innocent. Tragically, superpowers do not enjoy such luxury. An intellectually honest case can be made that it is better for the US to be a model of morality than an effective superpower. The point is that it cannot be both.

II

The accordion, bedecked with mysterious buttons and keys, is an intimidating instrument to behold. Once past the facade, the thing is found to be a naive assemblage of chromium sparkle and plastic designed to recycle air, and easily managed.

The Reagan administration's anti-terrorism policy is Hafez Assad's accordion.

In learning to play it, he has revealed not only the lethal emptiness of the promise of "swift and effective retribution" for acts of terrorism against the U.S., but the slapdash, improvisational character of our Middle East policy, particularly as it involves states that sponsor terrorism. . . .

Toward Iraq, our policy is merely fatuous, being built on the notion that a friendly face turned toward Baghdad, where the U.S. has virtually no serious interests at all, will somehow put Tehran at a disadvantage, which will somehow stem the tide of Shiite fundamentalism, which will somehow save our "moderate" Arab friends from being mau-maued by mullahs.

It Still Spawns

In the service of this notion, the U.S. more than two years ago removed Iraq from its list of states sponsoring terrorism. Following his recantation, Galileo muttered: "It still turns." Following its removal from the U.S. list of states sponsoring terrorism, Iraq is still sponsoring and spawning terrorism. Iraq hosted, among others, Abu Ibryhim, the gifted bomb-maker whose products have at least twice turned up on U.S. civilian airliners.

Abu Ibryhim took his skills to Damascus, where he was surely the inspiration behind, if not the source of, the bomb Nezar Hindawi gave his girlfriend at Heathrow Airport. There is little reason to doubt that the infrastructure of Abu Ibryhim's organization—the May 15 group—remains in place in Iraq.

In a more recent gesture of contempt toward the U.S., Baghdad has harbored Abu al-Abbas, PLO "mastermind" of the Achille Lauro hijacking and the Leon Klinghoffer murder. . . .

For five years the U.S. has talked tough and done virtually nothing about Middle East terrorism. More, we created for

113

Jeff MacNelly. Reprinted by permission: Tribune Media Services.

ourselves a number of excuses for doing nothing. One, popular at the National Security Council, has been the need to "internationalize" any response. Were we to act unilaterally, the authority of our action would be lessened or questioned, or so the argument has gone. (A nation so lacking in self-confidence that it needs international support for the proposition that its own citizens should not be kidnapped and/or murdered abroad is going to have a lot of its citizens kidnapped and murdered abroad.)

This argument comported nicely (or was thought to) with the perception of insufficient cooperation from our European allies. If our friends didn't do anything, how could we?

Intolerable Behavior

There was the argument for "balance" in our relations with the Arab world, meaning we should be as attentive to Arab interests and concerns as to Israel's. An unexceptionable proposition in the abstract. In practice, it has demanded toleration of behavior that civilized nations shouldn't tolerate. Part of an omnibus anti-terrorism legislative package two years ago would have required listing terrorist organizations. The State Department blocked that provision for fear the Palestine Liberation Organization would have been named, and this would have offended our Arab friends and violated the policy of "balance." The PLO has been implicated in anti-American terrorism from the murder of our ambassador in Khartoum in 1973, to the murder of Leon Klinghoffer on the Achille Lauro.

And there is the argument, especially popular in the Pentagon, that we must have a "smoking gun" before we act. What is intended is exactly the kind of evidence that linked Libya with the bombing of the LaBelle disco in Berlin, the sort of evidence it was never expected we would get and which we probably never will get again. The insistence on adherence to rules of evidence construed more rigidly than a court would require merely assures the unlikelihood of our being obliged to act against states sponsoring terrorism.

If, against all expectation, a "smoking gun" is found, we hasten to help its offending owner hide it, or explain it away. The unwillingness of our ambassador in Damascus to believe that his hosts could be involved in terrorism caused such exasperation in the administration around the time of the Libyan strike that it was decided to bring him home to set his head straight. (He's now on a separate recall.)

The idea was to have Robert Oakley, then head of the State Department's anti-terrorism office, go to Damascus to explain to the Syrians that we were losing patience with them. The plan foundered in part over concern that Mr. Oakley, known for being tough, courageous and direct, might upset the Syrians. (By far the most effective official the U.S. has had at the head of its efforts to fight terrorism, he also suffered from a congenital inability to dissemble; facts kept popping out of his mouth. Accordingly, Mr. Oakley is now on leave of absence at a think tank.)

Impotent in the War on Terror

The conviction of Nezar Hindawi in Britain strips away every fig leaf covering U.S. impotence in the war on terror. . . . We can accept Nezar Hindawi's smoking flight bag for what it has been shown to be in a British court, or we can persist in the delusion that Hafez Assad is a power whose transgressions must be tolerated at all costs, and that if we are extra tolerant, he might even squeeze out another American hostage or two for us as a reward.

Inviting Victimization

American foot-dragging in this matter reaffirms to Mr. Assad what he has known since the bombing of the U.S. Embassy in April 1983, and that is that there is no "swift and effective retribution" against terrorism and those who make it an instrument of their own national policy. There is rather a self-induced paralysis of will that, almost pleadingly, invites the victimization of American citizens and the national interest. The accordion plays on.

"Rather than ask why it is that some Lebanese are willing to volunteer for suicide missions in an effort to punish the United States, we become preoccupied with . . . security provisions in our embassies."

US Retaliation Ignores the Causes of Violence

Dale L. Bishop

Dale L. Bishop is Middle East executive for the United Church Board of World Ministries and a contributing editor to *Christianity and Crisis*, a weekly Christian journal. In the following viewpoint, he argues that US discussion of the Middle East ignores the people of the Middle East and the effect our foreign policy has on their lives. Middle Eastern radicals who use violence are protesting US policy and are striking out against repressive regimes. Bishop concludes that understanding the causes of violence is an essential step toward formulating an effective, humane policy.

As you read, consider the following questions:

1. Why does the author object to US policy that creates a buffer zone out of Lebanon?
2. According to Bishop, what are the wrong answers the West uses to explain violence in the Middle East?
3. What factor makes the Islamic revolution in Iran powerful, according to Bishop?

To the people of Lebanon the reaction of U.S. politicians to the September 20, [1984] bombing of the American Embassy "Annex" in East Beirut should have come as no surprise. Except for a brief period in 1982-83 when Lebanon became the "centerpiece" of U.S. policy in the Middle East, there has been little discussion of the impact of that policy on the Lebanese themselves. During a visit to Washington, for example, I heard a high-ranking official of the Reagan administration assert with all seriousness that the U.S. policy in Lebanon had been a success because we had created a buffer zone between Israel and Syria, thus preventing another major Middle East war. I doubt that anyone asked the Lebanese whether they wanted to be buffers. The official also said that "we" had gotten the PLO out of southern Lebanon. It was the Israelis who did the job, of course, and, according to Alexander Haig's much-disputed story of that bloody episode, "we" gave the Israelis a "green light" before the invasion. . . .

Reagan's Explanation

Reagan himself offered a curious version of recent Lebanese history:

> . . . the first time we went in [to Lebanon], we went at [the Lebanese government's] request because the war was going on right in Beirut between Israel and the PLO terrorists. Israel could not be blamed for that. Those terrorists had been violating their northern border consistently and Israel chased them all the way to there. Then we went in, with the multinational force, to help remove and did remove more than 13,000 of those terrorists from Lebanon. We departed and then the government of Lebanon asked us back in as a stabilizing force while they established a government and sought to get the foreign forces all the way out of Lebanon. . . .

The president went on to assert that it was the success of the American mission that prompted the terrorist attacks, and he hinted that Syria was one of the hostile forces supporting the terrorists. . . .

The president's statement enters into the realm of self-congratulatory revisionism. Aside from the fact that the oft-repeated justification for the Israeli invasion—that the PLO was consistently violating Israel's northern border—is simply false (the border had been quiet for a year before the invasion because of an agreement between Israel and the PLO, brokered by U.S. Ambassador Philip Habib), there is a notable omission in the president's narrative. Missing is any mention of the real reason U.S. marines returned to Lebanon: the massacre of hundreds of Palestinians and Lebanese in the camps of Sabra and Shatila, a massacre that took place despite Habib's solemn promise that following the departure of the PLO fighters the U.S. government would guarantee the safety of the camps' residents.

But the horror of that massacre has been neatly excised from the official account of the U.S. involvement in Lebanon, as if those Palestinians, nonpersons in their lives, are to be forgotten in death as well; as if the deaths of U.S. diplomats and marines were not connected to the deaths of Lebanese and Palestinians. . . .

Acknowledging Our Shortcomings

One of my roommates during our [444 days of Iranian] captivity pointed out, not for the first time, that our captors "want to take their country right back to the thirteenth century." By then thoroughly fed up with him, I shot back: "So what's so great about the twentieth?". . . . Had it been possible to pursue the matter, I would have questioned whether the course of events which produced the twentieth century, the last half of which has been America's century, necessarily represents progress. We have imposed our idea of "the good" on the Middle East. But if it is so "good," why are they so forceful in rejecting it? Perhaps it is because they have tried it and found it wanting, indeed harmful, in important respects. If we are to understand and come to terms with the factors that generate Middle East terrorism, we had better look into the mirror that terrorism holds up to us, for what it tells us not about the terrorists' shortcomings but about our own. Only if we are able to do something about our shortcomings can we hope to regain the respect and moral leadership we once enjoyed in the Middle East and in the rest of the Third World.

Moorhead Kennedy, *The Ayatollah in the Cathedral*, 1986.

There is a common thread in . . . discussions of Middle East policy. It is the absence, or invisibility, of the people of the Middle East. U.S. policy in Lebanon is discussed without reference to the fate of the Lebanese: They are the buffers. The word "Palestinian" is not to be used except as an adjective modifying the noun "terrorist." The Arabs who do put in cameo performances in these discussions are either "terrorists"—and there is general agreement that they (and any civilians foolish enough to live near them) are to be wiped out—or that elusive group known as the "moderate Arabs." Even the Israelis are most often mentioned only in terms of Israel's strategic value to the U.S.

Asking the Wrong Questions

It is, therefore, not surprising that in the wake of such tragedies as the bombing of the American embassy in Beirut the wrong questions inevitably are asked. Rather than ask why it is that some Lebanese are willing to volunteer for suicide missions in an effort to punish the United States, we become preoccupied with the technicalities of security provisions in our embassies overseas. The reasons for the rage that motivates such acts remain unexplored.

Or, when the right questions are asked, facile answers are given that tend to absolve the U.S. of all responsibility for the creation of such a poisonous atmosphere in the Middle East. After the September bombing of the embassy, for example, hardly anyone recalled that a few weeks earlier the U.S. government had cast the only negative vote, a veto, against a UN Security Council resolution condemning the Israeli occupation of southern Lebanon. This has been a particularly onerous occupation, which has cut off southern Lebanon from its markets in the north, and thus destroyed what was once a vigorous local economy. Families are separated, orchards destroyed, offenses against Islam are committed. That lone U.S. negative vote—none of our allies on the Security Council even abstained—belied our stated intention of getting all foreign forces out of Lebanon, and since it was seen by many Lebanese as a betrayal, was deeply resented. . . .

Getting the Wrong Answer

The "answer," then, is clear. "We" didn't do anything to prompt these attacks; they are rather the product of a hostile ideology, Islam, which is devoted to the destruction of the West and Western values. In this view, Islam has its own irrational dynamic, incomprehensible to the Western mind, a dynamic that motivates people to do crazy things. Islam has thus been restored to the demonology of the West, and takes its place alongside "godless communism" as a force to be reckoned with.

But serious questions deserve serious answers, and the demonization of Islam, as popular and convenient as it may be, is not a serious answer. We need to look not at the constructs of religion and ideology but at the concerns of people. Middle East issues, in short, must be humanized; they must be peopled with Lebanese, Israelis, Palestinians, Iranians, Iraqis.

Is it not relevant, for example, that although many people in the Middle East live in dire poverty, the region has the world's highest per capita expenditure for armaments? Isn't it relevant that roughly 50 percent of those armaments are sold or supplied by the United States and another 25 percent by our European allies? Should not a debate about U.S. policy in the area include a serious examination of one of the major tools of U.S. diplomacy in the Middle East, the sale of arms? Is it not relevant that U.S. foreign aid (much of it military aid) to Egypt, a country of 45 million people with a truly astonishing rate of population increase, is roughly equal to that provided Israel, a country of 4½ million people? Come the revolution in Egypt, how will people feel about the U.S.?

Which brings us back to those "moderate Arabs." The Arab world is a cauldron of political and religious extremism largely because the regimes courted, patronized, and armed by the super-

Steve Sack. Reprinted by permission of the Minneapolis Star and Tribune.

powers are unrepresentative and often oppressive and, precisely because they are so beholden to outside powers, are considered illegitimate by their own constituents. Herein lies the power of Khomeini's "radical Islam" and its threat to the "moderate Arabs." The Iranian revolution, whatever its faults, and they are legion, was a genuine indigenous revolution that had as its result the dethroning of an unpopular monarch and, more importantly, the expulsion of a superpower, without that superpower's replacement by another superpower. What many Middle Easterners saw as a deadly reciprocity—the exchange of oil for arms and superpower political control—was broken. The Iranian revolution, or, to be more precise, the Islamic revolution in Iran, pursued a course that was "neither East nor West," and such a course has growing appeal in a Middle East weary of superpower manipulation.

While it is true that the precise content of the Islamic alternative has yet to be determined—witness the extraordinary ferment in Iran—the symbolism of the Moses-Khomeini figure overthrowing the Pharaoh-shah carries great power. Nor are people fooled by the superficial "Islamization" proposed by leaders like Pakistan's Zia al Haqq or Sudan's Numeiri. The imposition of "Islamic punishment" for crimes, however popular for some benighted zealots, is no replacement for political and cultural independence.

Islam, once regarded as a conservative force reinforcing an unjust status quo, has become a revolutionary movement, and its legitimacy is largely determined by its revolutionary content.

Band-Aid Solutions

We heard nothing of this, of course, in our [1984] presidential campaign. Rather than deal with underlying issues, the candidates focused on security provisions and "international terrorism." And yet the prospects of world peace are much more likely to be affected by developments in Israel, Jordan, Syria, Lebanon, Iraq, Iran, and Egypt than they are by nuclear arms negotiations in Geneva. . . .

Middle Easterners bear a special curse. They live in an area regarded by the superpowers as critical. That the superpowers prefer to see the area as one in which they can seek and gain advantage through political manipulation and the supply of arms, rather than as an area in which the peace of the world is at stake, may be the final tragic irony of our times.

"[The Reagan administration] should press ahead with its efforts to develop a stable, long-term relationship with . . . Iran."

The US Should Have Diplomatic Relations with Iran

Robin Wright

Since the US-supported Shah of Iran was overthrown in 1979, US relations with revolutionary Iran have been tense. In November 1986 it was revealed that the Reagan administration had been selling arms to Iran in exchange for Iran's pressure on pro-Iranian militants holding American hostages in Lebanon. Robin Wright argues in the following viewpoint that the US should have a continued relationship with Iran, but it should not sell arms. The US can coexist with Islamic Iran, she argues, and relations with Iran will benefit the US. Wright has been a foreign correspondent for several news organizations and wrote *Sacred Rage: The Wrath of Militant Islam.*

As you read, consider the following questions:

1. What signs does the author point to that indicate Iran wants to end its isolation?
2. What did Iranians revolt against in 1979, according to Wright?
3. What are the appealing aspects of Islam, described by Wright, that have led to its current revival?

Robin Wright, "Our Overture to Iran Was a Misstep in the Right Direction," *The Washington Post National Weekly Edition,* January 13, 1987. Reprinted with the author's permission.

The Reagan administration should finish what it started with Iran. Specifically, it should press ahead with its efforts to develop a stable, long-term relationship with an Iran that is entering a new, post-revolutionary political phase.

The core of our new relationship with the Islamic republic shouldn't be arms sales, much less trading arms for hostages. That part of the Reagan policy was ill-planned and almost bound to fail.

A model for what the United States should be doing comes, ironically, from the Soviet Union. Last month, a Soviet delegation traveled to Tehran, ending a six-year suspension of economic cooperation, to sign a wide-ranging protocol on technological and industrial trade that Moscow heralded as "a prelude to strengthening relations."

Ending Isolation

Iran has been trying to end its isolation gradually since at least August 1984, when Iranian Foreign Minister Ali Akbar Velayati stood up before parliament and proclaimed, "The world is determined on the diplomatic scene. If we are not present, it will be determined without us."

That stunning statement from the isolationist and arrogant theocracy—whose foreign policy was reflected in the rhetorical catch-all "Neither East nor West"—symbolized a turning point in Iran's revolution: Because of a combination of convictions and circumstances, the Islamic republic was gradually preparing to open its doors again.

The next step for the Reagan administration, despite the fiasco over the Iran-contra affair, is to conclude quickly the talks at The Hague on the final financial claims of the 1981 Algiers accord that led to the freedom of 52 American hostages. Closing the book on that tragic episode, which has colored all rational U.S. thinking on Iran for six years, should now provide a symbolic new beginning for the Reagan administration.

Tehran's door still appears to be open. Five times since the "arms-for-hostages" scandal broke on Nov. 3, [1986,] Ali Akbar Hashemi Rafsanjani, the parliamentary speaker and the second most powerful man in Iran, has repeated an offer to intercede with the American hostages' captors if the U.S. releases $506 million left over from the Algiers accord and the weaponry paid for but not delivered during the shah's regime.

"If the Americans show good faith towards our revolution, it is possible that people in Lebanon who sympathize with our revolution will show good faith towards the Americans," Rafsanjani said, indicating a bit more flexibility than Iran's public posturing might suggest.

A "good faith" U.S. policy needs to be divided into two stages: First, develop a package of economic, political and social incentives to encourage detente with Iran. And second, initiate a broader effort to defuse the tension between the West and militant Islam, of which Tehran's theocracy is the most vibrant and visible symbol, but which is increasingly affecting Moslem communities far beyond the Middle East.

The single common denominator in Iran's frenzied diplomacy—which includes high-level talks with the Soviet Union, France, Britain, Pakistan and six African countries—is economics. Strapped as never before because of sagging oil prices and the draining costs of the Gulf war, only a fraction of which involve weapons purchases, the theocracy needs more foreign business and more foreign aid. And necessity breeds compromise.

The Islamic Revival

Islam represents the resurgence of the spiritual among hundreds of millions of people, who are finding in it a faith to guide their daily lives. . . . Devout observance endows the religious Moslem with a sense of identity, of dignity, and with a code which governs his life in the family, in his work and in society.

When the U.S. government adjusts its policies to the reality of this immense Islamic revival, Americans will find a welcome once again among the hundreds of millions of these faithful, who will look on them as friends.

Said Rajai Khorassani, interview in *The Spotlight*, December 24, 1984.

Moscow won over the historically-wary Iranians with a deal that involves everything from steel mills and gas purchases to fisheries and home construction. On many items Tehran would actually prefer to deal with the West because, as one Iran-born U.S. analyst explained, Iranians "unabashedly prefer the superior technology of the West to that of the East." Indeed, by 1985, economic and commercial ties between Iran and Western Europe had almost returned to prerevolutionary levels.

Technology Transfer

Instead of dealing in arms, the United States can offer to deal in equally important but nonlethal material: reconstruction supplies particularly for the devastated western provinces and homeless refugees, rehabilitation facilities for hundreds of thousands of wounded, and oil equipment for oft-targeted rigs, refineries and export centers.

Long-term, a technology transfer to boost Iran's flagging industry and limited social services makes sense for both Iran and America.

Since the revolution, . . . the mullahs have learned the painful realities of ruling the first purely Shi'ite theocracy since Islam was revealed to the prophet Mohammed. They need modern agriculture and hospital equipment, among many things, to feed and care for 45 million Iranians.

Modernization, not Westernization

Many western diplomats and reporters have erroneously claimed that the ayatollah's revolution seeks to take Iran back to the seventh century. The theocracy does want to restore the purity of original religious values—but in a 20th-century context. The 1979 revolution was not against modernization, but rather the westernization that had become synonymous with development.

This type of aid also serves a political purpose by demonstrating a sincere U.S. interest in Iran's future—and the bona fides the Iranians reportedly demanded in early exchanges that eventually led to arms sales. Washington must temper its approach, however, with a hands-off attitude, so as not to appear to be either too eager or too domineering. . . .

Politically, the United States needs quickly to sort out the contradictions in its policy on the six-year Iraq-Iran war. Washington should stop providing, directly or indirectly, military intelligence to Iraq, a story that became known only recently in the United States but about which Tehran has long been aware.

Rapprochement with Iran doesn't mean severing relations with Bagdad, which were restored in 1984 after a 17-year break. The United States has ties with many rivals, including Israel and Syria, which allowed Secretary of State Henry Kissinger to mediate a disengagement after the 1973 war.

Ready for Better Relations

There are abundant signs that Tehran is ready for closer relations with the United States. Indeed, one of the most striking aspects of the recent Iran flap is that rather than running for cover, the Iranian leadership—reportedly including Ayatollah Khomeini—appears to have blessed the secret dealings with the Great Satan.

The October arrest of Mehdi Hashemi, allegedly one of the chief architects of Iran's extremist plots, and dozens of his accomplices is one indication that Tehran may be trying to clean up its image as part of a larger effort to re-enter the world community. And with each gain through diplomatic channels, the theocracy may in turn feel less dependent on violence or subversion to achieve its aims. . . .

The Reagan administration can make short-term gains in rebuilding an economic and political relationship with Iran. But it will not be able to construct the foundation for a lasting policy without acting simultaneously on the broader challenge of establishing a balanced relationship with the 70 nation ''house of Islam.''

Coming to grips with militant Islam is difficult for a nation that is constitutionally secular, such as ours. Indeed, because our own values are so different, we tend to see Islam as alien to the western mind—far more than any other monotheistic or eastern faith.

We need to view Islam with greater understanding and tolerance. It is not simply a religion of zealots out to kidnap, hijack or terrorize American citizens and facilities. It is a religious polity, the only major monotheistic faith that offers a code of political conduct and a complete set of human laws. And the energy that it has ignited among Moslems—not only in Iran, but in Lebanon, Egypt and elsewhere—is in many ways constructive.

Moslems have returned to their faith after disillusioning experiences with foreign ideologies of both East and West. Since most Islamic states became independent after World War II, material life in only a few oil-rich nations has improved and spiritual life has been sterilized.

A Natural and Predictable Revival

No other religious revival of the late 20th century was as natural or predictable as the Islamic resurgence. Among its many goals are finding a way of life that restores dignity and independence, a political system that focuses on indigenous goals rather than imposed foreign priorities and an economic structure that redistributes wealth more equitably.

Islam also has capitalist traditions dating from Mohammed's stint as a caravan trader. Moscow's preemptory deal with Tehran is actually ironic, for communism is anathema because it is atheistic. The West at least has a strong religious tradition.

As Iran's revolution settles down, militant Islam is also less a force to be feared; coexistence is increasingly possible. But time is running out. Cementing the first phases of rapprochement is vital to help prevent the turmoil between Iran's religious and political rivals that has long been predicted for the era after Khomeini's passage.

"*Wisdom . . . would clearly dictate a policy of total non-negotiation with Iran.*"

The US Should Not Have Diplomatic Relations with Iran

Georgie Anne Geyer

When the Iran arms sales scandal broke in November 1986, many Americans bitterly remembered the 444 days that Iran held 52 Americans hostage in the US embassy in Teheran from 1979 to 1981. In the following viewpoint syndicated columnist Georgie Anne Geyer writes that the US should have no relations with an Iran that is hostile to the West. There is a fundamental cultural difference between the two nations, she argues. Until the US understands Iranian attitudes, Geyer believes, Iran will be able to manipulate the US at will, as it has successfully done in the past.

As you read, consider the following questions:

1. What does Geyer describe as the cultural symbol of the US and the cultural symbol of Iran?
2. Why are charismatic leaders uninterested in dialogue with the US, according to the author?
3. Why does the author believe the Iranians are able to manipulate the US?

The *New York Times's* front page headline [February 2, 1987] . . . about the two newest American hostages unwittingly revealed the incredible manner in which the cynical and sadistic Persia of the Ayatollah Khomeini still needs on this world stage a "reasonable" American willing to deal.

"U.S. Journalist Is Held by Iran: Reason Unclear," the headline about the "detainment" of respected *Wall Street Journal* correspondent Gerald F. Seib read. And next to it was an equally telling headline about Terry Waite, the hostage negotiator, which read: "Mystery in Beirut deepens on status of Anglican envoy."

The operative words to watch here are "reason" and "mystery," for they reveal the pathetic extent to which we still insist upon believing, even after all we've gone through, that there are reasons and that there is mystery about what is going on.

A Clash of Cultures

Our great weakness in dealing with the Iranians is that we persist in thinking that, if only we do indeed persist, we will find a way to have a dialogue with these folks, to come to an agreement and to find "the reason" to solve the problem. Of course, as in American union negotiating, that will lead on all sides to a happy "compromise," another key American code word.

My fear is that we actually will continue to engage in round after round of negotiations that will lead us only further into the ever-darkening shadows of the Khomeini-type bazaar. The symbol of America is the open and flowing superhighway, aiming ever at the freeing horizon; the symbol of the Persias of the world is the maze.

But is there not still some reason for the Iranians' and their Lebanese Shi'ite cousins' compulsive hostage-taking? Of course, but it is not at all the reason we seek, which is something specific that they want or feel they have been cheated of.

Knowing How To Manipulate

When the Iranians and the Shi'ites in general see that they can tie us up politically and militarily, they cynically take still more American and Western hostages to weaken us in power terms. They know our cultural propensities, if we do not know theirs.

They know we will do almost anything for individual citizens; they know that gives them ultimate power over us, and so they just keep taking hostages for no "reason," and we keeping looking for moderates and third forces in countries that have never known moderation.

There are related misunderstandings about the charismatic leaders of the world—and their true desires. As Mark Falcoff of the Amerian Enterprise Institute, a scholar on Latin America, has pointed out, charismatic leaders such as Fidel Castro do not seek

Bill Schorr. © 1986, Los Angeles Times Syndicate. Reprinted with permission.

compromise or dialogue in order to work things out; instead, they seek the ultimate and infinite "other" satisfactions of personal grandiosity in the world.

A few canny American diplomats do understand this. U.N. Ambassador Vernon Walters, after returning from meeting with Mr. Castro in 1982, told me wisely: "We don't have anything he wants. If he made peace with us, he'd be like the president of the Dominican Republic."

Ongoing Ignorance

So what worries me most in this whole sorry business with arms, hostages, and Iran is really the abysmal lack of even the most basic understanding of the Iranians. And, incredibly, the ignorance is ongoing.

Even after all these revelations, we are still being drawn in, with this new hostage-taking unquestionably being encouraged by exactly those arms deliveries that were supposed to free those other hostages (who are still imprisoned, in case anybody hadn't noticed).

The greatest lesson of this whole amateur-night performance is not even the criminality or the lying; the greatest embarrassment is the ignorance displayed for all the world to see—still being displayed.

What we need desperately if we are not to continue being "taken" in the world is the kind of sophisticated cultural understanding that anthropologists Ruth Benedict and Margaret Mead brought to American occupation policy toward Japan after World War II. It was their sophisticated wisdom that led directly to the great successes there, in great part through Ruth Benedict's book, *Chrysanthemum and the Sword.*

If their wisdom were to be applied today to Iran, it would clearly dictate a policy of total non-negotiation with Iran, a closing down of all relations with Iran, and a policy that would do everything possible to defeat it definitively in the Iraq-Iran war, which is the only way it will ever give up its viciously anti-Western hostage policy.

Vulnerable to Intrigue

The wily Parliament "speaker," Hojatoleslam Hashemi Rafsanjani, said something right after "Irangate" broke that has been largely missed but which is amazingly insightful. The Americans, he said, are "vulnerable to intrigue," and he invited other countries to trap us in this vulnerability. He was oh, so right.

And we will always be vulnerable—to intrigue and to every other humiliation and horror—if the other side continues to know more about us that we in our complacent ignorance know about them.

Recognizing Deceptive Arguments

People who feel strongly about an issue use many techniques to persuade others to agree with them. Some of these techniques appeal to the intellect, some to the emotions. Many of them distract the reader from the real issues.

Most appeals can either advance an argument in an honest, reasonable way or they can deceive and distract readers from important issues that weaken the author's argument. It is helpful for critical thinkers to recognize these tactics in order to rationally evaluate an author's ideas. Here are a few common ones:

a. *deductive reasoning*—claiming that since a and b are true, c is also true, although there may not be a connection between a and c

b. *patriotic appeal*—using national pride to sway the reader into favoring a position which flatters one's own culture

c. *scapegoating*—blaming complex problems on one faction involved in a dispute rather than exploring the dispute

d. *scare tactic*—the threat that if you don't do this or believe this something terrible will happen

e. *slanter*—trying to persuade through inflammatory and exaggerated language instead of through reason

The following activity will allow you to sharpen your skills in recognizing deceptive arguments. The statements are derived from the viewpoints in this chapter. *Beside each one, mark the letter of the type of deceptive appeal being used. More than one type of tactic may be applicable. If you believe the statement is not any of the listed appeals, write N.*

1. Despite three years of negotiations, no agreement was reached on Palestinian autonomy because of Israel's narrow, inflexible negotiating position.

2. The Middle East is the most dangerous region in the world. The failure of the US to launch a peace initiative could mean nuclear Armageddon.

3. Tehran would actually prefer to deal with the West because Iranians unabashedly prefer the superior technology of the West to that of Eastern bloc nations.

4. The US should negotiate with Iran. If Iran's diplomacy is successful in advancing the theocracy's national interests, Iran is less likely to use violence and subversion.

5. The conflict now puts Israel on the offensive against the Palestinians who have been stripped of even the right to self-defense.

6. The symbol of America is the open and flowing superhighway, aiming ever at the freeing horizon. The symbol of the Persias of the world is the stifling maze.

7. The Arab world is a cauldron of political and religious extremism largely because the US and the Soviets arm and support oppressive regimes that do not represent their people.

8. A nation so lacking in self-confidence that it needs international support for the belief that its own citizens should not be kidnapped and/or murdered abroad is going to have many of its citizens kidnapped and murdered abroad.

9. US foreign aid to Egypt, a poor nation of 45 million people, is equal to that of its aid to Israel, a nation of 4½ million people. Come the revolution, the Egyptian people will remember US stinginess.

10. The West imposed its idea of "good" on Iranians. Iran forcefully rejected what we define as "good" because for them it was harmful and violated their values.

11. The greatest lesson of this amateur night performance of selling arms to Iran is not the lying or the criminality. The embarrassment is the appalling ignorance displayed for all the world to see.

Periodical Bibliography

The following articles have been selected to supplement the diverse views expressed in this chapter.

Shaul Bakhash — "Iran and the Americans," *The New York Review of Books*, January 15, 1987.

Abolhassan Bani-Sadr — "U.S. Policy: Views of a Victim," *The Nation*, March 22, 1986.

Dale L. Bishop — "Two 'Nations of Hostages,'" *Christianity and Crisis*, March 16, 1987.

Brian Duffy — "Bloody Beirut—Trading in Lives," *U.S. News & World Report*, February 9, 1987.

Robert I. Friedman — "Selling Israel to America," *Mother Jones*, February/March 1987.

Ali Ghandour — "The Middle East in the Year 2000," *Vital Speeches of the Day*, May 15, 1987.

Richard N. Haass — "Paying Less Attention to the Middle East," *Commentary*, August 1986.

Jeane Kirkpatrick — "Wrong Message to the Terrorists?" *Conservative Chronicle*, February 18, 1987. Available from Hampton Publishing, 9 2nd St. NW, Hampton, IA 50441.

Paul N. McCloskey Jr. — "Harsh Truths, Harsher Realities," *The Washington Report on Middle East Affairs*, September 8, 1986. Available from American Educational Trust, PO Box 53062, Washington, DC 20009.

Walter A. McDougall — "A Short History of an Epic Blunder," *Los Angeles Times*, January 4, 1987.

Barry Rubin — "My Friend Satan," *The New Republic*, December 15, 1986.

Harold H. Saunders — "Arabs and Israelis: A Political Strategy," *Foreign Affairs*, Winter 1985/86.

George Shultz — "U.S. Interests in the Persian Gulf," *Department of State Bulletin*, March 1987.

Ronald Steel — "Hostage to Innocence," *The New Republic*, February 23, 1987.

Are Palestinian Rights Being Ignored?

Chapter Preface

The question of whether Palestinians are currently being persecuted and denied their rights arises, ironically, from a settlement originally meant to rectify grave injustices committed against another persecuted group, the Jews. After six million Jews were killed in Nazi concentration camps during World War II, international concern focused on the creation of a homeland for the survivors. The region called Palestine seemed a natural choice because Jews had historic ties to the land and because Zionist Jews had been immigrating to Palestine since the 1880s. The issue came before the newly created United Nations (UN) in 1947 and the state of Israel was proclaimed in 1948. This solution, however, created a new problem: there was a large population of Palestinian Arabs in Palestine. More than a half million of them were displaced at the end of a civil war between Arabs and Jews. Since then, there has been constant conflict, often bloody, between Israel and the Palestinian Arabs who feel they have been driven from their land.

In 1967, a war broke out between Israel and its Arab neighbors that dramatically changed the Palestinian issue. In six days, Israel defeated the Egyptian, Syrian, and Jordanian armies and took territory three times its own size from all three countries (see map on page 140). It gained the Sinai Peninsula and Gaza Strip from Egypt, the West Bank from Jordan, and the Golan Heights from Syria. (Israel later gave the Sinai Peninsula back to Egypt.) It also, consequently, acquired an even larger Palestinian population. After twenty years, Palestinians continue to struggle against Israeli rule over these areas. Yet for many Jews, these territories and Jerusalem in particular now seem an integral part of Israel.

The range of opinion among individual Palestinians and Jews is diverse. Some Palestinians argue that they can live in peace with Israel if they are given a homeland. Others argue that their homeland is Israel itself and that the state of Israel is an illegitimate entity which must be destroyed. Some Jews contend that the rights of Palestinians should be respected—either that they should have more rights in Israel or that they should be given their own homeland. But there is also a Jewish movement in Israel that believes the Palestinians threaten the state of Israel. To them, Israel must be a Jewish state, not a state with non-Jewish Palestinians in it. This chapter gives vent to these varying opinions.

"The 'purely Jewish State' and the exclusiveness of Zionism negate the Palestinians, deny their rights and their existence."

Palestinians Have a Right to a Homeland in Israel

Abdallah Frangi

Civil war broke out between Jews and Palestinians after Israel was created in May 1948. Many Palestinians argue that Israel, since its creation, has continually encroached upon Palestinian land. Abdallah Frangi, the author of the following viewpoint, traces Israeli settlement policies after the 1948 war and the 1967 war. By taking Arab land, he argues, Israelis try to deny the existence of the Palestinian people. Frangi is a member of the Al-Fatah Revolutionary Council and the PLO representative of the Arab League office in Bonn, West Germany.

As you read, consider the following questions:

1. Whom does Frangi call "the generation of resistance"?
2. How do the Israelis take Palestinian land, according to the author?
3. Why does the author disagree with the argument that the Israelis have raised the Palestinian standard of living?

The PLO and Palestine by Abdallah Frangi (translated by Paul Knight), published in 1983 by Zed Books Ltd., London and New Jersey.

The founding of Israel had two direct consequences: it led to the first war between Israel and the Arab states and it created the problem of 900,000 Palestinian refugees. . . .

After 15 May 1948, the Israeli army attacked countless defenceless Arab villages, blew up houses and entire villages and indiscriminately killed men, women and children. The survivors were driven out of the villages. News of these appalling massacres spread like wildfire and those who did not believe the reports were likely to become the next victims.

Psychological War

The Israelis' psychological warfare was based on shock tactics. Israeli radio was constantly calling on the Palestinians to flee 'to avoid a bloodbath.' Israeli army vehicles with loudspeakers drove through the streets of towns and villages pointing out escape routes. This happened, for example, at 5:15 on 15 May 1948 in Jerusalem and on 21 April just before the attack on Haifa. But rumours and radio reports were not the only reasons for panic and headlong flight. The Israeli army deliberately and systematically destroyed villages and drove out their inhabitants. . . .

From 1948 to 1956, Israel not only attacked towns and villages directly under its control, but also launched military attacks on neighbouring areas. Israel was condemned for such actions by the United Nations Security Council in 1951, 1953, 1955 and 1956.

One of the attacks for which Israel was condemned was that on the village of Qibya on the West Bank on 14 and 15 October 1953. Half a battalion of Israeli soldiers blew up 41 houses and a school and cold-bloodedly murdered 42 men, women and children. Even before the founding of Israel, the Israelis had adopted the tactic of bombing crowds of refugees to hasten their departure. In August 1954 the Israelis attacked the UNRWA [United Nation Relief and Works Agency] refugee camp at Bureij in the Gaza strip, killing 20 and injuring 62 people.

Yitzhak Rabin, former Chief of Staff and later Prime Minister of Israel, summed up this policy with brutal clarity: 'By razing villages to the ground and driving out the inhabitants we will ensure that there are no villages left for the Arabs to return to.'

A Helpless Population

These tactics nipped resistance in the bud and reduced the Palestinian population to helplessness. . . .

Right up to the present day, world opinion has taken little or no note of the atrocities Israel committed at that time. It would not and could not believe that the Jews, who had the whole-hearted sympathy of the entire world after their dreadful experiences under Nazism, could perpetrate such cruelties on

137

another people. The Israelis themselves sowed the seeds of armed resistance in the hearts of the Palestinians at this time. Many acts by the Palestinians which world opinion would later condemn as terrorism can be better understood in the light of this historical background.

> We came to this land which was inhabited by Arabs and established a Hebrew, i.e. a Jewish State . . . Jewish villages were built where Arab villages had once stood. You do not even know the names of these villages and I do not blame you, because the geography books with their names no longer exist—and the villages no longer exist.

The Palestinians had seen their villages destroyed, they had been forced to flee with nothing but what they could carry. Often enough, this meant only their children. Yet they took with them something else as a token of their determination to return: the keys to the doors of their houses. These keys can still be seen hanging above the doors of small houses in refugee camps in Jordan, Syria and Lebanon, bearing silent but eloquent witness to the expulsion from and longing for Palestine.

Living with Dignity

These five million Palestinians have the right to live as human beings. We are not asking for the moon. We want to live in peace, in our land, in our state, as free people and with dignity.

Yasir Arafat, *Journal of Palestine Studies*, Summer 1986.

From spring 1948 to spring 1949, streams of refugees left the country, with the Israeli army behind them and an uncertain future before them. Families would often walk on at night and hide from Israeli attacks by day. Children wept because they were hungry, their fathers remained silent and despondent, their mothers were too helpless and weak, too numbed by horror to comfort their children. They slept under trees and behind bushes till they came to a country which provided refuge against this first persecution. The tents they were given provided scant protection against the wind, the rain and the cold of winter. Their starvation rations did nothing to dispel their inner despair and deep sense of humiliation. They were a nation in exile. 900,000 individuals shared this collective fate—forgotten by the world, humiliated, insulted, despairing, silent. . . .

The violent expulsion and uprooting of the Palestinian people by the new State of Israel, the theft of their homes and the refusal to allow them to return—all this contained the seeds of a new confrontation. A new generation was growing up in the camps, the generation of resistance.

Year after year, the Palestinians in the camps went on hoping to return to their homes. But the hopes they had pinned on UN resolutions proved vain. Israel humiliated the United Nations, and the world made the Palestinians pay for its humiliation.

The Refugees' Progress

In the loneliness and obscurity of huts and tents, the Palestinians learned new laws of survival. They learned to rely on themselves and take their fate into their own hands. The queues for UNRWA rations disappeared. The Palestinians sought work throughout the world. They knew that the only chance was education. They wanted their children to be able to cope better with the future, to study and not to have to rely on others. Groups were formed in the camps and courses were started, even though the teachers themselves often had no school-leaving certificates or training. Small schools were set up. Mosques and churches were soon crammed with students and pupils studying hard, even at night, by the light of oil lamps. Illiteracy soon disappeared.

But no real change in their situation could be expected in the near future. The radio report for which they had waited so long in their tents and huts, telling them that they could return to their homes, did not come. But they were no longer resigned and hopeless.

The Palestinians had begun to take their fate into their own hands. A new chapter now began: resistance. . . .

> If one wishes to colonize a country in which people are already living, one has to establish a garrison in this country or else find a benefactor to establish this garrison for you. Zionism is a pioneer adventure and it therefore stands or falls with the question of armed force.

Zeev Jabotinsky, the great teacher of Israeli Prime Minister Menachem Begin, wrote these words in 1925. He was to be proved right. Great Britain provided the garrison until the founding of the Jewish State in 1948; and thereafter Israel ran its own garrison with support from the United States.

Occupation and "Liberation"

The State of Israel was created by force of arms in 1948. And in the war of June 1967, the West Bank, Gaza, the Golan Heights and Sinai were conquered and occupied by force of arms.

The Israeli occupying forces have ruled the West Bank and Gaza for 16 years. In the first years after 1967, Israel regarded itself as an occupying force, dubbing itself 'the most liberal occupying force in the world'. This view has now changed. Today the official Israeli terms for the West Bank are the biblical names of 'Judaea and Samaria'. The occupying force has now declared itself the 'liberator' of these areas.

The consequence of this liberation is that Israel has declared its intention never to leave the West Bank and Gaza.

This is today the official strategy of the Israeli government and the settlement department of the World Zionist Organization. For the past 16 years, Israel has massively increased its presence in the occupied areas, taking control of every sector. Politically, the areas are under military rule, and the Israelis have brought the industrial, cultural and educational systems completely into line with the requirements of the Israeli market, and of Israeli settlement and land acquisition policies.

The key feature of Israeli strategy has remained unchanged since the beginning of Zionist immigration to Palestine: land acquisi-

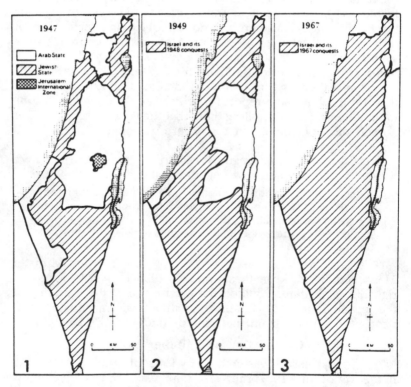

The takeover of Arab Palestine:
1. The U.N. Partition Plan of 1947.
2. Israel after the 1948 War.
3. Israel after the Six-Day War of 1967.

Alan Hart, *Arafat: Terrorist or Peacemaker?* London: Sidwick & Jackson Publishers, 1984. Reprinted with permission.

tion. Official propaganda cites military and strategic reasons for the Israeli occupation or else invokes, as it did before 1948, the familiar magic word 'security'. In reality, the Israeli goal is the gradual expulsion of the inhabitants and appropriation of the conquered lands. The trusted methods of the past are once again proving their worth. . . .

New Settlements

Even before the end of 1967, the Labour government started building new Israeli settlements in the occupied territories—mainly in strategically important areas. Their main purpose was to ensure a military and physical Israeli presence in those areas, which in the long run were to become part of 'Eretz Israel'. . . .

Israeli settlement policy is both means and end in this process of displacement. The building of new settlements robs the Palestinians of their land and brings Israel nearer to its goal of gradually replacing the native population with its own settlers. The method of land acquisition in the areas conquered in 1967 differed little from that of 1948: the use of armed force.

Today, 40% of the West Bank and Gaza has been appropriated and colonized by Israeli settlers or brought under Israeli army control. 85% of the land appropriated or confiscated in the occupied areas belongs to Palestinian farmers, for whom the loss of land means the loss of their livelihood.

The most common methods of appropriating Palestinian land is that of 'legal' dispossession, which operates as follows: the military commander of the area in question declares it a 'prohibited zone', for 'security reasons.' This procedure accords with Article 125 of the British mandatory government's emergency decrees of 1945. In issuing these decrees, the British aimed to limit freedom of movement in order to prevent conflicts and confrontations in 'restive areas.' Israel has been applying this decree since 1967 to prevent Palestinian farmers from having access to their land. After three years, the military administration found it convenient to apply a Jordanian law under which land left uncultivated for three years running had to be registered as state land. This enables the Israeli government to claim that it is merely using state land for the establishment of settlements. However, according to the Hague War Convention on Land, state land cannot become the property of an occupying power, whether the appearance of legality is kept up or not.

Another frequent pretext is that land has to be confiscated for military purposes (bases, barracks, etc.). The army then builds houses and barracks in the area; and after two or three years it leaves to make way for settlers.

Another method of land acquisition that seems tailor-made for Israeli requirements is that laid down in the law on 'absentees'.

141

According to this law, all land and buildings whose owners left before, during or after the June war are regarded as 'abandoned property', even if the owner was only away on a business trip. This law has been extended since 1978 to apply to Palestinians living abroad. As Israel refuses to allow Palestinians abroad or Palestinian refugees to return, Israel has been able to take a further 500,000 *dunam* of land under its 'trusteeship', and this is also used for Jewish settlements. A Jewish settler gives the following account:

> Here in the Jordan valley we are cultivating a thousand *dunam* of rich, fertile farmland. This is—let's be honest about it—Arab land . . . , the land of 'absentees', people from Nablus and Tubas who fled to Jordan during the six-day war. These people cannot come back to Judaea and Samaria because the troops at the bridges have lists of names. The people in charge at the bridges are strict, and if you are an absentee landowner they just won't let you in . . . Some of the absentees' land wasn't suitable for settlement, either it was too stony or too remote . . . so we exchanged it for the land of Arabs still living here. Do you think they wanted to move out? We put, as you might say, pressure on them—we, the government, the military administration, the army.

Obstacle to Zionism

To put it bluntly, the Palestinians witnessed the hijacking of a whole country—their own—and found themselves expected to acquiesce and approve. They did not. No one should have expected them to do so; indeed there was no good reason why they should submit to the giving away of their country. . . .

The Zionists did not want to live or co-exist with the indigenous population of Palestine, the Arabs. The Palestine Arabs had to go, since the Zionists could not expect Jewish immigration on a scale that would make them a majority in the land (their prerequisite for nationhood) if they remained. The Arab inhabitants, as they continued to live and work on the land of their forefathers, became an obstacle that had to be removed.

Hassan bin Talal, *Search for Peace*, 1984.

Another not infrequent method of Israeli settlement and occupation is the blowing up of Palestinian houses and villages. Since the foundation of the Israeli State on Palestinian territory, 478 villages have been completely destroyed. In the 16 years of Israeli occupation of the West Bank, more than 20,000 houses have been blown up—some as a collective punishment of Palestinian families.

Another common tactic is to demolish houses because of extensions for which no planning permission was granted. Thus the

Palestinians lose not only their land, but the roof over their heads.

It must be stressed that these are not 'regrettable incidents' or isolated acts of violence by the occupying forces. In *Mahanaim*, the official publication of the rabbinate to the Israeli armed forces, the strategy of expulsion is described as follows:

> We therefore have to carry out an orderly and humane policy of resettlement over a relatively long period—not abruptly. This should be done in accordance with the fertility of the Israeli population and its capacity to replace evacuees and thus ensure that the land is not left uninhabited . . . The Arabs who live in this country represent an essentially alien element in it and in its destiny and should be treated according to the rules by which foreigners were treated in ancient times; our wars with them were therefore inevitable.

This may have been largely theoretical in 1969. Today it is everyday practice in the occupied areas.

One of the direct methods of 'resettlement' is deportation. Since 1967, more than 2,000 people—mainly lawyers, teachers, doctors, town councillors and mayors—have been deported. One of the most effective methods of displacing Palestinians and depopulating the land is economic control over the occupied areas and political repression of Palestinians.

Israeli land acquisition deprives Palestinian farmers of their work and their livelihood, forcing them to emigrate or seek poorly-paid unskilled work in Israeli industry. . . .

Palestinians in the Israeli Economy

Israel has boasted for years that Palestinians under Israeli rule are far better off economically than they ever were before. And it is correct that the wage level of Palestinian 'commuters' has risen under occupation in a relatively short time, so that they can now afford refrigerators and televisions—imported from Israel of course. However, wage and price differences between Israel and the occupied territories have now practically disappeared—and with it the short-term material advantage.

Palestinians today have no prospect of any improvement in their material situation, which is still worse than that of the poorest sections of Israeli society.

There can no longer be any doubt that the Palestinian economy under Israeli occupation has been completely geared to Israeli requirements. The vast majority of goods are imported from Israel. The West Bank exports labour and produces only a limited range of agricultural goods, which are promptly bought up and exported by Israeli companies. The deformation and dependence of the West Bank and Gaza strip economies are the result of Israeli occupation. In the political context, the Israeli 'integration' of the Palestinian economy is an important step towards final annexation of the occupied territories. . . .

The 'purely Jewish State' and the exclusiveness of Zionism negate the Palestinians, deny their rights and their existence. Palestinian resistance in the occupied areas has confronted Israeli usurpation for the past 16 years. In these 16 years, the movement has been tried and tested—and has emerged all the stronger. It is now a broad popular movement. The Palestinians in the occupied areas are a political force which, despite repression, has successfully resisted collaboration and capitulation.

"The Arabs believe that by creating an Arab Palestinian identity . . . they will accomplish . . . the destruction of Israel."

Palestinians Do Not Have a Right to a Homeland in Israel

Joan Peters

The following viewpoint is an excerpt from the controversial book, *From Time Immemorial*, written by Joan Peters. Peters, a writer and former White House consultant on the Middle East, argues that many Palestinians who claim to have an historic right to land now occupied by Israel are themselves illegal settlers. They illegally immigrated to that land shortly before the state of Israel was created in 1948. Jews deserve the homeland of Israel, she argues, and Palestinians already have a homeland in the Arab state of Jordan.

As you read, consider the following questions:

1. How do Arab countries use the Palestinians to try to destroy Israel, according to Peters?
2. Why does the author believe that Palestinian Arabs have less of an historic right to Palestine than Jews do?
3. What does Peters mean by "turnspeak"? What examples of turnspeak does she cite?

The "Palestinian problem" is often asserted to be the "heart of the matter," which must be dealt with before any real Middle East peace or any solution can occur. Britain, for example, has never altered its policy. In 1980 the British Foreign Office proposed a "new" Middle East "line": the "Palestinian Question" must be settled before any peace can begin in the region. The British journalist Terence Prittie wrote:

> the media . . . contain many hard-hearted and fair-minded people . . . but [the new policy's] effects are undeniable. Just as water may eventually wear away stone, so Foreign Office arguments which are tirelessly expounded are wearing away doubts and scruples.

The British are still, wistfully, courting Arab "gratitude."

Palestinians Are Not the Issue

The "heart of the matter," however, is not the Arab refugees or the "Palestinian Arab refugees" or the "rights" of the "Palestinians"—or even Palestine. Were the Jewish-settled independent state on any area within reach of the Arab world—like the Christians in Lebanon, or the Kurds in Iraq—no matter how remote or how barren the location, there might well be another "problem." And very likely there would also be another group of *effendis* [the Arab upper class] to sell land to the Jews. There would be "landless" peasants anxious to better their lot who would migrate into the area of Jewish development. Perhaps they too would be goaded into claiming that the Jews displaced them from their "land since time immemorial." But the chances of the *dhimmi* [practicing] Jews gaining independence among Arabs in an Arab country, where Islam is the state religion, are not even arguable. Even in the Jews' own Holy Land it took two thousand years and millions of Jewish lives to accomplish the political rebirth of Israel.

The Arabs believe that by creating an Arab Palestinian identity, at the sacrifice of the well-being and the very lives of the "Arab refugees," they will accomplish politically and through "guerrilla warfare" what they failed to achieve in military combat: the destruction of Israel—the unacceptable independent *dhimmi* state. That is the "heart of the matter."

Arab Myths

All the myths surrounding the Arab "Palestinians" are based on the same premises: 1) the "Palestinian people" have had an identity with the land; 2) that identity has been present for "thousands of years"; 3) the alien Jews "returned after 2000 years" in 1948 to "displace" the "Palestinian Arabs" in the "new" Jewish state; 4) the Arabs were there first—it was Arab land; 5) the Jews "stole" the Arabs' land; 6) the Jewish terrorists forced the peaceable Arabs to flee from "Palestine"; 7) Palestine is Israel,

146

Israel and the occupied territories

From A STRANGER IN MY HOUSE: JEWS AND ARABS IN THE WEST BANK by Walter Reich. Copyright © 1984 by Walter Reich. Reprinted by permission of Henry Holt and Company, Inc.

and Israel constitutes all of Palestine—"In 1948 Palestine became Israel"; 8) only Jews immigrated into "Palestine," while Arabs were natives there for millennia; 9) there are no places for the "homeless" Palestinian "refugees" to go; 10) the Jews were living in equality and tranquility with the "Palestinian Arabs" before Israel became a state, just as Jews had lived traditionally in peace and harmony throughout the benevolent Arab world; 11) the Arab "Palestinians," like other Arabs, have "nothing against Jews—only Zionists."

Arab "Refugees"

Contrary to those Arab propaganda claims, 1) in the late nineteenth and early twentieth centuries, Arabs or Arabic-speaking migrants were wandering in search of subsistence all over the Middle East. The land of "Palestine" proper had been laid waste, causing peasants to flee. 2) Jews and "Zionism" never left the Holy Land, even after the Roman conquest in A.D. 70. 3) The traditional land of "Palestine" included areas both east and west of the Jordan River. 4) The Arabic-speaking "masses" in "Palestine'—what few there were—thought of themselves as "Ottomans or Turks," as Southern Syrians or as "Arab people'—but never as "Palestinians," even after *effendis* and the Mufti [ruler of Jerusalem] tried to incite "nationalism," and even after T.E. Lawrence had made herculean attempts to inject the Arabic-speaking residents of "Palestine" with nationalism. 5) Imbued with religious prejudice, the Muslims of Palestine erupted into anti-Jewish violence often, and at the call of the Muslim leaders, long before Israel. 6) Those anti-Jewish, apolitical acts were later, by the British, ascribed to "Nationalism." 7) The bulk of all "Arab" peasantry in the area—East-Palestinian, Syrian, Iraqi, Egyptian, and others—were rendered "landless" by feudal-like societal structures, natural disasters, extortionate taxation, and corrupt loan sharks. Yet the Jews were cynically charged with creating "landless" Arabs in "Palestine." The British gave state domain lands, allocated for the "Jewish National Home," to those "landless" Arabs who claimed they were being "displaced by Jews" in Western Palestine. 8) All the land outside the limited Jewish-settled area of Western Palestine was treated as "Arab" land: more than eighty percent—including even part of *Western* Palestine—was diverted to the Arabs. 9) The overwhelming bulk of Palestine called "Eastern Palestine," or "Transjordan," became the Arab independent state within Palestine, despite the fact that all "Palestine" had been designated as a "Jewish National Home." 10) The "homelands" to which Arab refugees moved in 1948 included lands that many Arab refugees had only recently left in order to gain the economic advantages of the small Jewish region within Palestine. Those "homelands" where many Arab refugees of 1948 originated included the greater part of "Palestine"—Jordan today—to which the Jews claimed historic rights: "Jordan" was no less a "Palestinian state" than was the Jewish-settled fraction named "Israel." 11) Those who deprived the Arab "refugees" of homes among families and within their own Arab nation are the Arab-Muslim leaders. 12) The Arab "refugees-émigrés," who by tradition had been migrating into the Jewish-settled areas, *were* accepted as citizens of Palestine-cum-Jordan, because Jordanians acknowledge that their country is "Palestinian soil." 13) All other adjacent Arab states *refused* to grant the dignity of citizenship to those whom they called their Arab brothers. The migrants had left their nearby Arab homelands to share the new prosperity in the Jewish-settled area of Western Palestine, that fraction of the original Jewish homeland retained by the Jews. . . .

The Arab Strategy

Why is the obvious fact that Jordan is a Palestinian Arab state not generally accepted? The main reason is that by such acceptance the Arabs will lose a major leverage for their main objective—the elimination of Israel. Since the efforts to accomplish this goal by force have failed, they must do it by other means and in stages. A most important step is to get the Israelis out of the West Bank, which will place the majority of the population of Israel within range of rockets and artillery. The best way to get world support for such a move is to promote the notion of a "Palestinian" nation, which is exactly what the Arab states have been doing.

E.B. Ayal, position paper from the Jordan Is Palestine Committee, New Hyde Park, New York.

Today's twelve- or twenty-year-old "Arab Palestinian people" were not yet born when the Arab exodus from Israel occurred. Most have no notion themselves of the prior history of in-migration and immigration to the Jewish enclaves of settlement within Western Palestine. They do, however, know that to verbalize out loud the thought that it was their Arab "brothers" who kept them in a suspended state of animation called "refugeehood" would bring ostracism and perhaps worse. The Arab Palestine "Liberation" Organization "eliminates traitors," as the PLO's United Nations "observer" Terzi declared in 1978.

The injustices done to the "Arab Palestinian refugees" have been perpetuated by the Arab world, which has also masked and denied the "Palestinian state" that exists. By fanning intolerance toward Jews as "infidels" into violence against Israel as "the enemy," the PLO, or "Palestinian revolutionaries," have taught the twelve-year-old Arab born in a refugee camp that his oppressor is Israel. He knows not about the Arab *effendi* or sheikh who may have stolen his grandfather's or his father's land, through graft or usury; he knows nothing of the thousands of his Arab brothers who had, in the years before 1948, been "landless" peasants, streaming into the newly reclaimed wastelands of the Jewish-settled areas from the very countries where some are still in camps; he has not learned that the Arab world's oil wealth has been used to keep his hatred directed against Israel, by keeping him and his family from the dignity of citizenship in the "brother" country where he is encamped. Moreover, he does not know what many Arabs have admitted: that the Arab world which has rejected its responsibility for his plight must eventually undertake it.

The violent opposition by PLO strongmen and the Arab world in general toward rehabilitation and resettlement of the Arab refugees has brought confusion, frustration, and a state of suspended animation to the lives of some younger Arab "refugees." While a number of the Arab refugees by now actually possess citizenship in countries such as Kuwait, some families have been absorbed in one or another of the Arab countries *except* for the formal identity of citizenship, which is still withheld; there are also others whose families belong to the hard-core nucleus of militant "revolutionaries." In that small fanatical group which has become the main source and the conduit for Arab propaganda, to assume any role other than the sacrificial one slotted for them by their leaders would be interpreted as "treachery" by his or her peers. . . .

Turnspeak

The "Palestinian Problem," no new phenomenon, is but the pan-Arab enmity by another name. The Arab refugees' manipulation at the cruel whim of leaders in the Arab world is traditional; in earlier days, too, Arabs were periodically whipped into fanatically anti-Jewish onslaughts. What is new is the sophisticated use of Middle-East turnspeak, twisted rhetoric artfully aimed at the hearts and minds of the West, originated by the Arabs, and rivaling the Soviets, who are veterans of "semantic infiltration" and the word war. Just as, in their lexicon, totalitarianism translates into "democracy," and degradation becomes "freedom," so has the flawed but democratic Israel been branded "Zionist imperialist" and "racist." So has the carving of Jordan out of the internationally Mandated "Jewish National Home" during the Mandatory period been transformed into the notion that "Israel is all of Palestine"—the "homeland" of all the Arab refugees. It is *1984*, where as George Orwell wrote, "War is peace; freedom is slavery; ignorance is strength."

According to *turnspeak*, those Arab migrants and immigrants who, in Sir John Hope Simpson's words, committed the "injustice" of "taking the places" of Jews in the "Jewish National Home" are today's "displaced" Arab Palestinian people, "excluded" from the Jewish-settled area of Western Palestine, their "homeland since time immemorial." The free world is targeted for deception by the twisted speech of Arab propaganda.

Arab Attack on Jews

From past history it is apparent that the Arab-Muslim world would not, without prodding and pressure, perhaps, from the rest of the world, accept an infidel or non-Muslim minority community as equals; as Arabs say, the land is forever Arab. Arab writers frankly recognize that the world, however cynical, would not take kindly to an abrupt or "quick" destruction of Israel. By promoting "Palestinian nationalism" through the publicized and orchestrated violence of "guerrilla attacks," as the Arab writer al-Ayubi wrote in the early 1970's that they should, the Arabs had *changed the perception* of reality *from the xenophobic and powerful Arab world pitted against the tiny Jewish state* into the image of *one tiny nation of Israel against an equally tiny nation of "Palestine."* Israel is portrayed, then, as *all* of "Palestine," the giant "aggressor." . . .

Little Wealth, Little History

The Arab refugees who fled Israel left little wealth and little history, since most of them had not come to "Palestine" until Jewish settlers opened economic opportunities in what had been a desolate country for centuries. But the Jews of Arab lands have a history going back thousands of years. When forced to flee, they left behind land, wealth, and a long history. They arrived in Israel, quite literally, only "with their shirts on their backs." They now make up 55% of the vibrant and productive population of Israel. What have the Arabs, the richest people in the world, done with "their" refugees in almost 40 years? They have kept them in misery, on the dole of the world, have taught their hopeless youth the "skills" of suicide missions and of slaughtering defenseless and unarmed men, women, and children.

Advertisement for Committee for Accuracy in Middle East Reporting in America, February 9, 1987.

In the name of humanitarianism, the Arab refugees have been bred to believe that the fraudulent history they learn by rote is true: their "dream" of "identity" can only materialize, they believe, at the cost of the destruction of a people. The young "Palestinian refugee" of twelve or thirteen or even twenty has no choice. All persons must dream, and the only dream that has been drilled into the Arab refugee child—in or out of the camps—is "to return to the Palestinian homeland." That they and their families may have little desire to "return" themselves, that a legitimate

151

Palestinian homeland in Jordan already exists, which has been open to them, or that many of them can claim origins and legitimate rights to citizenship in Syria, or Egypt, or Algeria, or wherever their families came from—none of these options for identity has even the slightest chance of gaining credence among them under present conditions of thought control. Merely to verbalize such an idea would bring rejection, if not violence. . . .

A Humanitarian Solution

One must care about the "Palestinian" peoples, whatever their heritage. They are Arabs and Jews and "others" who have been long abused in a world misled by its torturous misconceptions. Instead of permitting those Arab "refugees" who are outside of Jordanian Palestine to suffer the planned discrimination of adamant Arab governments in lands where many "refugees" have lived for a generation or more, the free world might begin a fair and realistic effort to solve the problem.

The possibility of solution is there. An Arab Palestinian state already exists in Jordan. The other Arab states can be encouraged to make room for those among the Arab refugees who have not yet been absorbed, and to give citizenship in their respective states of asylum to those outside Jordan. There is no bromide here for a facile solution, or one that would not be fraught with bitterness and antagonism. Before the India-Pakistan exchange of refugee populations was resolved, years of rancor and violence elapsed.

What must not continue, what cannot be allowed to continue, is the cynical scapegoating of the Jewish state and the Jewish refugees therein, or the sacrifice of the Arab refugees who are, in the name of "humanitarianism," being employed inhumanely as a war weapon against Israel by the Arab world. In the face of these major problems, too many politicians and persons of influence choose to shut their eyes to the facts. Too many refrain from critical analysis of propaganda in order to preserve their illusions about the price of oil. And far too many, the overwhelming bulk of us, had never been furnished with enough data to understand what the problem really was.

3

"The more the Israeli government tries to subdue Arabs, the more it sacrifices its own moral independence."

Ignoring Palestinian Rights Threatens Israeli Democracy

Bernard Avishai

A 1984 poll of teenagers in Israel uncovered opinions that shocked many Israelis. The poll found that young Jews were opposed to allowing Palestinians to exercise full democratic rights and that many of them would not want to live near or work with an Arab. In the following viewpoint Bernard Avishai argues that these attitudes are harmful to Israel's interests. Palestinians must be given equal rights if they are to be integrated into Israeli society and feel loyal to Israel. Avishai lived in Israel for three years. He currently teaches writing at the Massachusetts Institute of Technology (MIT).

As you read, consider the following questions:

1. According to the author, what factors contributed to an atmosphere that made Israel "a meaner place" to live?
2. What does Avishai believe Israel should do to more fully integrate Palestinians into Israeli society?
3. How do Palestinians view Israeli democracy, according to Avishai?

Before 1984, poll after poll disclosed that about 90 percent of Israeli youth called themselves democratic, and to be sure, the majority have been greatly influenced by the styles of the Western industrial democracies—Yale T-shirts, Sony ghetto blasters. The question remained, however, whether Israeli youth have had any profound understanding of what living in a democratic country entails; what are the arguments to justify democracy, what are the laws to ensure civility and tolerance? A poll in 1984 revealed that some 60 percent of Israeli youth would have curtailed the rights of Israeli Arabs and that 57 percent thought Arabs in the occupied territories who refused Israeli citizenship ought to be expelled. Not surprisingly, among those who expressed such stridently anti-democratic views, most favored annexing the West Bank over any territorial compromise. Insofar as the new Zionist program called for annexing the West Bank and Gaza, it alienated Israeli adolescents from the Palestinian community as a whole and deeply estranged them from nearly 18 percent of Israel's enfranchised population, who are themselves of Palestinian Arab origin. . . .

Racist Stirrings

A.B. Yehoshua has compared the West Bank to a tar baby; the more the Israeli government strives to subdue Arabs, the more it sacrifices its own moral independence. Most Israeli Jews have indeed become accustomed to living in what Meron Benvenisti, the former deputy mayor of Jerusalem, has called *Herrenvolk* democracy, with first-class citizenship for Jews and second-class citizenship for Arabs. If the former are pushed to an even more extreme situation—a violent rising in the West Bank, say, or a bloody stalemate with Syria—there is bound to be a collapse of faith in the slow, centrifugal workings of parliament. Would more wars not create a yearning for *achdut leumit*, the national solidarity and transcendent power which tolerance only obstructs? Since 1967, there has been polarization, a coarsening of political rhetoric, the stirrings of racism; one poll in *Ha'Aretz* during 1984 revealed that 32 percent of Israelis felt violence toward Arabs, even terrorism, was either "totally" justified or had "some justification." Over 60 percent of young Israelis believe Arabs should not be accorded full rights in the state. (The last student essay of "Peace Now" activist Emile Greensweig was an analysis of just this trend, about how political violence could subvert the spirit of Israeli democracy; he submitted it a few days before he was murdered by a grenade thrower during a demonstration against General Sharon.)

Significantly, the West Bank is ruled under British emergency regulations from 1946, which one former Israeli Justice Minister, Yaacov Shimshon Shapiro, has called Fascist; preventive detention is common. Amnesty International reported that, from January to June 1979 alone, some 1,500 youths were taken into custody. Tens of thousands more were interrogated or intimidated during the period of the general strike in the spring of 1982. Under Sharon there was no freedom of the press on the West Bank, no freedom of assembly, no freedom to organize political parties. Nearly every elected mayor was deposed by the military government. Instead of enjoying municipal government, the towns have been firmly controlled by IDF [Israeli Defense Forces] patrols. During strikes, shops have been forced to open, campuses closed down.

Eroding Israeli Values

The continuation of Israeli rule and oppression in the West Bank will ruin the last chance for a peaceful resolution to the conflict. It is also the road to Israel's self-destruction.

The circle of violence caused by resistance and oppression leads to an erosion of Israeli moral and social values and to the emergence of fanatic, chauvinist, terrorist elements that defy the authority of the state's jurisprudence and government, destroy Israeli democracy, and erode the unity and solidarity of the Jewish people.

Simha Flapan in *Prescription for Conflict: Israel's West Bank Settlement Policy*, 1984.

The Arab town of Nablus has some 70,000 residents. It is nestled in a valley surrounded by several eroded mountains, and as of 1983, there were Jewish settlements on every summit. Some are pathetic, isolated outposts, to be sure, but the roads to the settlements are more impressive than the housing, and they entirely bypass the Arab dwellings. Settlements and housing are portents of a Jewish presence that does not so much annex the territory as graft a thin layer of control over the top of it. . . . Ever since the mayor of Nablus, Bassam Shaka, was fired by Professor Milson, the town has been run by low-ranking Israeli officers. Public housing construction has been stopped. Roads are deteriorating. Families who protested by not paying taxes had their electricity shut off. Arab youths (including Shaka's own teenage son) have been political prisoners, and they report living with fifteen others in rooms seventy-five feet square, with a few blankets, no books, nothing but time to talk about the "struggle." Israeli investors and contractors, meanwhile, have not failed to profit from the situation. Benvenisti points out that hundreds of private speculators and builders have made fortunes here; the total amount of private capital invested may add up to some $250 million a year, according to the government's own reckoning.

Granted, the rhetoric of former Justice Minister Shapiro may have been too much. Patrols, settlements, interrogations, profiteering—this is the stuff of the British Raj, not Fascism. Indeed, if the Palestinians had one Gandhi instead of a hundred Garibaldis, the Israeli occupation might be put in serious difficulty. There are few well-documented cases of torture in Israeli military prisons, and no executions; when two terrorist prisoners were discovered to have been beaten to death in custody, their assailants were arrested. . . .

A Meaner Place To Live

Still, it would be terribly complacent of Israelis to take satisfaction in Israel's comparatively humane record of occupation. Fascist states did not have a democratic character to lose. IDF patrols and Gush Emunim vigilantes became increasingly trigger-happy during Rafael Eitan's tenure as Chief of Staff; the Israeli government extended Israeli law to Jewish settlements on the West Bank, and it also extended its high-handed control of West Bankers to some Israeli dissidents. Groups of Israeli professors and students who demonstrated for academic freedom at Bir Zeit University during the winter of 1982 were arrested and beaten. The head of the state television authority, the Likud-appointed Yosef "Tommy" Lapid, ran a campaign against "non-Zionist" reporting. One correspondent, Rafik Halabi, an Arab graduate of Hebrew University, claimed that as many as 120 people were on unpaid leave from the broadcast authority around the time of the Lebanon War, many of them in protest against political restrictions. In this atmosphere, Israel became a meaner place to live. A new extremist discourse emerged from the war, but also from the daily confrontation of Arab laborers and Jews, the first walking to jobs, while the latter averted their eyes. In Jerusalem, Israelis feared to walk near Arab neighborhoods at night. Soldiers were mobilized as if part of a deadly routine. Begin, and especially General Sharon, brought out the very worst instincts of Israeli young people: the desire for domination, lock-step, revenge. (Defending Sharon's role in the Sabra and Shatila massacres during the winter of 1983, one taxi driver insisted that the only way to deal with the Palestinians was to shoot them: men, women, and children. "I was in Lebanon," he said. "Twelve-year-old boys can kill you with an RPG [a rocket-propelled grenade] as easily as a man." True, a little resistance, a little scolding, and the cabbie took much of it back. The point was that this rhetoric was not an embarrassment to him.) . . .

Social and Economic Conditions

In 1948 the 175,000 Palestinian Arabs who stayed in the territory that became Israel were almost all peasant farmers. Unlike the professional people, merchants, workers, and other urban Arabs who fled cities such as Haifa and Jaffa in panic—or were driven out of towns such as Lod and Ramle by the Haganah—the Palestinians who became Israeli citizens lived mainly in rural villages in north central Galilee or in the Little Triangle between Haifa and Nablus, which the fighting did not quite reach. With the exception of Christian Nazareth, these were among the most backward places in the territory that became the state of Israel. About half Israel's Arabs still live in nearly isolated towns and serve as a work force for Israeli Jewish industries. A quarter work on Jewish farms and construction sites.

Zionism's Democratic Tradition

Annexation of the West Bank would increase Israel's global isolation. The possible loss of U.S. support would gravely endanger the security of the State of Israel.

100,000 Jewish settlers on an annexed West Bank will perpetuate the Arab-Israel conflict for generations to come. The intention of settling Israelis on the West Bank, in order to realize the goal of territorial annexation, arises from the "Greater Israel" idea, which maintains that only one people can be sovereign in the land of Israel and which perceives the Arab-Israel conflict as a head-on clash with no room for compromise. The settlement of 100,000 Jews on the West Bank would turn this chauvinistic philosophy into a self-fulfilling prophecy; the conflict would intensify as each side fought for absolute control. . . .

Massive Israeli settlement of the West Bank would create a dual society in which Israelis, having elected local councils and exercising full political rights, would live side by side with a Palestinian Arab population under military administration and deprived of meaningful political rights. This situation would have profound moral consequences for Israel and would endanger the integrity of Zionism's democratic tradition.

Everything You Didn't Want To Know About Settlement on the West Bank, pamphlet from Peace Now, Jerusalem, Israel.

These figures convincingly show that the Israeli Arabs are dependent upon and dominated by the Jewish economy, that Arabs have become a segregated industrial proletariat in Israel and will remain one unless some of Israel's political institutions are reformed. Yet the changes in the social conditions of the Arabs in these regions have not all been for the worse. In 1944 about 11 percent of the Arab population was employed in "commerce and services," as compared with only 8.2 percent in 1963. But most of the urban Arabs who had commercial jobs fled in 1948; a great many working in services in 1944 were clerks in the Mandate bureaucracy. In contrast, the number of Arabs working as "traders, [commercial] agents, and salesmen" in Israel actually

doubled from 1963 to 1972 and was roughly equal to the propor-
tion of Jews doing the same work during the same years. . . .

To grasp the full implication of changes in the Arab sector, one
ought to consider the resistance of rural Palestinians to modernization. One of the few Israeli academics to have done this successfully is Professor Sami Mar'i, an Israeli Arab whose major
study, published in 1978, pertained to Arab education in the Jewish
state. Mar'i was born and educated in Israel; he attended Hebrew
University, where he studied sociology. In 1984, he was one of
a handful of Arabs teaching social science at Haifa University, the
only university in Israel whose number of Arab students is pro-
portionate to the Israeli-Arab population.

Mar'i's central point is that Arab citizens will have to have far
greater social and economic opportunities in Israel if their children
are to feel loyal to the state and their teachers are not to feel like
quislings. Of course, it may be asked why the Israeli school system
is not more fully integrated, why kibbutz schools still exclude
Sephardi children from nearby development towns, or why Jewish
urban schools exclude the Arabs from nearby villages. But Mar'i
makes a forceful case that the Arab educational system ought to
be run by Arab educators, that it should teach more about Palestinian national culture and history. Will cultivating Palestinian identity inevitably lead to anti-Zionism? Mar'i thinks not.

True, there is contempt among the Israeli Arabs for what
Zionism represented and more for the spirit of Greater Israel.
Israel's Arabs have had bitter claims against their government,
arising out of the years of Israeli-Palestinian bloodshed. They often
bore the brunt of the turmoil and have not forgotten the violence
done them by Israeli forces: between 1949 and 1956, the state ex-
propriated about half of all Arab land for Jewish settlement, often
resorting to specious claims that the land was abandoned or was
required for state security. During the Sinai War in 1956, Israeli
soldiers shot forty-three people for breaking the curfew at Kfar
Kassem. (The Israeli commanders were court-martialed, and par-
doned after a number of years.) The Israeli defense apparatus
resorted to high-handed "security regulations" to suppress the
emergence of any national Arab party, such as the El-Ard ("the
Land") Party of the early sixties, which threatened to field candidates for election to the Knesset. In 1976, six young men were
killed by soldiers during demonstrations against new Israeli plans
to expropriate land in the Galilee. The government would not hold
public inquiries into these killings. . . .

A Relatively Free Culture

Yet Mar'i has pointed out that Israeli Arabs appreciate what they
can share of Israel's libertarian style of life. If Hebrew culture falls
short of English with respect to liberal freedom, it is incomparably

more liberal than that of the Arabs; Zionism may be conquering, humiliating, and hostile, but Israel has been a source of rapid progress for some Arabs in their knowledge of technology and their sense of women's rights, economic equality, and the values of individualism. So whatever their current enthusiasm for the "Palestinian cause," Arab students have taken a place in the modern world by means of a Hebrew education. They have ceased viewing membership in a powerful, patriarchal clan as central to their lives and have grown accustomed to co-educational arrangements outside school as well as within it. According to the research Mar'i cites, Israeli Arab children have become impatient with rote learning and have shown a much stronger predisposition for independent and creative thinking when compared with children in West Bank schools. There is, moreover, an ambivalence toward Hebrew literature itself since, during four years in high school, Arab students have to study 768 hours of Hebrew language and literature (including Bialik, Alterman, and leading Zionist writers), as compared with only 732 in Arab studies. However, Israeli Arabs have developed an affinity for the Hebrew culture they have had to master; they are certainly more drawn to actual Israeli life than Diaspora Jews.

Democracy vs. Daily Life

Daily life in Israel teaches just the opposite of democratic values. The 1.5 million Arabs in the territories have been living under Israeli occupation for 18 years—living alongside Israelis without sharing their rights. Our young people have grown up believing that nationalist struggle, terrorism and lawful discrimination are facts of life. Under such circumstances, how can one hope to teach democracy?

Danny Rubinstein, *The New York Times*, July 16, 1985.

Mar'i's most discouraging finding is that, nevertheless, 90 percent of the Arab students he interviewed in 1977 doubted they had a future in Israel. (Some 40 percent of young Israeli Jews concurred with this assessment of Arab prospects. More recent studies have found that 60 percent of Israeli Jewish teens would refuse to live in the same apartment building as an Arab, and 40 percent would not want to work with one.) Such attitudes might change if progress could be made on peace between Israelis and the Palestinians beyond Israel's border. . . .

The problem obviously is not simply that Israel is a Zionist state, as some ultra-left critics of Israel have charged. Israeli Arabs know better than most that they live in an incipiently democratic state which accords important civil rights to all. Yet old Zionist institu-

159

tions still reserve the principal economic benefits only for the Jews, and this must stop if Israeli Arabs are to be integrated. By 1980, for example, the Jewish Agency had spent some $5 billion to develop the Jewish economy and advance the prospects of Jewish families. No Arab had access to any of those funds. Land expropriated from Arabs by the Israeli Land Authority for "public use" is still consigned to Israeli citizens according to the exclusionary regulations of the old Jewish National Fund. Again, Israeli Arabs may not reside on about 95 percent of cultivated Israeli land.

Regulations of this sort create a particular hardship for Israeli Arabs in towns such as Nazareth and Acre, which are critically short of housing. But the Israeli state apparatus itself has not been free of overt discrimination in favor of Jews—a pattern which intensified under the pressure of the new Zionism. In the 1984 budget for Arab and Jewish areas, the Arab city of Nazareth received the equivalent of $629.40 per capita, compared with $1,688 per capita for Upper Nazareth, the largely Jewish town next door. The Arab town of Kfar Kara got $231.17 per capita, while the neighboring Jewish town of Pardes Hana received $1,540.90 per capita. The state still refuses to draft Arab men into the Israel Defense Forces, though Israeli Arab youths have paid a high added cost for their military exemptions: national service is not only the prerequisite for being socially accepted in Israeli cities; it is also necessary for benefits upon discharge, such as low-interest mortgages, jobs which require security clearance, welfare payments to parents with many children, and so forth.

Loyalty Depends on Democracy

In fairness, since Israeli Arabs live in a rural economy they have often avoided paying full income tax; they can eat better than poor Jewish Israelis and get services for less. Would they move to the cities and go to work in the advanced economy? And would Israeli Arabs want to take an active part in the life of Israel while receiving a greater share of social benefits as they did so? After all, conscripting them into the IDF would mean that they would have to fight other Arabs; perhaps the state deserves some credit for refusing to insist that they serve. Still, it seems of critical importance to reiterate here what some Israeli Arab intellectuals—the television journalist Rafik Halabi, for instance—have insisted all along: that the loyalty of Israeli Arabs to Israel derives from what democracy it has achieved.

"I am prepared to use every possible means to insure that [Arabs] . . . will never again murder Jews and threaten the existence of my state."

Giving Palestinians Rights Threatens the State of Israel

Meir Kahane

The author of the following viewpoint, American-born Rabbi Meir Kahane, emigrated to Israel in 1973 and was elected to the Knesset, Israel's parliament, in 1984. In Israel Kahane founded Kach, a right-wing political party which advocates expelling Arabs from Israel. In the following viewpoint, Kahane argues that it is futile for Israeli Jews to try to coexist with Arabs by giving them democratic rights. Palestinians want their own Arab state, he contends, not equal rights in a Jewish state. Kahane concludes that Israel is the fulfillment of Jewish destiny and it would be madness for Jews to allow democracy to thwart that destiny.

As you read, consider the following questions:

1. Why does Kahane insist that it is impossible for Israel to be both Jewish and democratic?
2. What do Arabs want, according to Kahane, and why are economic and social development programs for Arab villages useless?

Jewish terror awakens at the terrible thought—and sub-conscious realization—that western democracy is simply incompatible with Zionism and its central idea of a Jewish State. . . .

What in the world does this "Jewish State" mean? What is its minimal and fundamental definition, the one that every Zionist—religious or not, rightist or leftist, whatever his political, social and economic hue—will agree upon? Why surely it is the definition of a Jewish State as one *with a majority of Jews.* Of course this is the most basic and bottom-line definition possible.

Only a state with a majority of Jews guarantees all the things that Zionism and Zionists dreamed of, worked for, demanded. Only a state with a majority of Jews guarantees Jewish sovereignty, and independence. Only a state with a majority of Jews guarantees that the Jew will be captain of his ship, master of his fate, free from dependency on and prostration before strangers.

Only a state with a majority of Jews will insure that, never again, will we enjoy such dubious benefits as Crusades and Inquisitions and pogroms and holocausts—small and very large. Only a state in which the Jew controls his destiny will free him from both gentile Church *and* State, from both the intolerance of the non-Jew as well as his humiliating "tolerance." A Jewish majority *is* a Jewish State and a Jewish State is the repudiation of the ghetto, the Exile, humiliation, degradation, weakness and the shame of raising our eyes unto the stranger, "from the gentile shall come forth our salvation. . . ."

Anything less than a Jewish majority is not a Jewish State. Surely Brooklyn has many, many Jews but it is not a Jewish State for it. It is not a sovereign, independent one, and this is what Zionism and its founding fathers understood and fought for: A Land of Israel with a majority of Jews in it. A Jewish State.

This being so, what is one to do with western democracy? What is one supposed to do with a concept that demands that anyone, regardless of religion or national background, has the right to sit quietly and peacefully, have as many babies as possible, and become the majority? The question, simply put, the question that explodes terror in the hearts of the Jew is: *Do the Arabs in Israel have a right to quietly, peacefully, democratically, equally, and liberally become the majority?* . . .

Arab National Pride

For years, Jews and their leaders were able to deceive themselves and everyone else except the Arabs with a breathtaking contempt for Arabs that sounded amazingly like some paternalistic, colonialist high commissioner marching to a Kiplingesque tune of noblesse-oblige. How many cabinet ministers (and prime ministers) and how many guided tour guides and how many speakers at UJA [United Jewish Appeal], Jewish National Fund,

Israel Bonds and other meetings, patted themselves glowingly on their Jewish-Israeli back as they described how much they had done for the (backward) Arabs. "Their villages had no electricity—and we lit them up. They had no sanitary facilities—we gave them indoor toilets. They were illiterate—we not only gave them education but thousands learn in our universities."

Was there ever greater contempt for Arabs? Was there ever greater blindness by Jews? The words sound like some grotesque echo of a British imperialist in Kenya shaking his head in puzzlement and asking: "What do the natives want? We came here and found a jungle and turned it into a garden. . . . " The answer of the "natives" was, of course: "True, but it was OUR jungle and now is it YOUR garden. . . ." And, of course, that is exactly the answer of the Arab to the absurd and paternalistic contempt of the schizophrenic Jew: "True. You came and found a desert and turned it into green fields. But it was OUR desert and the green fields are now yours. . . ."

The Eternal Possession of Jews

In the democratic age we live in, it is a difficult task to openly adopt what seems like a non-democratic position. But it is nowhere provided that non-Jews will enjoy full equal rights as a national community. After all, the Land is the eternal possession of the Jewish people alone. . . .

This inexorable reality will move on and impress itself more deeply on the Israeli consciousness. This would become a smoother process if people realized that pouring Western liberal ideas into Jewish vessels, and serving them up as Jewish, is dishonest and dangerous.

Mordechai Nisan, *Jerusalem Post*, January 18, 1983.

Is there an honest person alive who believes that one can buy the Arab's national pride with an indoor toilet? Is there anyone with a minimal intelligence who does not understand that it is precisely the educated Arab, the university graduate of whom the schizophrenics boast, who is precisely the most dangerous of all Arabs? That the head of the PLO-supporting Progressive List in the Knesset, Muhamad Miarai, is a graduate of Hebrew University? That revolution never comes from the numb and the dumb but precisely from the educated? That Israel, with its own schizophrenic hands, is creating the new leadership of the PLO?

Equality Is Not a Solution

Is there anyone who does not understand that the Arab is not a fool, and that you cannot create a modern, educated, rising generation and tell them that they can have everything except the right to rule in what they consider their own country? Is there no one who grasps the elementary fact that a country which is defined as a Jewish State *cannot* be anything except a foreign concept for the non-Jewish Arab? . . .

Because they desperately fear to look at the reality of Arab hostility, the two-legged lemmings of the Mosaic faith proclaim that the root of the Jewish-Arab problem is, firstly, a lack of social and economic equality, but even more important, because there is no contact between Jews and Arabs, there is a "lack of understanding." *A lack of understanding.* We must, therefore, rush to break down "stereotyping, fear and suspicion," as Arabs and Jews work together, play together, create together. And so the liberal vision of happy and equal Jews and Arabs spending summers together in a camp, visiting each other's homes, laughing at each other's jokes in a cafe. Break down the barriers and peace and tranquility will reign as we put an end to the "lack of understanding."

If I were an Arab I would fairly shake the walls with my disgust and anger. *This* is the problem and *this* the solution? The fact that Jews and Arabs do not "understand" each other? That there is no social contact?

The truth is that the Arab understands the Jew and the State of Israel very well. And that is precisely what makes him hate it and oppose it. The Arab understands very well that his ultimate complaint, anger and inability to accept the State of Israel is the fact that it is a Jewish State and is so defined officially in the Declaration of Independence. . . .

A "Moderate" Arab Village

Mi'ilya is a prosperous village. Construction goes on constantly as the Arabs there build homes or add rooms to their present ones. Nearly every family has a vehicle and many are new ones. It is a Christian Arab village, for the most part, hence according to existing Jewish mythology, "moderate." Many of its inhabitants possess a higher education. In short, it is the very model of the modern, progressive Israeli Arab village, which, thanks to liberal, humane, progressive Jews, will produce "good" Arabs.

And so, meet Salim. Salim lives in Mi'ilya and does quite well, thank you. He is an attorney, as are his wife and his brother, all three sharing an office in the Jewish city of Nahariya. He speaks Hebrew fluently (being a graduate of Hebrew University) and, in his jeans, no one could possibly know that he is not an Israeli Jew. But when asked by the Israeli weekly *Newsview* (October 16, 1984) to describe himself, this is what the Christian, educated, prosperous attorney, beneficiary of Jewish liberalism and coexistence, had to say:

"First of all I'm a Palestinian. Then I'm an Arab. Last, I'm a

Christian. I also happen to live in Israel but I don't feel I'm an Israeli citizen. I can't be a real citizen of Israel as long as it's a Jewish State which discriminates against non-Jews. . . .

"We're against Arabs participating in Israeli elections because this legitimizes the Jewish State." And, again: "We could accept a West Bank state only as far as a first step to the liberation of the Galilee."

Liberation of the Galilee? Surely, our educated, enlightened Christian Arab, the beneficiary of the Jewish largesse, and darling of the United Jewish Appeal and Hadassah women, must be joking. *The Galilee*? Of course, all progressive Jews join with him in deploring Israeli occupation of areas that do not belong to her, such as the West Bank (Judea-Samaria) and Gaza, the Biblical areas where Jewish ancestors lived and created their own Jewish states. But to speak of the liberation of the *Galilee*? An area that is part of the State of Israel, that is *Jewish*? How can Salim say such a thing?

Israel's Purpose

It's our country . . . and it's our destiny to live in our land as a 'nation of priests.' . . . We invite the Arabs to live everywhere. But we don't believe they have the right to change the idea, the purpose, of the state. For that reason, I believe that they shouldn't be able to vote in national elections for the Knesset, because if they could then they would vote to change the purpose, the Jewish nature, of the state.

Moshe Levinger, quoted in *A Stranger in My House* by Walter Reich, 1984.

Easily. For Salim does not believe that the Galilee is "Jewish." For Salim, like countless other Israeli Arabs who live in Israel, does not believe that "Israel" should be Jewish. He does not believe that Israel should *be*. And this is what he says, in the same interview:

"We are against Arabs participating in Israeli elections because this legitimizes the Jewish State." . . .

The Myth of Coexistence

I can imagine that the ordinary Jew, simple and naive, a captive of the absurd and deceitful Jewish Establishment propaganda concerning Jewish-Arab co-existence in Israel, in reading Salim's words, is shocked and depressed. I am too, I am shocked and depressed that any Jew is shocked and depressed. I am shocked and depressed that any Jew is so blind and obtuse and ignorant of Arab national pride that he should be shocked and depressed upon reading Salim's words. They are so logical, so obvious, so self-explanatory. They are the words of an Arab who has no need for "understanding." He understands perfectly. He understands that Zionism believes in a *Jewish* State in which the Jew rules and that he wishes a Palestinian state in which the *Arab* rules. Even if he were not an attorney with an LLB from Hebrew University he would understand that. It is only the two-legged lemmings of the Mosaic persuasion who persist in fleeing in terror from the terrible (for them) reality. . . .

Rights of the Non-Jew

The non-Jew has no share in the Land of Israel. He has no ownership, citizenship, or destiny in it. The non-Jew who wishes to live in Israel must accept basic human obligations. Then he may live in Israel as a *resident stranger*, but never as a citizen with any proprietary interest or with any political say, never as one who can hold any public office that will give him dominion over a Jew or a share in the authority of the country. Accepting these conditions, he admits that the land is not his, and therefore he may live in Israel quietly, separately observing his own private life, with all religious, economic, social, and cultural rights. Refusing this, he cannot remain. Those are the conditions for the gentile who wishes to remain in the Land of the People of Israel, of the *Jewish* people. A stranger who is allowed to reside as a resident but never with citizenship, never with anything to say about the country.

Then, by all means, he must not be ill-treated or oppressed. *Then*, by all means, we should treat him properly, kindly, heal his sick and support all his needs. *Then*, we must treat him with the same kindness we would show any decent human being who is not Jewish if we lived in the Exile outside of Israel.

Then he is entitled to personal rights, economic and cultural and social rights within Torah law. But *national rights*, the right to say anything about the structure, the character, of the state—never!

Jewish Sovereignty Must Be Accepted

And certainly nothing of even this to one who does *not* accept the Jewish sovereignty over the land, the tribute and servitude that *goes along with it*. And a thousand times never to a gentile, the Arab, who is the *enemy*, who claims the country is really his, and who declares his right to retake the country through war or through population growth and democracy! And concerning those who do not accept the permanency and legality of Jewish sovereignty, the Torah clearly commanded: "And you shall drive out all the inhabitants of the land from before you. . . . But if you will not drive out the inhabitants of the land from before you, then it shall come to pass that those which you let remain of them, shall be thorns in your eyes and thistles in your sides and shall torment you in the land wherein you dwell. And it shall be that

I will do to you as I thought to do to them" (Numbers 33:53-56). . . .

That is Judaism, and if it be painful to the western secularized Jew because of its all-too-obvious contradiction of western political democracy, so be it. . . .

Ending Jewish Guilt

I feel no guilt. Not the slightest. I feel no guilt about the fact that I am a Jew. I feel no guilt about the fact that I believe *and know* that the Jew is a Chosen person who stood at Sinai and was selected to be G-d's elected. I feel no guilt over the fact that I believe *and know* that the Land of Israel is the exclusive home of the Jewish people, and that no other people has the slightest right to it. I feel no guilt over my knowledge that Arabs are thieves who entered my land when the Jewish people was forceably exiled from it, and I feel no guilt over the fact that I am prepared to use every possible means to insure that they will never again murder Jews and threaten the existence of my state. I feel no guilt over the fact that I prefer winning wars to losing pogroms, that I choose living over dying. It is infinitely more satisfying to win. *I feel no guilt over feeling no guilt.*

The Land Belongs to the Jews

You can compromise about unimportant things, but you can't divide your wife, you can't divide your children, you can't divide your Bible, and you can't divide your holy earth. And if a man is ready to divide his son, it means he doesn't believe that it *is* his son. To compromise on our own home, a home that belongs not only to us but also to God, is abnormal! You can't do it! It's the same as if you had a home and another man came in and said that a part belonged to him. You wouldn't compromise. You would fight until you possessed your beloved home. And all the more your beloved country.

Moshe Levinger, quoted in *A Stranger in My House* by Walter Reich, 1984.

Having lost, been losers for so many centuries, too many Jews have difficulty dealing with winning. I have no such problem. It is infinitely more satisfying to be a winner than a loser. It is exceedingly more pleasant to live than die; there is little of any positive value in Holocausts or pogroms. And I totally prefer a powerful and proud Jewish State that is hated by the entire world than an Auschwitz that is loved by one and all.

"Israel must accept in principle the Palestinians as a political entity."

Israel Must Recognize the Rights of Palestinians

Nafez Nazzal

Nafez Nazzal is a professor of Middle East history at Birzeit University, a Palestinian university near Jerusalem which has often been the site of protests against Israel's occupation of the West Bank. In the following viewpoint, he argues that the long-term interest of both Israelis and Palestinians is peace. Although Israel gains short-term benefits from the current stalemate in negotiations, Nazzal contends that it is only prolonging the day when it will have to recognize the Palestinian right to self-determination.

As you read, consider the following questions:

1. What is the position of the Likud party regarding the West Bank, according to Nazzal?
2. Why does Nazzal believe a Palestinian state is the only way to gain peace?
3. What does the author argue is the main objective of West Bank and Gaza Strip Palestinians?

Nafez Nazzal, "The Palestinian Perspective on the Future of the West Bank and the Gaza Strip," from *Peace-Making in the Middle East*, edited by Paul Marantz and Janice Gross Stein, 1985. Permission granted by Barnes & Noble Books, Totowa, New Jersey.

It is obviously in the interest of all the peoples of the Middle East that peace should prevail. There can be no military solution to this conflict. Arab honour and dignity cannot be restored by further wars, bloodshed and an eventual military victory. No Arab state at present has the capability to destroy Israel, nor is any major power willing to help the Arab states to eliminate Israel. Consequently, Israel must cease talking of "security" and "defensible borders." Israel's argument for maintaining control over the occupied territories to ensure its security should be rejected. No Arab leader can be expected to relinquish sovereign territory for the sake of Israel's security, nor can Arab governments be expected to agree to the safeguarding of Israel's territory through the acquisition of territory by force. Israel's security concern cannot prevail over Arab rights to their land.

Israel Must Accept the Palestinians

Nor can Israel's dream of a "permanent peace" with its Arab neighbours be achieved by denying Palestinian nationality. It follows that Israel must accept in principle the Palestinians as a political entity. The Palestinians must have the right to self-determination, leading to the establishment of an independent state in the West Bank and Gaza Strip. Such a solution surely falls far short of justice—but one cannot possibly do full justice now to the victims of this long tragedy.

The Arab defeat of June 1967 and the consequent Israeli occupation of the West Bank and Gaza Strip triggered a dual process within the Palestinian community; commando operations against Israel, which at times were counter-productive, but nevertheless forced the international community to notice the Palestinians' plight; until the mid-1960s, the Palestinians had been largely passive observers of their fate. A second related trend, one which is particularly predominant among the Palestinians in the occupied territories, supports the establishment of a Palestinian state on the West Bank and Gaza Strip, alongside Israel. This state must be independent and autonomous; it cannot be established in a package deal at Palestinian expense in order to normalize conditions in the Middle East. The Palestinian National Council during its 13th and 16th sessions of 1977 and 1982, accepted in principle the establishment of a Palestinian state on any territories evacuated by Israel. Nothing is more important to the Palestinians in the occupied territories than the withdrawal of Israel from the territories occupied in June 1967 and the establishment of an independent Palestinian Arab state.

Except for marginal groups, like the Peace Now movement, *Rakah* (the Israeli communist party) and *Shelli*, no group in Israel is willing to contemplate a total Israeli withdrawal from the West Bank and Gaza Strip. The *Likud* Party supports the Jewish right to occupy and settle the land of Israel. As far as they are concerned, the Palestinians in the West Bank (Land of Israel) are Jordanian citizens and temporarily resident in Israel. The Labour Alignment adopted the "Jordanian Option," a more sophisticated position based on an updated version of the Allon Plan; it would allow Israel to control the security of the West Bank and continue Jewish settlement as well as affirm the right of Jews to settle anywhere in the occupied territories, but would return to Jordan's King Hussein civil and administrative control of the densely populated areas of the West Bank. In effect, the Labour program returns to King Hussein the responsibility of policing the Palestinians, a responsibility which he unilaterally rejected.

Equitable Settlement

The two nations, the Israeli and the Palestinian, are faced with a choice: Either we continue to bloody each other, to struggle against each other; or we decide to reach an equitable settlement. For an equitable settlement we once again have a choice: Either we accept to partition this land between us as two equal peoples; or we choose to partition political rights in the government which runs this land equally.

This is what a just settlement is. And I submit to you that we, the Palestinians, are ready to accept either option.

Sari Nusseibeh, *Al-Fajr*, March 6, 1987.

The present stalemate on the Palestinian issue favours Israel. It allows Israel to create new realities in the form of settlements and further expropriation of Arab land. This, coupled with the continuing emigration of the Palestinian intelligentsia since 1967, has convinced many Israelis that, given time and a decade of continuing stalemate, they would be able to transform the character of the occupied territories, both demographically and politically, from an occupied to an annexed territory. Such a conclusion assumes:

1. Israel's ability to implement its policies in the occupied territories without tangible Palestinian resistance.
2. Continued U.S. military and political support and the failure of the PLO to gain U.S. support.
3. Continued military and technological superiority of Israel over the Palestinians and the Arab states, individually and collectively.
4. Continued failure of the Arab states to unite against the de-Arabization of the occupied territories.

This policy of Israel however, is very shortsighted over the long run. If there is no settlement, a change in any one of these assumptions could plunge the Middle East into a state of turmoil and jeopardize not merely Israel's security but larger western interests in the Middle East as well. The present configuration of forces within the region permits Israel to negotiate from a position of relative strength and arrive at a formula which, within a two-state framework, would assure its security.

The framework for peace in the Middle East, signed at Camp David, speaks of a "just, comprehensive and durable settlement." Such a settlement is possible only if the Palestinians become a party to the negotiating process. But if the Palestinians are to join the process, their legitimate rights must become more than words. Israel can no longer claim sovereignty over the West Bank and Gaza Strip when it has clearly agreed, both in accepting UN Resolution 242 and in signing the framework for peace, to the "inadmissibility of the acquisition of territory by war."

Restoring Self-Respect

At the heart of the Middle East conflict which has dominated the body politic of the area for thirty-five years lies the Palestinian problem; the attempt by a twice-occupied and twice-exiled people to regain their political independence through the establishment of a state which would restore some measure of political self-respect and provide some degree of psychological compensation. Only such a state, sovereign and independent, endorsed by the PLO, is likely to end the anonymous ghost-like existence of the Palestinians as a non-people. It would terminate their dependence on the mercy, charity, or tolerance of others. It would be a centre of hope and achievement.

Of all peoples, the Jewish people are historically qualified to understand the demands of the Palestinian people. . . .

Israel claims that it has been in a state of siege throughout its existence and that its children have known nothing but war. Yet here now is a chance for peace. Peace requires a return to boundaries that Israel itself was more than willing to accept prior to the Six Day War, and the acceptance of the principle of Palestinian self-determination in territory then controlled by Jordan. Israel presumably would have had little to say or do if King Hussein had granted self-determination to the Palestinians in May 1967.

Not all Palestinians in the West Bank and Gaza Strip are of the same opinion about the appropriate form of political settlement. The majority of the Palestinians residing in Palestine would welcome any settlement that would end Israel's military occupation. They are willing to recognize and live side by side with Israel, if Israel is willing to withdraw from the territories occupied in June 1967 and recognize the Palestinians as a political entity. Israel must do so if it is to breed respectability and responsibility.

171

"Grassroots Palestinian opinion . . . has yet to reconcile itself to Israel's permanent existence."

Palestinians Must Recognize the Rights of Israel

Ze'ev Chafets

Since the Palestine Liberation Organization (PLO) was created in 1965, it has refused to recognize the nation of Israel. In the following viewpoint Ze'ev Chafets argues that although this strategy perpetuates conflict, it remains the one most Palestinians favor. To support his argument, he points to the murder of a moderate Arab mayor by radical Palestinians. Demonstrators at the mayor's funeral supported the PLO and rejected the position of Arab leaders who favor moderate proposals for peace. Chafets is a journalist and the author of *Heroes and Hustlers, Hard Hats and Holy Men: Inside the New Israel*. He grew up in Michigan and, after going to Israel as a college student in 1967, decided to become an Israeli citizen.

As you read, consider the following questions:

1. Why does the PLO refuse to recognize Israel's right to exist, according to the author?
2. What distinction does Chafets make between the PLO's position and the political views of Palestinians on the West Bank and Gaza Strip?

Ze'ev Chafets, "The PLO's 'No' Must Turn Into A 'Yes,'" *Los Angeles Times*, March 5, 1986. Reprinted with the author's permission.

The assassination of Nablus Mayor Zafer Masri by rival Palestinian gunmen and the frenzied demonstration in favor of the Palestine Liberation Organization at his funeral are the latest events in a dramatic fortnight of Palestinian political activity. . . .

Jordan's King Hussein reshuffled the deck with a televised address in which he blamed the PLO for the breakdown of the peace process in the Middle East. The king implied that the PLO should be replaced, and obliquely volunteered for the job. The anti-Hussein slogans at the Masri funeral provided the Palestinian answer.

The Key Questions

But two key questions are left unresolved: Why did the PLO torpedo the peace process, and, with the process dead, what can the Palestinians expect now?

According to Hussein, the PLO had received an indirect American promise to include it in an international peace conference. In Hussein's words, it was an Arab achievement that had previously seemed impossible; it would have given the PLO instant recognition, respectability and a chance to raise its demands in a presumably friendly forum.

The price of the invitation? A public declaration that the PLO "has accepted U.N. Resolutions 242 and 338, is prepared to negotiate peace with Israel and has renounced terrorism." (The resolutions implicitly recognize Israel's right to exist within secure boundaries.)

Hussein believed that the PLO would pay the price. Yasser Arafat assured him of it in private talks. And it seemed reasonable. For a decade the PLO leader has hinted that he might make such a deal. But when Hussein came up with what Arafat claims to have wanted—inclusion in a peace negotiation that could well yield a large part of the West Bank and Gaza—the PLO boss unexpectedly said, "No."

"How stupid of Arafat," thundered dozens of editorials in the Western press. "Doesn't he realize that he is missing the chance of a lifetime?" But Arafat is hardly stupid. He turned down the deal because he isn't free to accept it.

Irreducible Goal

When the PLO was formed, two years before the Israeli occupation of the West Bank began, its stated purpose was to destroy Israel and replace it with a Palestinian state. More than two decades later, that is still its strategic aim. Only this week Arafat told a Kuwaiti newspaper that his irreducible goal is "a Palestinian flag flying over a liberated Jerusalem, capital of a united Arab Palestine."

For years Arafat's Western sympathizers have dismissed this

173

kind of talk as mere rhetoric. But the PLO's rejection of the Jordanian-American offer makes it clear that the rhetoric is the reality.

Why? Politics. The PLO's strength is that it expresses the will of its constituents, the Palestinian people. And grassroots Palestinian opinion, especially outside the West Bank and Gaza, has yet to reconcile itself to Israel's permanent existence.

Unrealistic Demands

In seeking understanding [of their plight], the Palestinians' greatest failure is in Israel and the United States, among the very people who may well hold the key to their future. Their willingness to resort to terrorist acts, their refusal to make any clear acknowledgement of Israel's right to exist in harmony with its neighbors, their reluctance to permit King Hussein or other representatives to explore opportunities for peace and the assuaging of grievances, and their uncompromising demands that are patently unacceptable to Israel and its supporters have all served to prevent the official recognition of their leaders and the marshaling of further backing for their cause.

Jimmy Carter, *The Blood of Abraham*, 1985.

The majority of Palestinian refugees live in Lebanon, Syria, Jordan, the West Bank and Gaza, but they come originally from areas within pre-1967 Israel. For them the West Bank and Gaza may be a part of the homeland, but these areas are not the "home" that they dream of reclaiming. Their goal is Galilee, Jaffa, Ashkelon and Jerusalem. It may be an impractical dream, but no Palestinian leader can sign it away in return for a West Bank state next to Israel and expect to retain the support of the refugees.

Good for Politics, Bad for Palestinians

Seen in this light, Arafat's refusal to recognize Israel's right to exist is not fanaticism but political self-preservation. It may be good for the PLO leader, but it has disastrous consequences for the Palestinian cause. This same all-or-nothing approach led the Palestinian leadership to reject the 1947 U.N. partition resolution, which would have created a Palestinian state.

In the 1970s, when Arab oil muscle created an international consensus for a Palestinian entity in the West Bank and Gaza, the PLO squandered it by refusing to utter the magic numbers: 242 and 338. Today, given the pace of Israeli consolidation in the West Bank, King Hussein is almost certainly right when he says that Arafat's rejectionism has caused him to miss another historic opportunity.

The Palestinians with a real interest in dealing with Israel are in the West Bank and Gaza. Among them are thousands of moderate, able people who clearly understand the implication of Arafat's "no." But they lack the will to act. Partly it is fear: Zafer Masri's was the 24th political murder in the occupied territories in the past eight years. Partly it is the result of Israel's refusal to allow moderates to organize politically. But mostly it is the moderates' own fault.

After all, the PLO has established a network of supporters and institutions in the West Bank and Gaza without Israeli permission; the moderates have not, for the most part, even tried.

A Palestinian "Yes"

Ever since the Rabat summit in 1974, Arab diplomacy has maintained that the PLO is the sole legitimate representative of the Palestinian people. . . . [The] West Bank demonstration [at Masri's funeral] indicates that this is true.

But the PLO can only say no, and the Palestinians will achieve nothing until they have produced leaders who can challenge Israel with a Palestinian "yes."

Evaluating Sources of Information

A critical thinker must always question sources of information. Historians, for example, distinguish between *primary sources* (eyewitness accounts) and *secondary sources* (writings or statements based on primary or eyewitness accounts or on other secondary sources.) The account of a peasant who watched as her village was attacked by hostile forces is an example of a primary source. An historian evaluating the incident by using the peasant's account is an example of a secondary source.

To read and think critically, one must be able to recognize primary sources. This is not enough, however, because eyewitness accounts do not always provide accurate descriptions. Palestinian villagers and Israeli soldiers remembering the same incident may differ in their reports of what happened. The historian must decide which account seems most accurate, keeping in mind the potential biases of the eyewitnesses.

Test your skill in evaluating sources of information by completing the following exercise. Imagine you are writing a report on how the lives of Palestinians have changed since Israel took over the West Bank. You decide to include an equal number of primary and secondary sources. Listed below are a number of sources which may be useful for your research. *Place a P next to those descriptions you believe are primary sources.* Second, *rank the primary sources* assigning the number (1) to what appears to be the most accurate and fair primary source, the number (2) to the next most accurate, and so on until the ranking is finished. *Next, place an S next to those descriptions you believe are secondary sources and rank them also, using the same criteria.*

If you are doing this activity as a member of a class or group, discuss and compare your evaluation with other members of the group. Others may come to different conclusions than you. Listening to their reasons may give you valuable insights in evaluating sources of information.

P = *primary*
S = *secondary*

176

_____ 1. The diary of a Jewish woman who settled on the West Bank in 1968. _____

_____ 2. An article in a scholarly journal by a specialist on the Middle East who teaches at Yale. _____

_____ 3. A memoir of childhood in the West Bank before the Israeli invasion, written by a Palestinian now working on an oil rig in Saudi Arabia. _____

_____ 4. A memoir of childhood in the West Bank before 1967 written by the president of Middle East Associates, a major US consulting firm. _____

_____ 5. Viewpoint 2 in this chapter. _____

_____ 6. An ABC news report on a PLO attack on an Israeli village. _____

_____ 7. A book entitled, *An Oral History of Palestinians and Jews in the Occupied Territories.* _____

_____ 8. An editorial in *The New York Times* on the PLO. _____

_____ 9. A report by Israel's Ministry for Economic Affairs on economic conditions in the West Bank. _____

_____ 10. A newspaper story about reactions to a report on economic conditions on the West Bank. _____

_____ 11. An article in the Soviet magazine *New Times* on Israel's treatment of Palestinian teenagers. _____

_____ 12. Viewpoint 3 in this chapter. _____

_____ 13. An American minister's account of his visit to the Holy Land. _____

Periodical Bibliography

The following articles have been selected to supplement the diverse views expressed in this chapter.

Ezra Bowen	"Classes in Coexistence," *Time*, June 10, 1985.
Ido Dissentshik and Mahmud Abu Zalaf	"Two Editors, Two Views: An Israeli and a Palestinian with a Common Goal," *World Press Review*, July 1987.
Ibrahim Fawat	"The PLO: Key to the Middle East Crisis," *AfricAsia*, October 1986.
Glenn Frankel	"The Six-Day War's Volatile Legacy," *The Washington Post National Weekly Edition*, June 15, 1987.
Thomas L. Friedman	"Israeli in Disguise Learns the Anguish of an Arab," *The New York Times*, May 5, 1986.
Erich Isaac and Rael Jean Isaac	"Whose Palestine?" *Commentary*, July 1986.
Scott MacLeod	"An Interview with Yasser Arafat," *The New York Review of Books*, June 11, 1987.
Menahem Milson	"How Not To Occupy the West Bank," *Commentary*, April 1986.
The New Republic	"The West Bank Bust," June 25, 1984.
Edward Rothstein	"Israel's Alienated Intellectuals," *Commentary*, February 1987.
Edward Said	"Interpreting Palestine," *Harper's*, March 1987.
Yezid Sayigh	"The Politics of Palestinian Exile," *Third World Quarterly*, January 1987.
Tikkun	"Twenty Years on the West Bank," volume 2, number 2. Available from The Institute for Labor and Mental Health, 5100 Leona St., Oakland, CA 94619.
Patrick E. Tyler	"Yessir, Arafat Is Back," *The Washington Post National Weekly Edition*, May 11, 1987.
Bernard Ullman	"Israel at Odds with Itself," *World Press Review*, November 1986.
Michael Walzer	"Israel's Great Victory," *The New Republic*, June 8, 1987.

Is Peace Possible in the Middle East?

Chapter Preface

The following chapter focuses on two conflicts: first, the long-term conflict between Israel and the Palestinians; second, the war between Iran and Iraq.

Generations of Jews and Palestinians have fought for the land which both sides claim as their own. In his book *Conflicts and Contradictions*, Israeli author Meron Benvenisti reflects on the number of times his mother has seen her family at war. Her husband fought against the Turks for the British army in 1917 and against the Arabs in 1920, 1929, and 1936. He was wounded in the 1948 war. Her son fought in 1956, 1967, 1973, and then in 1982 in Lebanon. Two grandsons were drafted to fight in the 1982 war. The Benvenistis have fought in nine wars. What is significant is that they are representative of the Jewish and Palestinian families who have fought each other for decades.

The war between Iran and Iraq, although of much shorter duration, has also been devastating. Observers estimate that 500,000 soldiers have died. This high mortality rate makes the Iran/Iraq war the third deadliest since World War II. The cost in weapons, destruction, and lost income has been $500 billion, and the war continues with no end in sight.

The authors in this chapter debate whether peace is possible and advance the proposals they believe are necessary for peace.

"There are increasing numbers of Israelis and Arabs who have become convinced that warfare cannot resolve the Arab-Israeli conflict."

Peace Is Possible in the Middle East

Rami Khouri

Rami Khouri is a Palestinian who was born in New York City. Khouri is an editor for the *Jordan Times* and the Jordan correspondent for several British and American news organizations. In the following viewpoint, he contends that the political positions of Arabs, Israelis, and the United States have become more conducive to peace. Arabs now are talking about resolving the conflict, Khouri writes, and if Israel takes advantage of the opportunity, peace is possible.

As you read, consider the following questions:

1. In what ways does Khouri believe the Arab position has changed in the past twenty years?
2. What is the international consensus on how the conflict can be resolved, according to the author?
3. What decisions does Khouri believe the Israelis will have to make to take advantage of the opportunity for peace?

Rami Khouri, *For Those Who Share a Will To Live*, 1985. Reprinted by permission of the Resource Center for Nonviolence, 515 Broadway, Santa Cruz, CA 95060.

When the state of Israel was created in 1948, the Jewish people realized a dream they had carried in their hearts since the destruction of the Second Temple, some 2,000 years ago. Their years of wandering, persecution and struggle had come to an end. Or so it was thought to be.

The reality is rather different, for since the establishment of Israel in 1948 Israel and the Arabs have fought five major wars. Israel has not had genuine peace and security. It has, thanks to massive American aid and the fervor of its own people, only enjoyed a military advantage. It has been able to defend itself, but not to find a place among the nation-states of the Middle East.

For the four million Palestinian people, the establishment of Israel as a Jewish state in 1948 marked the start of the Palestinian diaspora, of Palestinian homelessness and political disenfranchisement.

Let us forget, for the moment, the rights and wrongs of the past, and apportion neither guilt, nor righteousness, in the history of Arab-Israeli warfare.

The challenge before the people of the Middle East today is not how to ascribe blame for the horrors of the past, but rather how to reconcile conflicting Arab and Israeli claims in order that we may all share the land of Palestine—and the promise of the future.

Positive Trends

On the surface, political circumstances in the Middle East and further afield suggest that Arab-Israeli reconciliation is a distant and naive dream. But beneath the surface, things may be slightly less discouraging. Consider the following:

1. In 1967, the Arab summit at Khartoum rejected negotiations, recognition or coexistence with Israel. In the 1982 Arab summit at Fez, the Arab world proposed a peace plan based on negotiations with Israel, leading to ultimate coexistence on the basis of an Israeli state living side-by-side with a Palestinian state. The shift in the Arab peace posture since 1967 has been dramatic, but insufficiently appreciated in the West.

2. In Israel, public opinion polls since 1967 have shown a consistent trend toward more and more Israelis who are willing to make peace with the Palestinians and the other Arab states on the basis of an Israeli withdrawal from parts or all of the occupied West Bank and Gaza. A small but growing number of Israeli politicians and peace groups have accepted the principle of the mutual and simultaneous self-determination of Israelis and Palestinians. The Israelis have realized most recently in Lebanon that military force can never resolve political disputes.

3. In the United States, the traditional concern for Israel's security has been increasingly matched by an appreciation of Palestinian rights. The Reagan initiative of September 1982 was

a step forward in this respect, though it was immediately rejected by the Israeli government, and also failed to satisfy the Arab demand for Palestinian self-determination.

Direct Negotiations Are Possible

Efforts now taking place in the Middle East again aim to reinvigorate the forces of peace on both sides. Jordan and the Palestine Liberation Organization (PLO) reached agreement on February 11, [1985] on a joint position that envisages a peaceful settlement of the Arab-Israeli conflict, based on Israeli statehood and security, and Palestinian self-determination. Egypt has made some specific proposals. Israel's response has left the door open for direct talks with a Jordanian-Palestinian team. The United States has tried to keep the momentum for peace alive.

Mutual Security

The time is ripe for a just and lasting settlement of the Arab-Israeli conflict. The prerequisites are clear. The Palestine Arabs, under Israeli occupation and in the diaspora, must be allowed the right to national self-determination. The international community, including the United States, and implicitly even Israel, has recognized that the Palestine problem is at the core of the continuing Middle East tragedy. If it is to be solved, Israel must withdraw from territories occupied in the 1967 war. Withdrawal must be accompanied by the introduction of security measures and guarantees. . . . Such exchanges, however, must come about as a result of negotiations aimed at mutual security and not through the use of force or the threat of permanent occupation. Whatever happens, the search for peace must go on, not only for the sake of Arab and Jew, but for that of the whole world.

Hassan bin Talal, *Search for Peace*, 1984.

The prospects for direct negotiations between Arabs and Israelis are distant, as always, but perhaps less distant than they were a few years ago. The opportunity that now challenges us all is nothing less than peace among all the children of Abraham—Christians, Moslems and Jews.

Guns Cannot Bring Security

The Jewish people have secured their state, and fortified it militarily. But they have not secured that which should be more dear to them than anything else in this world—the acceptance of their Arab brothers and sisters, their Semitic cousins, their Abrahamic family.

History has taught us all that genuine security does not come from the strength of guns, but rather from the mercy, forgiveness and acceptance of one's adversary. There are increasing numbers of Israelis and Arabs who have become convinced that warfare cannot resolve the Arab-Israeli conflict. It can only be resolved by assuring the rights of both Israelis and Palestinians, in the historical land of Palestine they both covet. . . .

The Arab Vision

An international consensus has emerged in recent years that envisages the resolution of the Arab-Israeli conflict through the satisfaction of Israeli demands for recognition and security, and of Palestinian demands for self-determination and security. In the Fez peace plan and the Jordan-PLO accord, the Arab world has outlined its vision of a Middle East at peace, with security guaranteed for Israel, a Palestinian state confederated with Jordan, and all the other Arab states.

The people of Israel and their many supporters in the West must soon decide: Is their objective the false security that comes from occupying Arab lands and denying Palestinian rights? Or is their objective the genuine security that can only emanate from a peace that satisfies Palestinian as well as Israeli demands?

For the first time since 1948, the Arab world is talking in terms of a negotiated, peaceful and permanent resolution of the conflict with Israel. We are talking about international guarantees for the security of all states in the region, including an Israeli and a Palestinian state.

Short-Lived Opportunities

The opportunity before us today will not remain on the table for very long. The history of the Arab-Israeli conflict is one of short-lived opportunities that have been missed because of inflexible political attitudes, and invariably replaced by a resurgent extremism on both sides.

A new opportunity now presents itself: An opportunity to satisfy Palestinian demands for the promise of national self-determination that Woodrow Wilson articulated for all the people of the free world in 1918. An opportunity for Israel and the Jewish people to enjoy the kind of genuine security they have sought unsuccessfully for two millennia. An opportunity for the Arab states to get on with the challenges of nation-building and fulfilling the vast potential of their people.

If this opportunity is to be seized, reasonable people on all sides will have to reinforce the conviction that peace, security and the right of self-determination, like liberty, are indivisible, and must be granted to both Israelis and Palestinians. If balance and reciprocity are our guidelines, the dream of a just peace can be attained. And the legacy of Abraham can be realized at last.

"At this point in our conflict, maps . . . turn into an act of faith, a call for action, for revenge. I'll destroy your map as you have destroyed mine."

Peace Is Not Possible in the Middle East

Meron Benvenisti

In his most recent book, *Conflicts and Contradictions*, Meron Benvenisti analyzes the problems facing Israeli society. Benvenisti's vantage point is that of a Jew living on the border between an Arab and a Jewish neighborhood in Jerusalem. In the following viewpoint, an excerpt from that book, Benvenisti argues that both sides have created their own sacred maps of Palestine, maps that correspond to their histories in the land. Since neither side can recognize the other side's map, he argues, peace is unlikely. Benvenisti was formerly the deputy mayor of Jerusalem.

As you read, consider the following questions:

1. What does the author mean by the expression, *"geographia sacra"*?
2. Why does Benvenisti believe that both Jews and Palestinians have their own *geographia sacra* and how does this make peace less likely?
3. What questions does Benvenisti believe need to be asked before the conflict can be resolved?

A little while ago, just before the Passover vacation, my son Yuval came home with the itinerary for his school outing. My father, who was there at the time, asked to see it. Glancing through it, I could see something was making him angry. "Why are all the place names in Arabic?" he demanded. "Don't they know in the Scouts that these places have Hebrew names?" His reaction was not surprising. My father, eighty-seven, a teacher and a geographer, has devoted his whole life to one thing: creating a new Hebrew map of Eretz Israel and instilling in young people a love of country. For years he has been a member of the official "naming committees" whose task it was to Hebraize all the names on the ordinance map of Eretz Israel and to name new Jewish settlements. His maps can be seen on the walls of classrooms throughout Israel. In fact the huge blue-brown-and-green wall map he drew is imprinted in the visual memory of hundreds of thousands of Israelis. . . .

The Jewish Map

Changing place names in order to arrive at a Hebrew map of Eretz Israel was considered by my father a sacred task. He was one of Israel's first geographers—awarded the Israel Prize for his life's work. And now, after sixty years, that his own grandson should come to him with Arab names instead of Hebrew ones seemed to him tantamount to sacrilege. Like all immigrant societies, we attempted to erase all alien names, but here the analogy becomes complicated because we were not simply an immigrant society or an army of conquerors. At our coming, we reestablished contact with those same landscapes and places from which we had been physically removed for two thousand years but whose names we had always preserved. We carried around with us for centuries our *geographia sacra*, not only biblical names but all the mishnaic and talmudic names. Wherever we were dispersed—in France, Germany, Egypt, Persia—we would study texts and learn about the rosters of priestly duty in the Temple enumerating by turn their home villages in the Galilee. People who knew nothing about the physical reality of those villages knew their names by heart. So when we returned to the land it was the most natural thing to seek out those ancient places and identify them. . . .

Arab Names Cannot Be Erased

From a very early age, perhaps four or five, I and my brother would accompany my father on his Sabbath expeditions. And so it was that the Arab names of villages and mountains, groves and springs became those of my childhood. I remember the names perfectly—they became second nature to me—and when I travel around the country I unfailingly recall the previous names. The

Arab names. I have a friend who lives in a Jewish village in the Jerusalem corridor. When he mentions the Hebrew name Shoevah, I immediately think of it as Saris, the Arab name. . . .

Taking One's Eyes Off the Map

Peace between Egypt and Israel could be accomplished through a change in the map, along with some soothing rhetoric. But peace between Israel and Jordan and the Palestinians can only be accomplished through a change in sensibilities. . . . The only peace process with a future is one in which peoples on both sides can be convinced, educated or cajoled to take their eyes off the map for a moment and to take a few small steps toward each other. It is also the only approach that can create options which now seem unavailable.

Thomas L. Friedman, *The New York Times Magazine*, January 26, 1986.

The Hebrew map of Israel constitutes one stratum in my consciousness, underlaid by another stratum of the previous Arab map. Those names turn me and anyone who was born into them into sons of the same homeland—but also into mortal enemies. I can't help but reflect on the irony that my father, by taking me on his trips and hoping to instill in me the love of our Hebrew homeland, imprinted in my memory, along with the new names, the names he wished to eradicate.

The Palestinian Map

This brings me, strangely enough, to the Lebanon war. I was aware for quite some time that Palestinian research institutes in Beirut were compiling files on each Palestinian village in Israel. Since the beginning of the war I wondered about the fate of those files. I was fairly sure that General Sharon and General Eitan would search them out, seize them, and destroy them in order to complete the eradication of Arab Palestine. This is what eventually happened when the Israeli Army entered West Beirut. I knew that some of the information in those files was purely imaginary and was used as propaganda against my country. Every refugee, even the lowliest, is convinced that he used to own at least a hundred acres of orchards and a large house in Israel. It is an understandable tendency to magnify the scale of what they lost. But the point is—and there lies the irony and the tragedy— that they have created their own *geographia sacra*, just as we did in our Diaspora. Their map-making is the answer to our Hebrew, Israeli map. They are trying by an act of will to recreate and preserve the old reality, the one we erased in order to create our own. Their map-making is as far removed from reality as our memorizing the list of villages of the priestly roster.

187

Not only are the refugee camps organized by sections according to the villages in Palestine from which the refugees originated, their children are taught exclusively with reference to the pre-1948 map of Palestine. On their maps hundreds of Palestinian villages, long since destroyed, are shown, but the Jewish cities, settlements, roads, and ports are omitted. Everything that happened subsequent to their departure is perceived as an aberration. Their refusal to cope with the stark and cruel reality causes them to believe that what the Jews print on their maps is sheer fiction. . . .

A Zero-Sum Game

At this point in our conflict, maps cease being geographical and turn into an act of faith, a call for action, for revenge. I'll destroy your map as you have destroyed mine. A zero-sum game that is played out not only in words and symbols, but in concrete deeds of destruction.

There is no point in asking who started. It is true that my father had started his Hebrew map to gain symbolic possession of his ancestral land. But he believed that he was doing so peaceably, not disinheriting anybody. Indeed he and most of his generation genuinely believed that there was enough room in the country for everybody. The Palestinians did not take him seriously. For them he was a romantic Westerner, just like the British and German explorers who came before him and left, with their strange compasses, sextants, and theodolites. They did not realize that his map-making was of a different sort, that he intended to settle down and teach his children the names he invented, and by so doing, to perpetuate them and thus transform symbolic possession into actual possession. When the Arabs realized the danger, it was too late. They tried to destroy my father physically, but they failed. He offered them compromises, but they rejected them. Finally an all-out war decided the issue; they were driven out, and his map triumphed. Then we set out to transform the land, to construct our own edifices, to plan our own orchards. But we also deliberately destroyed the remnants our enemies left lest they come back and attempt to lay claim to it. We knew that had they won they would have destroyed our work. But we won, so we became the destroyers. Who is the victim? Who is the culprit? Who is the judge? . . .

Almost two million Palestinians still live on their land, cherish it, and are determined to preserve their own map and physical forms. It is impossible to erase their contribution to the landscape of our shared homeland, no matter how hard people try. Someone, someday, will raise the question and will demand an answer. Are we ready to merge the two maps? Are we ready to stop eradicating each other's names? When such questions can be asked, perhaps the dissonance and conflict that plague so many Israelis will be

© Kirk/Rothco

resolved.

When at a certain stage I left my own immediate surroundings to seek out a more universal dimension to my experiences, I found myself in the Grand Opera House of Belfast. The first performance of Brian Friel's *Translations* was given in the Opera House—rebuilt after twenty-four bombing incidents—to an all-Catholic audience. The play dealt with the substitution of an English map of Ireland for the original, the ultimate symbolic expression of possession. When the play ended, I said to my friend, a Catholic, "You know what? We've been doing the same thing all along—translating, changing names, creating a new reality." My friend regarded me for a moment with an expression of the utmost sadness and said at last, "Well, if that's the case, may God have mercy on you all!"

"Today there is simply no alternative to an international conference on the Middle East."

An International Conference Is Necessary for Peace

Alexei Vasilyev

In 1984 the Soviet Union proposed that an international conference be held to work for peace in the Middle East. The conference would include members of the United Nations Security Council, representatives of Middle Eastern nations, and Palestinian representatives. The following viewpoint is by Alexei Vasilyev, a Soviet historian and the assistant director of the Africa Institute at the USSR Academy of Sciences. Vasilyev argues that previous negotiation efforts by the US have failed because they were unfair to Arab countries. He believes that a successful international conference would create a system to protect the interests of all parties and end the conflict.

As you read, consider the following questions:

1. What does Vasilyev believe has been wrong with the peace settlements offered by the US and its allies?
2. What position does the author believe the Arab nations must take to work for peace?
3. What is required for the conference to be successful, according to Vasilyev, and who will benefit from a successful conference?

Alexei Vasilyev, "Middle East: A Solution Is Feasible," *New Times*, No. 8, March 2, 1987.

For a long time now perennial conflicts, which have carried off tens and even hundreds of thousands of human lives, have become well-nigh standard items of press and TV news. The Arab-Israeli conflict, now more and more often overshadowed by the bloody and protracted Iranian-Iraqi war, is a case in point. That conflict is dangerous not only because it could at any moment flare up with renewed violence, but because it is an obstacle to the solution of cardinal international problems without which it is impossible to safeguard humanity from destruction.

Separate Deals vs. Collective Effort

Numerous plans for finding a way out of the crisis have been advanced. The "settlements" offered by the U.S.A., Israel and a number of West European countries have boiled down to nothing more than attempts to conclude separate deals between Israel and neighbouring Arab countries, invariably at the expense of the Palestinians.

Soviet diplomacy has always placed the emphasis on collective effort, on the convening of an international conference on the Middle East. In the light of current developments this has become an urgent necessity. Today there is simply no alternative to an international conference on the Middle East. Even those unwilling to take part in it have begun to speak of a conference as a practical possibility. True, they are prompted not so much by a striving for peace as by the intention to use it as a means of putting through the same old separate deals on their own terms—in the interests of the aggressor and his powerful backer.

UN Support

U.N. General Assembly resolution 41/43D reaffirms the urgent need to convene an international peace conference to work out a comprehensive resolution of the Middle East problem acceptable to all. The call contained in it to set up a preparatory committee with the participation of all the permanent members of the U.N. Security Council is the first practical step in this direction. In adopting the above resolution by 123 votes the United Nations endorsed the Soviet proposal on this issue. Thus, the question now is not whether to hold such a conference but what methods are most constructive for holding it and ensuring its success.

The Soviet proposals lay down no hard and fast rules for the preparation and conduct of the conference. It is not imposing its own point of view on others. The conference must be the product of the efforts of many, and this implies both compromise and diplomatic methods of reaching agreement.

The need for an international Middle East conference is recognized both in the Arab countries and in many West European capitals. The lack of any progress has to be a characteristic feature of the present situation. But there is a growing realization that this stagnancy is becoming increasingly dangerous for the parties to the conflict and the region as a whole. The malignancy of the crisis has been brought home sharply in recent weeks by the shooting down of peaceful Palestinian Arab demonstrators in the West Bank, the intensification of hostilities in Lebanon and the latest Israeli air raids on Palestinian refugee camps and Lebanese towns and villages. And, of course, by the latest U.S. moves—the dispatch of naval forces to the Middle East coast with obviously aggressive intentions.

Disunity Among the Arabs

The tragedy, perhaps the main tragedy, lies in the disunity of the Arab countries, their inability to find the strength and courage to put an end to the internecine strife and to the contradictions which, of course, pale before the main problem facing them all—the need to take a united stand against the American-Israeli conspiracy, to take joint action to achieve a political settlement. The

Ed Stein, reprinted with permission.

Arabs need resolution and consistency also for coordinated actions to resolve the Palestine question. The two are inseparably linked. For any agreement on a Middle East settlement must provide for the establishment of an independent Palestinian state. To evade the issue is to stop halfway and perpetuate the likelihood of even more bloodshed. The tendency of some Arab states described as "moderates" to accept the situation when the coals of the conflict continue to smoulder, threatening to flare up into another military conflagration may be explicable but by no means justifiable.

Israel's Uncompromising Position

Now about Israel's position. Formerly Tel Aviv, in unison with Washington, rejected out of hand the idea of a Middle East peace conference, counting on its military superiority, its ability to continue to "run the show." But on February 1, [1987] the Israeli government held a meeting at which, according to Reuters [news service] for instance, Israel's participation in an international peace conference on the Middle East was discussed. Prime Minister Itzhak Shamir and Foreign Minister Shimon Peres reportedly argued at length about the advantage or disadvantage for Israel of participation in such a conference. The Foreign Minister said that Israel should not reject the proposal outright. Why? Because the idea was favoured by Egypt and Jordan, with which Israel wished to "improve relations"—to the detriment, naturally, of the rest of the Arab world. The Prime Minister, on the other hand, objected that "accepting an international forum would put Israel under pressure to make concessions." And it of course did not intend to make any concessions whatever.

The whole "argument," however, rang false. Peres advanced his own plan, every point of which was an ultimatum. An ultimatum to the Arabs—under no circumstances was the Palestine Liberation Organization to be allowed to take part in the conference. Instead, the "authentic Palestinians," i.e., those who live in Israeli-occupied territory and collaborate with the occupation authorities, could be admitted but without being given any independent role. This means denying any say to those who for decades had been living in exile. An ultimatum to the entire international community was the stipulation that "the conference must be of short duration." In other words, a mere formality, for a problem of such magnitude cannot be resolved at one sitting. This was in effect confirmed by Peres who said that "the conference cannot impose a solution to the Arab-Israeli conflict."

As you see, the Israeli position is as before aimed at excluding any possibility of a political settlement in the Middle East.

One thing is clear. The conference can be successful only on one condition: if the interests of all concerned—the Arab countries and Israel—are taken into account. It should not be just a matter of reconciling them for one moment only for the guns to start speaking again the next. The important thing is to establish a system in the Middle East that would ensure stable peace and guarantee the sovereign rights of all the peoples who live there. This, incidentally, would accord with the vital interests of the United States, which is still adding fuel to the flames of military confrontation. And it would accord with the no less vital and important interests of the Soviet Union in a region situated in such close proximity to the U.S.S.R.

4

"The only way to achieve progress is through negotiations."

Direct Negotiations Between Arabs and Israelis Are Necessary

Kenneth W. Dam

After the June 1967 war between Israel and its Arab neighbors, Egypt, Syria, and Jordan, the United Nations unanimously passed Resolution 242. The resolution called for Israel to withdraw its armed forces from the territories it occupied during the war. It also affirmed that all countries in the Middle East should have secure borders, free from attack from their neighbors. Deputy Secretary of State Kenneth W. Dam argues in the following viewpoint that US policy is based on Resolution 242. Israel, with the support of the US, must negotiate peace with each of its Arab neighbors.

As you read, consider the following questions:

1. What reasons does the author cite for US involvement in the Middle East?
2. How has the Soviet Union excluded itself from peace negotiations, according to Dam?
3. What, according to the author, constrains moderate Arab nations from directly negotiating with Israel?

Kenneth W. Dam, "Negotiations: The Path to Peace in the Middle East," a speech before the American Law Institute in Washington, DC on May 16, 1985. Published by the US Department of State, Bureau of Public Affairs.

The Middle East is a region of diversity, complexity, and turbulence. It is a strategic crossroads, a source of vital energy supplies, and the birthplace and confluence of three great religions. No wonder it has long been a focus of the world's attention. No wonder its challenges have a particular urgency. The dramas of the Middle East have a special compelling quality—in human and moral terms, as well as strategic. . . .

The Arab-Israeli conflict, of course, receives the lion's share of our attention, but we should bear in mind that it is but one element of a broad set of issues. Today, we must also be concerned about the continuing dangers of the Iran-Iraq war, the widespread use of state terrorism, the outlaw behavior of Qadhafi, the rise of religious extremism, the Soviet threat, chronic instability in Lebanon, and many other problems—all in a large and volatile area where the United States and the West have an enormous strategic stake. . . .

The US and Israel

Our involvement in the Middle East stems, above all, from our close relations with the peoples of the region. Since the founding of the State of Israel, for instance, the American people have been committed on both moral and strategic grounds to the security of that nation. In the aftermath of the Holocaust, we have all felt deeply the justice and necessity of helping preserve a land where Jews can live as Jews in a nation of their own. Our close ties to Israel are reinforced by that nation's commitment to ideals and principles that are the foundation of our own society: freedom, democracy, and the rule of law. As the years passed, Americans also came to see the growing importance of Israel as a strategic partner in a region of superpower contention. Today, Americans know that Israel is a staunch and reliable friend in a dangerous world. . . .

We also know that durable peace and security for Israel can only come when it is recognized and accepted by its neighbors. Our commitment to a secure Israel, therefore, is indissolubly linked to our search for peace.

The US and Arab Nations

Our close friendships in the Arab world are another reason for our deep involvement in the Middle East. Like the people of Israel, the Arab world is heir to a proud history and civilization that have enriched mankind. The United States has had a long association with the moderate Arab states. American companies, universities, hospitals, and private voluntary organizations have a long history of constructive activity in the region. Extensive military and economic cooperation and assistance have helped assure mutual security and well-being. The friendship, security, and economic and political stability of the moderate Arab states are important to us.

Finally, our involvement in the Middle East is grounded in our strategic interests. The Middle East is a region of vital importance to the West, a target of Moscow's efforts to expand its influence, and an arena in which hopes for peace and moderation are challenged by radical forces hostile to us. . . .

The American Role

The question, then, is how do we promote peace? What should our diplomatic role be?

We have long been a key factor in the search for peace. Both sides have sought our help. Such an American role is indispensable—and it is unique. The Soviet Union has excluded itself from any possibility of playing a constructive role. It has failed to maintain relations with Israel; it has not tried to moderate its clients; indeed, it has supported the forces of radicalism and violence.

Negotiating a Lasting Peace

We believe—and have consistently maintained—that a just and lasting peace in the region can only be worked out through direct negotiations between Israel and her Arab neighbors. And we will persist in our efforts to help the parties involved work out the means by which these direct negotiations can be begun—and pursued successfully.

Richard W. Murphy, speech to the U.S.-Arab Chamber of Commerce, April 3, 1987.

America's unique position as an honest broker trusted by both sides has resulted in a number of successes. Our diplomacy helped secure the Sinai disengagement agreements of 1974 and 1975, the Israeli-Syrian disengagement of 1974, and most important, the Camp David accords and the Peace Treaty Between Israel and Egypt. Our goal for the future is to build on these past successes to secure a lasting peace between Israel and *all* of its neighbors.

But as we seek this goal, we must be guided by the lessons of the past.

One of the most important lessons we have learned is that a strong, visible, and permanent American commitment to Israel is essential in the search for peace. History demonstrates that movement toward peace can come only when no one in the Arab world or elsewhere has any doubt of the central reality that America's support for Israel can never be weakened.

Israel has shown that it will not change its policies in the face of military or terrorist threats; nor will the policies of the United

States ever yield to terror or intimidation. Let no one miss the point: there are no military options. There are no terrorist options. The only way to achieve progress is through negotiations. . . .

We also know that Arab nations and individuals willing to move toward peace take risks. Radicals in the region use terrorism and threats of war not only against Americans and Israelis but against Arabs and Palestinians who work for negotiations. Those who take risks for peace should know that the United States will continue to support all who seek peaceful solutions against those who promote violence and oppose peace.

Direct Negotiations

America's task is to help the parties find ways to enter into direct negotiations. Our role requires persistence and active engagement. But the key decisions must be made by the parties themselves, willingly and free from coercion. Once the parties themselves have made the all-important decision to negotiate, we will participate actively, as we have in the past.

In preaching the efficacy of negotiations, we have urged our Israeli and Arab friends to avoid seeking guarantees, in advance, of the outcome of negotiations. There should be no preconditions. The place to negotiate is at the bargaining table.

As President Reagan said on September 1, 1982: "We base our approach squarely on the principle that the Arab-Israeli conflict should be resolved through negotiations involving an exchange of territory for peace." The land-for-peace formula was enshrined in UN Security Council Resolution 242 and remains the basis of our effort.

As the President spelled out in his initiative, ". . . the United States will not support the establishment of an independent Palestinian state in the West Bank and Gaza, and we will not support annexation or permanent control by Israel." We see self-government by the Palestinians of the West Bank and Gaza in association with Jordan as offering the best chance for a durable, just, and lasting peace. We foresee a transitional period, "during which the Palestinian inhabitants . . . will have full autonomy over their own affairs."

The President expressed the fervent hope that the Palestinians and Jordan, with the support of their Arab colleagues, would accept this opportunity. . . .

Moderate Forces for Peace

There has been a growing cooperative spirit and unity of purpose among the moderate Arab states that favor progress toward peace. Egypt, once ostracized for making peace with Israel, is regaining its leadership position in the Arab world—without compromising its commitment to peace. King Hussein's bold decision last September [1984] to restore relations between Egypt and Jordan was a key step in this process. Our re-establishment of relations with Iraq last November [1984], together with our improving relations with Algeria symbolized by President Bendjedid's visit here in April [1985], represent tangible steps toward greater and wider cooperation.

This coalescing of moderate forces in the region has improved the conditions for progress. . . .

An Honorable Solution

Nobody brought more tragedy on the Palestinians than PLO terrorism. . . . We know that there is a Palestinian problem. We recognize the need to solve it honorably. We are convinced that there is no solution but through diplomatic means. From this rostrum, I call upon the Palestinian people to put an end to rejectionism and belligerency. Let us talk! Come forth and recognize the reality of the State of Israel—our wish to live in peace and our need for security. Let us face each other as free men and women, across the negotiating table.

Shimon Peres, speech to the General Assembly of the United Nations, October 21, 1985.

The health of the Egyptian-Israeli relationship is vital to the overall peace process. When relations between Egypt and Israel are improving, it reminds both Arabs and Israelis of the efficacy of negotiations.

The challenge now is to translate the desire of Israel, Jordan, Egypt, and many Palestinians for movement toward peace into a concrete agreement for direct negotiations based on Resolution 242.

The United States has played an active part in that effort. . . . One goal has been to explore more deeply the prospects for direct negotiations between the Jordanians, Palestinians, and Israelis on terms that all can accept. Another goal has been to help strengthen ties between Israel and Egypt. . . .

Committed to Peace

To be sure, there is still much distance to be traveled. But the way is open for progress if the parties in the region have the will and the courage to forge ahead. . . . We have faith in the commitment and determination of our friends in the region to find a way toward peace. We will settle for nothing less.

"Iran has before it a criminal, aggressive and occupying regime that has violated all recognized international laws."

Iraq Prolongs the Iran/Iraq War

Ministry of Foreign Affairs of Iran

In September 1980, war broke out between Iran and Iraq. The following viewpoint is an excerpt from a book published by the Legal Department of Iran's Ministry of Foreign Affairs. The author explains that Iran values good relations between countries and respects international law as set forth in the United Nations Charter. The author then contrasts Iran's policies with Iraq's to argue that if international law is to be upheld, the Iraqi government of President Saddam Hussein must be punished for its invasion of Iran.

As you read, consider the following questions:

1. How does Islam affect Iran's relationship with other countries, according to the author?
2. Why does the author believe the government of Iraq is unfit to rule the Iraqi people?
3. What must be done before a just peace between Iran and Iraq is achieved, according to the author?

A Review of the Imposed War by the Iraqi Regime Upon the Islamic Republic of Iran. Published by the Legal Department of the Ministry of Foreign Affairs of Iran, February 1983.

The Islamic Republic of Iran, with its commitment to the lofty principles and teachings of Islam, deems itself as bound to implement the divine orders and exalted values which set the criteria in the relations between states and between the states and their nationals and, in the entire human society. . . .

The Charter of the United Nations Organization is among those treaties ratified by the Government of Iran and is as valid as any internal law passed by the legislature, and any interested person may demand its implementation and, when necessary, refer to internal courts. . . .

Iran's Peaceful Intentions

The pacifism of the Islamic Republic of Iran and its desire to follow a nonaligned policy without joining any military or political block for military or warlike objectives is very well reflected in Article 146 of the Constitution: "No military base shall be set up in Iran by foreign countries even if such bases are to be used for peaceful purposes."

"Negation of all forms of domination," which is repeatedly stipulated in the Constitution, is clearly indicative of the fact that the Government of the Islamic Republic of Iran cannot and should not embark on any aggressive act and should not have any nonpeaceful intention. It is, therefore, evident that if a dispute arises between this Government and any other government, it deems itself found to act in accordance with Paragraph 1, of Article 33 of the United Nations Charter that reads: "The parties to any dispute, the continuance of which is likely to endanger the maintenance of international peace and security, shall, first of all, seek a solution by negotiation, enquiry, mediation, conciliation, arbitration, judicial settlement, resort to regional agencies or arrangements, or other peaceful means of their own choice."

Inspired by the words and the spirit of this commitment, and impelled by its allegiance to its dictates, the Islamic Republic of Iran did from the outset insist that in the face of Iraq's preconceived schemes for invading Iran and notwithstanding widespread propaganda by the racist regime in Baghdad for promoting the notion of racial and ethnic superiority of Arabs, all disputes with the Baghdad regime must be resolved by peaceful means and in keeping with the provisions of the UN Charter and mutual treaties. . . .

The Government of the Islamic Republic of Iran has before it a criminal, aggressive and occupying regime that has violated all recognized international laws and principles, and which is led by Saddam Tekriti and his Ba'athist henchmen. There exists, between the government and people of the Islamic Republic of Iran and the tyrannized and oppressed people of Iraq, no feeling but one of brotherhood and equality and both nations share the same religion, which feeling will also be felt toward any government in Iraq coming to power upon the will of the people of that country. The Government of Iran, without having the least designs on Iraqi territory, will cooperate with such a government in all fields. This commitment has been repeatedly stated by the leaders of the Islamic Republic of Iran, which is an integral aspect of the general strategy of the Iranian Government.

Iraq's Criminal Government

The fascist and racist Ba'athist Party of Iraq, which has excelled all criminals in human history, . . . lacks the necessary competence to rule over Iraq and be the representative of the people of Iraq. Therefore, if the Government of the Islamic Republic of Iran, which is still exposed to Iraqi aggressions since the beginning of the aggression of the Ba'athist regime of Iraq and is still suffering from irreparable financial and human losses, wants the international community to punish the aggressor. It is because this regime, similar to other criminals, who commit acts against the peace and security of the international community, lacks, from the viewpoint of international law, the necessary good will to continue its rule. As an historical example, we may cite Nazism and the crimes they (the Nazists) committed against humanity and the world's reaction to it. . . .

Iran's Rights

The U.N. Security Council, upon a proposal extended by Jordan, and backed by the U.S., the Soviet Union and European countries, held a session on discontinuation of the war. After studying the proposal by Jordan, the Security Council passed a resolution calling for a cease-fire to be observed by the belligerent parties and demanding withdrawal of troops by both sides from each others' territories. . . .

Naturally, considering the fact that the United Nations has always backed Iraq and has never pressed it for the restitution of Iran's rights, it would never succeed in getting the approval of both parties, and therefore, the war will continue as the only way for Saddam's defeat.

Islamic Revolution's Guards Corps, *A Glance at Two Years of War*, 1982.

The Government of Iran, as the victim of this aggression, does not have any ambition to the other [country's] territories and believes that the Iraqi territory belongs to the Muslim and brotherly people of Iraq and that it is the Iraqis who should determine their own future and the form of government they prefer.

The criminal responsibility of the leaders of the present Iraqi regime emanates from their resort to force. This resort to force has been in violation of all international regulations. Hence, in accordance with these regulations, the perpetrators, and thereby the ruling regime in Iraq, becomes liable for its breach of these regulations. . . .

International Principles

The principles of the Nuremberg Court have been unanimously adopted in Resolution 95 of the UN General Assembly of December 11, 1946, as accepted principles of the international law. Some of these principles are as follows:

Principle 1: Whoever commits an act which, in accordance with international law, is considered a crime (e.g., preparing a war of aggression or commanding armed forces to attack a neighbouring country) is deemed as responsible and should be prosecuted. Article 19 of the project of the Commission on International Law is also applicable in this case. . . .

Principle 3: In this case, the perpetrator of the international crime is the head of a state (Saddam as head of the ruling regime in Iraq), who will be not be exonerated from his international responsibility. . . .

Iraq Must Be Punished

It is on the basis of these principles and other undeniable principles of public international law and accepted customs, that the Government of the Islamic Republic of Iran insists upon the punishment of the aggressor as a principal condition for the establishment of a just and lasting peace between the two countries.

"[Iran] aims at . . . creating a new political, military and economic situation in the region as a whole—one that would serve Iran's expansionist objectives."

Iran Prolongs the Iran/Iraq War

Tariq Aziz

In February 1986 the United Nations Security Council passed a resolution calling for an immediate ceasefire between Iran and Iraq. In the following viewpoint, Tariq Aziz argues that Iran uses peace negotiations to stall for time so that it can strengthen its military and invade Iraq. UN negotiations can be successful only if Iran is called to fully abide by international law and respect Iraq's territory, Aziz contends. He is the Deputy Prime Minister and Minister for Foreign Affairs of Iraq.

As you read, consider the following questions:

1. How does Aziz use the example of Iran's policy on civilian targets to support his argument that Iran is not serious about peace?
2. What is the fundamental rule of international law, according to the author?
3. What does Aziz believe has been wrong with peace negotiations to date?

Tariq Aziz in a speech given before the 2,663rd meeting of the United Nations Security Council in New York on February 18, 1986.

Iran, as it has declared openly in its military communiqués and in statements of the President of the Iranian Republic, aims at occupying the northern part of the Arab Gulf and creating a new political, military and economic situation in the region as a whole—one that would serve Iran's expansionist objectives. That is what led to the outbreak of the war on 4 September, 1980; that is why the war has continued ever since. That expansion is aimed not only at Iraq but also at the other States of the region. Hence, concern over this invasion, both Arab and international, is greater now than at any other time, despite the continuous calls for an end to the war and the achievement of peace in the area. . . .

Iran Attacks Cities

If we go back a little in history, we find that Iran began its aggressive war against Iraq on 4 September 1980, by shelling cities and densely populated areas. When the scale of military operations increased, Iraq did not use its air force to hit any population centre. Iranian jets, on the other hand, carried out dozens of raids daily on Baghdad, Mosul, Basra and other cities in Iraq, killing civilians and destroying houses, hospitals, schools and anything else that its bombs could reach. Iran's air force continued, despite the great destruction it had suffered, to carry out raids whenever it could against our towns and villages in order to hit population centres. . . .

Following the withdrawal of the Iraqi forces from the Iranian territories in June of 1982, and the concentration of Iranian forces along the borders, a regular and continuous shelling began to be carried out against all Iraqi towns and villages within range of Iranian artillery. . . .

On 7 June 1983, the President of the Republic of Iraq proposed the conclusion of a special agreement between Iraq and Iran, under the auspices of the United Nations, to abstain from attacking population centres. That proposal was rejected by Iran. Resolution 540 (1983) of the Council contained a specific paragraph calling for the immediate cessation of all military operations against civilian targets, including cities and residential areas. But Iran rejected that resolution too, as is well known. . . .

There is a basic conflict of intentions between the international community—of which we are a part—and the Iranian régime on the question of abstaining from attacks on purely civilian population centres. While the international community hopes to spare civilians the ravages of war and considers this a doorway to a comprehensive settlement of the conflict, the Iranian régime exploits this sensitive question without any moral constraint in order to create circumstances favourable to continuing the war and carrying out invasion. . . .

International law is founded upon fundamental rules, the most

205

important of which are respect for the sovereignty and independence of other States, the right of the State to self-defence in the face of aggression, and resort to peaceful means for the settlement of disputes. International law also contains subsidiary and supplementary rules, but it is not correct in law to adhere to subsidiary and supplementary rules and to persist in violating the fundamental rules. International law as a whole grants rights to States and imposes obligations upon them. It is not legally correct for a State to adhere to its rights without at the same time honouring its obligations and respecting the rights enjoyed by another State under international law. In the conflict it is now considering, the Security Council is faced with a strange and grave situation in which one of the parties to the conflict insists on violating all the fundamental rules of international law while adhering to the substance of the subsidiary rules. And even in adhering to those subsidiary rules, that party, while maintaining its own rights under them, omits to recognize the rights that the same rules give the other party. . . .

Iran's Aggression

Iran has violated the fundamental principle upon which international relations rest: the principle of non-interference in the affairs of any other country, which is universally recognized as the *conditio sine qua non* for peaceful coexistence between nations. In fact, the practice of any form of interference is not merely a violation of the letter and spirit of the United Nations Charter and the principles of international law concerning friendly relations and cooperation among States, . . . but it is also a step towards the creation of situations threatening international peace and security.

Chedli Klibi, speech to the United Nations Security Council, February 18, 1986.

The [UN] Organization has engaged itself in dealing with certain aspects of the war without placing any strong pressure upon Iran to put an end to it through peaceful settlement. That policy has in effect helped the Iranian régime to realize its objective of continuing the war and has served its endeavours to occupy Iraq; it has thus contributed to the continuation of the threat to security and stability in the Arab Gulf region.

Since the inception of that policy in 1983—a policy based on the hope that the scourge of war can be gradually reduced to the point at which the achievement of a comprehensive peaceful settlement might be possible—the Iranian régime has exploited it to the greatest possible extent. The concrete outcome of that policy is that the Iranians have been given time to prepare for repeated invasions of Iraq. . . .

I declare in this forum, with full candour and firmness, that Iraq will not accept any course different from that prescribed in the Charter and international law and consecrated in State practice to resolve international disputes. Enough of the policies of selective and divisible treatment, of ambiguous formulas; enough of not focusing our efforts upon the central point of the settlement—namely, putting an end to the war in accordance with the norms that have been established internationally.

Erroneous diplomatic interpretations have resulted in streams of blood, brought about untold destruction and encouraged the Iranian régime to persist in waging war with an arrogance unprecedented in the history of the United Nations. Iraq will not accept, participate in or assume the responsibility of any interpretation which does not focus clearly and unambiguously upon the means for ending the war. . . .

Complying with International Principles

Iraq is presenting to the Security Council its conflict with Iran, and is acquainting the Council with the Iranian aggressive schemes and the attempts of the Iranian régime to occupy its territory, not out of weakness or powerlessness but in excercise of its rights and responsibilities as a Member of the United Nations and out of its concern to establish peace and security with its neighbours and its respect for the rules of the Charter and international law. Hence, it is incumbent upon the Council to shoulder its responsibilities which are provided for in the Charter. The Council should confront the Iranian régime with its responsibilities in a decisive manner. Either it accepts these principles which were drawn up to regulate relations between nations in the modern age or it should isolate itself from the international community. It is for the international community, through the Security Council, which is entrusted with the task of the maintenance of peace, security and stability in the world, to take the measures appropriate to the situation.

"Responsibility . . . rests with the two belligerents, who started the war and are steadfastly perpetuating it."

Neither Iran nor Iraq Wants Peace

Mansour Farhang

Mansour Farhang is a professor of politics at Bennington College in Vermont. He was the Islamic Republic of Iran's first ambassador to the United Nations but resigned to protest Ayatollah Khomeini's policies during the American hostage crisis. He was also involved in international negotiations on the Iran/Iraq war. In the following viewpoint, Farhang argues that Iraqi leader Saddam Hussein and Iranian leader Khomeini are using the war to gain supremacy in the Persian Gulf. Despite the hardships the war has caused their countries, neither leader will end the war because it would mean losing face. Farhang concludes that the war will end only when Hussein and Khomeini are replaced.

As you read, consider the following questions:

1. What has been the effect of what the author calls the "cult of personality"?
2. How does Farhang believe the superpowers and their allies benefit from continued war between Iran and Iraq?
3. In what ways is the war contrary to the interests of both countries, according to Farhang?

Mansour Farhang, "The Iran-Iraq War: The Feud, The Tragedy, The Spoils," *World Policy Journal*, Fall 1985. Reprinted with permission.

The war of attrition between Iran and Iraq calls to mind Hegel's famous proposition: the real is absurd but the absurd is rational. Human wave tactics, suicidal behavior, poison gas, attacks on oil tankers, air raids on civilian targets—both sides have endured and inflicted horrible suffering and loss, yet neither seems to have any chance of gaining a clear victory. Outside powers have only encouraged this stalemate: a cluster of economically and politically diverse states have found it in their interests to fuel the fighting rather than take steps to end it. Thus both the origin of the war and the failure of attempts at mediation are rooted in the superpower competition and arms race in the region, as well as in the suppressed or unresolved conflicts and contradictions of the sociopolitical order within each country. Ultimately, though, responsibility still rests with the two belligerents, who started the war and are steadfastly perpetuating it.

A Personal Feud

The Iran-Iraq conflict bears all the classic earmarks of a personal feud. Despite the oil income that produced substantial economic growth and modernization and integrated the two countries into the world market system, the internal political structures of Iran and Iraq have remained autocratic and feudal. Iraq's President Saddam Hussein and Iran's Ayatollah Ruhollah Khomeini hold absolute power. These men's hatred and fear of each other has only intensified their countries' historical struggle for dominance in the Persian Gulf. At different times, both Khomeini and Hussein have rejected honorable third-party mediation proposals because of their own misperceptions and miscalculations. By now they know they cannot win, but neither—or so they seem to believe—can they afford to lose. Personal vendetta has led to massive suffering.

Thus it is not fair to blame outside actors for this tragic situation. But the industrial countries in general, and the superpowers in particular, have done virtually nothing concrete to encourage the belligerents to end the conflict. The United States, the Soviet Union, and their arms-exporting and oil-purchasing allies all claim to want peace in the Persian Gulf. Yet in relation to this tragic war between the region's two most important states, outside powers have behaved in a hypocritical and manipulative fashion, using the war to further their own economic or geopolitical interests. Weapons sales make good business; letting Iran and Iraq stay bogged down with each other keeps a check on whatever regional expansionist designs they might have. What is tragic in all this is the enormous amount of waste—human lives, natural resources, and the stability and strength of the two nations at war. . . .

What finally explains the senseless destruction and prolongation of the war is not the cult of martyrdom but the cult of personality. For it is the cult of personality—*not* the supposed desire to become a martyr—that is an endemic feature of the Iranian and Iraqi political cultures. By cult of personality, I do not simply mean a political system that emphasizes leader-worship, but rather the establishment of one individual's personal control over the apparatus of state. The cult of personality manifests itself when an uncontested and exalted leader becomes the sole source of authority for an entire political system. In both Iran and Iraq, the absolute ruler's cult of personality has become so fused with the official rationale behind the war that to question the wisdom of continued intransigence in the conflict is equivalent to committing a crime against the state. . . .

Despotic Leaders

Why do Iran and Iraq continue to fight a war that not only fails to achieve any of its stated objectives, but shatters their societies and devastates their economics? The border dispute over the Shatt al-Arab estuary that helped ignite the war rapidly receded into the background, but the rivalry for hegemony in the region and the historical strains that run between the two societies continue to fuel the conflict. . . . The continuation of the war has strongly reinforced a strand of despotism, intolerant of any opposition, in the political cultures of both societies. The leaders see the continuation of the fighting as a sign of their countries' sovereignty and nonaligned status. Iran and Iraq are incapable of ending this war on their own.

Robert C. Johansen and Michael G. Renner, *Christianity and Crisis*, December 9, 1985.

The Iranian and Iraqi states do not differentiate between politics and daily life. Back in the days when both countries were under traditional despotism, politics was merely one component of life; it did not interfere with the thought and being of the passive or uninterested citizen. But under the totalitarian regimes of Khomeini and Saddam Hussein, politics provides the method of constructing a supposedly organic society in which every aspect of life is to be integrated with the basic purpose of the state. As Khomeini and Saddam Hussein define this basic purpose, no citizen is allowed to stand apart. Constant propaganda, pervasive terror, character assassination, the presence of organized gangs in the streets, the perpetuation of big lies—all tools of modern totalitarianism—are used to maintain order and to exalt the cult of personality. . . .

Men like Khomeini and Saddam Hussein may be bold in praising martyrdom and ruthless in repressing their critics, but they are not at all reckless when the stability of their regimes is at stake.

As leaders who believe they hold historic or religious missions, they may exclude rational consideration of the costs and consequences of their actions; yet as pragmatists, they pay close attention to what can be accomplished within a given situation.

Thus both of them have alternated between ideological and pragmatic paths. During the first two years of the war, when Iraqi troops occupied Iranian territory, Khomeini was demanding no more than a return to the status quo ante; it was only when Iran gained the upper hand that he began to insist on the removal of Saddam Hussein from power as a precondition to ending hostilities. In addition, many of Khomeini's domestic policy decisions over the past six and a half years show him retreating from rigid ideological or messianic positions in order to meet the requirements of running the state and balancing the competing interests and claims within the Islamic Republic. Saddam Hussein operates in the same fashion. He used to regard the present rulers of Saudi Arabia, Kuwait, and Jordan as the enemies of the "Arab nations," but now that he needs their help he has established good relations with all of them. The urgency of the effort to resist Khomeini has forced Saddam Hussein to completely realign Iraq's economic, diplomatic, and military ties, both within and beyond the region.

One cannot argue, then, that Khomeini and Saddam Hussein are inherently irrational, or immune to pressure from without. What is important to understand about the mind-set and behavior of these men is that in the absence of any credible external imperative, they tend to be dogmatic and single-minded as they pursue their objectives. Habitually, they see politics, at home and abroad, as a zero-sum game with an enormous element of conspiracy. For example, both Iran and Iraq attribute the root cause of their conflict to a U.S.-Israeli collusion: the official spokesmen of Iran describe Saddam Hussein as a puppet of the Zionist-imperialist aggressors, while Iraqi authorities portray Khomeini as a groomed agent of international Zionism. . . .

Iran and Iraq, at different times, have been reluctant or afraid to make settlements that, in the eyes of their own countries and in the eyes of the region, might appear to put them at a disadvantage. Beyond that, however—and this may have been the more important factor—the industrial nations have failed to appeal to Saddam Hussein's and Khomeini's pragmatic sides by exerting effective economic and political pressure during the process of negotiation. . . .

Neither Side Can Win

The tremendous toll of human suffering is one of this war's greatest tragedies: hundreds of thousands of lives have been lost in a conflict that neither side can win. There has also been massive

The Gulf War الحرب

Reprinted with permission from AL-FAJR.

material destruction. After the initial outbreak of hostilities, Iraq announced its intention to refrain from attacking oil facilities. But Iran rejected this gesture and bombed Iraqi installations; Iraq retaliated in kind. On both sides, major export facilities, pumping stations, and important refining and petrochemical complexes have come under aerial and artillery fire. The physical damage has caused each country's oil output to fall drastically. . . .

Over the past five years, social welfare and economic development in both Iran and Iraq have been sacrificed in favor of fighting a war that is blatantly against the interests of the two societies. In 1980 Iraq had more than $30 billion in reserve. Today the country is deeply in debt and depends on external borrowing to meet its important needs. Iran cannot secure international credit or loans; to make its war expenditures possible, it has had to drastically cut nonmilitary spending. Khomeini used to criticize the Shah for his massive arms purchases. Now the Ayatollah has become a principal cause of the region's unprecedented militarization, and his own agents seem the most insatiable customers in the international black market for arms.

War Hinders Development

Consequently, the governments of Iran and Iraq have become so desperate to sell oil in order to buy weapons and food that they have lost their capacity to bargain with their trade partners or initiate any long-term plans for economic development. The massive task of reconstructing after the damages of the war still lies somewhere in the future. These revived conditions of impairment and dependency have forced Saddam Hussein and Ayatollah Khomeini to justify their feud in terms of elusive ideological or security concerns. But these claims have not succeeded in subduing popular resentment against the war. Thus the two regimes have had to greatly expand their internal security apparatuses to prevent active antiwar opposition.

Under these circumstances, the war of attrition between Iran and Iraq is likely to go on as long as Khomeini and Saddam Hussein—the parties primarily responsible for the start and continuation of the conflict—remain in power. Given the political history of their countries, these leaders will be in power as long as they are alive.

From What to When

When the Shah's regime collapsed in 1979, Khomeini was a popular hero, widely regarded in Iran as a unifying figure and moral guide. At that time, the Iranian people were deeply concerned with the question of *what* would happen when the 78-year-old ruler died. Once his regime was firmly established, though, the question's emphasis shifted from *what* to *when*. Now, after six and a half years of the Ayatollah's brutal puritanism and five years of war with Iraq, the question remains open, but the tormented Iranian humor has replaced the *when* with *if*.

President Saddam Hussein, on the other hand, has never enjoyed the popularity that Khomeini did at first. So, unlike the Iranians, the Iraqis do not regard their ruler as the betrayer of their hopes and aspirations. Nevertheless, the people of Iraq are eager to see Saddam Hussein leave his seat of power as their neighbors in Iran are to envision their country without Khomeini. For only the disappearance of these two men can bring their pointless and calamitous feud to an end.

213

Recognizing Stereotypes

A stereotype is an oversimplified or exaggerated description of people or things, usually focusing on a few characteristics rather than looking at the whole person or thing. Stereotyping can be favorable but it tends to be highly uncomplimentary, and at times degrading.

Stereotyping grows out of our prejudices. When we stereotype someone, we are prejudging him or her. Stereotypes are often applied to people of ethnic backgrounds different from our own. For example, some people look at conflicts occurring in the Middle East and draw the conclusion that all Middle Easterners are violent people who enjoy fighting. That is a stereotypical belief because it is an oversimplified prejudgment of a whole group of people.

The following picture was taken during a Shi'ite Muslim siege of Palestinian refugee camps in Beirut, Lebanon. Shi'ites and Palestinians have been fighting one another in Lebanon and are considered mortal enemies. Yet the photo shows a Shi'ite soldier feeding a Palestinian baby in a refugee camp. What stereotypes does the photo challenge? Does it support any stereotypes?

Wide World Photos

This exercise will help you recognize stereotypes and encourage you to think about how they affect you and other people.

Part I

Each student should examine the following statements, some of which are derived from this chapter. *Mark S for statements that are stereotypes, N for statements that are not stereotypes, and U for statements which cannot be clearly decided whether they are stereotypes or not.*

S = stereotype
N = not a stereotype
U = undecided

1. The Zionist response to peace negotiations is typical: they are interested only in a peace that furthers their militarist designs.

2. Money-grubbing Palestinian refugees, even the lowliest of them, are convinced they used to own at least a hundred acres of orchards and a large house in Israel.

3. The Middle East is a region of diversity, complexity, and turbulence.

4. Iran desires a just end to the war. So far, none of the peace proposals have been just.

5. Saddam Hussein is Iraq's leader because he represents the Iraqi mentality—irrational and unstable.

6. The Arab world is heir to a proud history and civilization.

7. Arabs are superior to Iran's lowly Persian peasants.

8. Those radicals with their unreasonable demands are the ones who are preventing peace.

9. Although Khomeini and Saddam Hussein are power hungry, they have a pragmatic side as well and might be willing to compromise if an appropriate offer were made.

10. All Jews are part of the international Zionist conspiracy, which promotes the war between Iran and Iraq.

11. We have already seen the havoc a few Israeli militarists wreaked in Lebanon.

12. Any agreement on a Middle East settlement must consider the rights of the Palestinian people.

Part II

Based on the insights you have gained from this activity, discuss these questions in class:

1. Why do people stereotype one another?
2. What are some examples of positive stereotypes?
3. What harm can stereotypes cause?
4. What stereotypes currently affect members of your class?

Periodical Bibliography

The following articles have been selected to supplement the diverse views expressed in this chapter.

Abbas Alnasrawi — "Economic Consequences of the Iraq-Iran War," *Third World Quarterly*, July 1986.

Meron Benvenisti — "The Second Republic," *Journal of Palestine Studies*, Spring 1987.

Michael Brzoska — "Profiteering on the Iran-Iraq War," *Bulletin of the Atomic Scientists*, June 1987.

Christianity and Crisis — "Hanging on to Hope in the Middle East," June 11, 1984.

Scheherazade Daneshkhu — "Gulf War Guilt—Another View," *Middle East International*, June 12, 1987. Available from PO Box 53365, Temple Heights Station, Washington, DC 20009.

Thomas L. Friedman — "No Illusions: Israel Reassesses Its Chances for Peace," *The New York Times Magazine*, January 26, 1986.

Harper's — "Prophets of the Holy Land," December 1984.

Hassan bin Talal — "Return to Geneva," *Foreign Policy*, Winter 1984/85.

Morton Kondracke — "Peace Nix," *The New Republic*, June 8, 1987.

Conor Cruise O'Brien — "Why Israel Can't Take 'Bold Steps' for Peace," *The Atlantic*, October 1985.

Vladimir Petrovsky — "Mideast Peace Conference Is Possible," *Los Angeles Times*, May 29, 1987.

Nita M. Renfrew — "Who Started the War?" *Foreign Policy*, Spring 1987.

Edward W. Said — "Interview: An Exile's Exile," *The Progressive*, February 1987.

Milton Viorst — "Ending the 20-Year War," *Newsweek*, June 15, 1987.

Milton Viorst — "Iraq at War," *Foreign Affairs*, Winter 1986/87.

Mark Whitaker — "Prelude to a 'Final Offensive'?" *Newsweek*, January 26, 1987.

Chronology of Events

1881	Russian pogroms force thousands of Jews to move west. This migration is an impetus to Zionism.
1897	Theodor Herzl convenes First Zionist Congress which designates Palestine as an appropriate Jewish homeland. Less than ten percent of Palestine's population is Jewish.
1914	World War I begins. Dissatisfied with Turkish rule over much of the Middle East, Arab nationalists cooperate with Britain against Turkey.
1916-1918	Turkey's Ottoman Empire collapses.
1917	British Foreign Secretary A.J. Balfour declares Britain's support for a national homeland for the Jewish people in Palestine, a declaration that conflicts with promises to the Arabs.
1920	France seizes Syria and Mount Lebanon after collapse of the Ottoman Empire and creates Lebanon out of the mountain and Syrian provinces.
1920-1948	Britain rules Palestine under agreement with the League of Nations. The British Mandate approves limited immigration for Jews.
1921	Military officer Reza Khan rules Iran after a coup and begins a secularization campaign that abolishes many Islamic customs. Khan begins the Pahlavi dynasty which rules Iran for 58 years, until overthrown by a revolution inspired by Ayatollah Khomeini.
1928	The Muslim Brothers establish themselves in Egypt as a movement of fundamentalist reform among Sunni Muslims.
1929-1939	Arabs rebel violently against British rule; Jews and Arabs fight each other for the right to live in Palestine.
1933-1939	Hitler takes power in Germany and begins segregating Jews. In these six years, he forbids marriage between Jews and Germans, demands that Jews wear yellow stars and encourages the destruction of synagogues and Jewish property.
1939	The British tighten limits of Jewish immigration into Palestine.
1939-1945	World War II. Six million Jews are killed by Nazis and the Jewish population in Palestine swells to 608,000 by 1946.
1941	British and Soviet forces, concerned that Reza Khan is allied with Hitler, invade Iran and depose the monarch, replacing him with his son, Muhammed Reza Khan Pahlavi.

November 1943	Lebanon achieves independence with government posts given to members of each of the main religious groups. Because Christians outnumber the other groups at this time, the president is a Christian.
March 1945	Egypt, Iraq, Jordan, and Lebanon found the Arab League.
1945-1948	Zionist organizations wage campaign of violence to end immigration restrictions in Palestine; thousands of Jews enter Palestine illegally.
November 29, 1947	United Nations (UN) General Assembly votes to partition Palestine into Jewish and Arab states with Jerusalem being an international city. Arabs refuse.
May 14, 1948	State of Israel is proclaimed. Five Arab League states attack Israel. At the war's end, Israel takes more land than originally assigned. More than one-half million Palestinians flee Israel.
September 17, 1948	Jewish terrorists assassinate UN mediator Count Folke Bernadotte.
March 1949	Egypt and Britain sign agreement for Egypt to be more involved in the management of the Suez Canal.
January 1, 1950	Israel names Jerusalem its capital despite protest from Arab states and the UN.
1952	A group calling themselves the "Free Officers" of the Egyptian army overthrow King Farouk and replace him with their leader Gamal Abdel Nasser.
July 1956	US and Britain refuse to support a loan to Egypt to build the Aswan Dam; in retaliation, Nasser nationalizes the Canal. After Britain freezes Egyptian assets held in England, Egypt closes the Suez.
October 1956	The Israelis, with military aid from Britain and France, invade Egypt. They take the Gaza Strip and the Sinai Peninsula which they later return in a peace settlement.
November 1956	Soviet Union puts pressure on Britain, France, and Israel to withdraw from Egypt.
1956-1958	First Lebanese civil war. Pre-war conditions are restored by US after a stalemate between warring religious groups.
January 1957	Suez Canal partially reopens; US President Eisenhower issues a doctrine "to deter communist aggression in the Middle East."
August 1959	Jordan offers citizenship to all Palestinian refugees.
January 1961	Iran, Iraq, Kuwait, and Saudi Arabia found the Organization of Petroleum Exporting Countries (OPEC).
May 1964	Palestine Liberation Organization (PLO) is established. It vows to return Palestine to the Palestinians.
1966	Muslim Brother Sayyid Qutb is condemned to death for revolutionary activity in Egypt.

May 1967	Nasser orders UN emergency forces to withdraw from the Sinai, declares a state of emergency along the Gaza Strip, and closes the Strait of Tiran to shipping both to and from Israel. Israel and the US warn Egypt to remove blockade; the US Sixth Fleet moves toward the Middle East; the USSR warns that it will help resist aggression in the Middle East.
June 5-10, 1967	Six Day War. Israel attacks Egypt, Jordan, and Syria and captures the Sinai, Gaza Strip, West Bank, and Golan Heights.
November 22, 1967	UN Security Council Resolution 242 calling for peace in the Middle East is adopted. The resolution asks that Israel return land acquired in the Six Day War and that Arabs respect Israel's boundaries.
1969	Yasir Arafat and Fatah (the largest Palestinian group) take over the PLO and give it a more aggressive role.
1969	Muammar el-Qaddafi overthrows King Idris I of Libya.
1970	Egypt's President Nasser dies at the age of 52. Vice President Anwar el-Sadat takes over.
1970	Libyan leader Qaddafi removes British and US military bases from Libya.
1970-1971	Jordanian civil war. King Hussein crushes Palestinian guerrillas and invading troops. Palestinians move offices from Jordan to Beirut in Lebanon.
1971	The Shah celebrates the 50th anniversary of the Pahlavi dynasty by crowning himself Emperor. The pomp draws attention away from continuing protest against the Shah and its brutal suppression by the Shah's secret service, SAVAK.
July 1972	Soviet military advisers, welcomed under Nasser, are expelled by Sadat.
October 6, 1973	Yom Kippur War. Egypt and Syria surprise Israel in a two-front attack. The US and USSR, who are both involved, urge a cease-fire.
October 18, 1973	First day of five-month Arab oil embargo; Libya starts by cutting off all exports to the US. Other Arab nations soon follow, cutting off or sharply curtailing oil exports to countries that support Israel.
October 22, 1973	Security Council Resolution 338 calls for immediate cease-fire in Yom Kippur War and establishes a peace-keeping force.
November 11, 1973	The war ends when Egypt and Israel sign a cease-fire.
February 28, 1974	US and Egypt renew full diplomatic relations after a seven-year hiatus.
May 15-16, 1974	PLO guerrillas attack a school in the Israeli border town of Maalet; the Israeli army kills the guerrillas and retaliates with air raids on Palestinian camps in Lebanon.

October 1974	The UN grants the PLO observer status and allows it to participate in debates on the Palestinian question.
April 1975	In Lebanon, Christian Phalangists attack Palestinians, touching off large-scale confrontations between Christians and Muslims. Syria participates on the side of the Muslims.
June 10-20, 1976	Tensions escalate in Lebanon; two US officials are shot and most US citizens are evacuated with the help of the PLO.
November 11, 1976	UN Security Council objects to Israel's establishment of settlements in the territories it has occupied since the Six Day War.
January 1, 1977	Committee of the US House of Representatives criticizes Iranian human rights violations under the Shah.
March 16, 1977	President Carter endorses the idea of a Palestinian homeland.
November 6-11, 1977	PLO refuses to move out of Lebanon as previously agreed. Israel bombs Palestinian camps in retaliation for shelling of villages in northern Israel.
November 9-21, 1977	Egyptian President Sadat makes the first visit of an Arab leader to Israel to promote renewed peace talks.
December 31, 1977	Carter visits Iran to talk with the Shah about the Arab-Israeli conflict and calls Iran "an island of stability" in the Middle East.
February 18-19, 1978	Khomeini-sparked riots in Qum, Iran result in killings and extensive damage to banks, cinemas, and government property.
March 21, 1978	UN troops move into southern Lebanon to enforce a cease-fire called by Israel.
May 8, 1978	Country-wide rioting intensifies in Iran. Regime leaders call for a day of mourning.
June 18, 1978	Ayatollah Khomeini, living in Paris, calls for an overthrow of the Shah.
September 5-17, 1978	Camp David summit meeting between Carter, Sadat, and Israeli Prime Minister Menachem Begin leads to an Egyptian-Israeli peace agreement and accords on the Palestinian question. Most of the Arab states, the Soviets, and the PLO denounce the agreements.
January-February, 1979	After months of unrest, the government of Iran is overthrown. The Shah, Iran's ruler for 37 years, takes an "extended vacation" and his newly-installed civilian regime is replaced by Muslim fundamentalists led by Khomeini.
November 4, 1979	Militants storm the US embassy in Tehran and hold 52 Americans hostage for the next 14 months.
November 20, 1979	In Saudi Arabia the Ka'bah mosque in Mecca is seized by fundamentalist Muslim rebels who declare themselves the new leaders of the nation. They hold the mosque for 15 days before being ousted by Saudi Arabian forces.

221

June 7-10, 1980	Israel bombs a nuclear reactor in Iraq "to prevent another holocaust." The US refuses to deliver promised military equipment to Israel.
September 1980	Iran makes air artillery attacks on Iraqi towns. A few weeks later, Iraq invades Iran, driving into Khuzistan province and capturing the port of Khuramshahr.
September 1981	Sadat imprisons 1500 people in a crack-down on political dissent.
October 1981	Sadat is assassinated by members of the Egyptian army. Vice President Hosni Mubarak takes over the government.
January-March 1982	As fighting intensifies, Iran drives Iraq out of its territory and crosses the Iraqi border for the first time in the Gulf war.
February 1982	Syrian leader Hafez Assad's troops crush a Muslim Brotherhood uprising in the city of Hama, killing more than 10,000 people.
June 1982	Arab assassin kills the Israeli ambassador to Great Britain; Israel retaliates by invading Lebanon.
July-September 1982	Fighting in Lebanon escalates with Syrian planes joining the battle against Israel; Israel moves into Beirut and demands that the PLO leave the city. US Marines help patrol the PLO evacuation. PLO establishes its headquarters in Tunisia.
August 23, 1982	Bashir Gemayel, a Maronite Christian, is elected President of Lebanon.
September 1, 1982	Reagan announces a US plan for Mideast peace including "self-government" by the Palestinians in the West Bank and Gaza in association with Jordan.
September 21, 1982	Lebanese President Bashir Gemayel is assassinated. His brother, Amin, is elected. Christian militia massacre hundreds of Palestinians in Sabra and Shatila refugee camps.
April 18, 1983	Sixty-three people are killed in the bombing of the US Embassy in Beirut.
May 17, 1983	Lebanon and Israel sign an agreement to withdraw Israeli forces from Lebanon. Israel refuses to withdraw completely until Syria also withdraws.
October 23, 1983	A pro-Iranian suicide bomber drives an explosive-laden truck into US Marine headquarters in Beirut, killing 241 people.
December 1983	US attacks Syrian positions in Lebanon.
January 1984	Reagan administration officially lists Iran as a supporter of international terrorism and cuts sales to Iran.
February 6, 1984	Radical Muslims take control of West Beirut.
February 7, 1984	The US peacekeeping force leaves Beirut and is redeployed offshore.

March 16, 1984	William Buckley, CIA station chief in Beirut, is kidnapped by pro-Iranian Muslim group.
February 11, 1985	Jordan's King Hussein and Yasir Arafat sign the Amman Agreement which affirms their mutual desire for an independent Palestine.
June 9, 1985	Thomas Sutherland, an American University professor in Beirut, joins five other Americans kidnapped and held hostage in Lebanon since March 1984.
June 14, 1985	Two Shiite gunmen hijack TWA flight 847 holding its 153 passengers hostage. They beat and kill a US Navy passenger on board the plane. In the next two days, most passengers are released except for 39 Americans who are taken to Beirut.
June 30, 1985	Iranian officials help negotiate freedom for the 39 American hostages originally on board TWA flight 847.
July 1985	Israeli Foreign Minister David Kimche tells Reagan's National Security Adviser Robert McFarlane that some Iranians would be willing to obtain the release of US hostages in return for shipments of US arms to Iran.
August-September, 1985	Israel makes clandestine shipments of US arms to Iran.
October 7, 1985	Four Palestinians hijack the Italian ship *Achille Lauro* and hold 400 hostages. They kill Leon Klinghoffer, an elderly American Jew.
December 1985	Radical anti-Zionist groups attack Israeli airline ticket counters in Rome and Vienna.
January 17, 1986	Reagan signs secret order authorizing direct US arms shipments to Iran through the CIA. The order instructs the CIA not to tell Congress of the operation.
April 14, 1986	Reagan, arguing that Libyan leader Qaddafi supports anti-American terrorism, orders the bombing of the Libyan cities of Tripoli and Benghazi. Hundreds of Libyans die and many homes are hit, including Qaddafi's.
July 1986	The US makes another shipment of arms to Iran.
July 26, 1986	American hostage Father Lawrence Jenco is released by Shiite Muslim captors.
August 14, 1986	US State Department Diplomat Richard Murphy, unaware of covert US arms sales to Iran, declares that an Iranian victory in the Iran/Iraq war would be a major setback for US interests.
October 31, 1986	Beirut magazine *Ash Shiraa* publishes a story asserting that McFarlane made a secret trip to Iran.
November 13, 1986	In a nationally televised speech, Reagan acknowledges that a "secret diplomatic initiative" involving shipments of "small amounts of defensive weapons and spare parts" to Iran took place. He denies that the sales were meant to free American hostages.

November 20, 1986	CIA Director William Casey admits that Israel delivered to Iran 2008 TOW missiles and 235 Hawk anti-aircraft missile batteries, for which $10 million was received and deposited in a Swiss bank account.
November 22, 1986	Justice Department lawyers uncover information in Lieutenant Colonel Oliver North's office indicating that Iranian arms sales proceeds were diverted to Nicaraguan contras.
November 25, 1986	Israeli government admits that Israel "helped supply defensive armaments and spare parts from the US to Iran following a request by the US." In the US, North is fired and Deputy Security Adviser Vice-Admiral John Poindexter resigns.
December 9, 1986	In separate appearances before Investigative Committees, Poindexter, North, and Secord refuse to testify.
December 15, 1986	White House and State Department officials disclose that the US has been providing Iraq with military intelligence about Iran for the previous two years.
December 17, 1986	Attorney General Edwin Meese reasserts that only North, Poindexter, and McFarlane knew of the diversion of Iranian arms-sales funds to the contras. FBI begins inquiry into why Meese delayed the bureau's investigation of the private contra supply operation.
January 20, 1987	Hostage negotiator Terry Waite is, himself, taken hostage while seeking the release of two Americans.
April 20, 1987	The PLO Executive Committee officially cancels the Amman Agreement, an agreement signed by Arafat and King Hussein in 1985.
May 17, 1987	An Iraqi fighter plane fires a shot that disables patrolling US warship Stark and kills 37 members of its crew.
June 1, 1987	A bomb explodes on board a plane carrying Lebanese Prime Minister Rashid Karami, killing him instantly.

Organizations To Contact

The editors have compiled the following list of organizations which are concerned with the issues debated in this book. All of them have publications or information available for interested readers. The descriptions are derived from materials provided by the organizations.

American-Arab Anti-Discrimination Committee
1731 Connecticut Ave. NW, Suite 400
Washington, DC 20009
(202) 797-7662

This organization protects the rights of people of Arab descent within the US and challenges defamation, discrimination, and disenfranchisement. It publishes the monthly *ADC Times* and bimonthly *Background Papers*.

American Friends Service Committee (AFSC)
1501 Cherry St.
Philadelphia, PA 19102
(215) 241-7000

AFSC was the first US-based peace organization to develop a peace education program on the Middle East. Through its information and educational materials and programs, AFSC aims toward greater public understanding of the Arab-Israeli-Palestinian conflict and the role the United States plays in shaping events in the Middle East. The Committee has published two books on the Middle East, as well as program literature and booklets.

American Jewish Congress (AJC)
Stephen Wise Congress House
15 E. 84th St.
New York, NY 10028
(212) 879-4500

AJC is an organization founded during World War I to support Jewish rights in different countries and the right of Jews to their homeland. It promotes human rights, civil liberties, and denounces all forms of discrimination on any grounds. It publishes *Judaism* and *Boycott Report*, in addition to other pamphlets.

Americans for Middle East Understanding
475 Riverside Drive, Room 771
New York, NY 10115
(212) 870-2336

This group's purpose is to foster better understanding in America of the history, goals, and values of Middle East people, the rights of the Palestinians, and the forces that are shaping American policy there. Its publications include the newsletter, *The Link*, a pamphlet series, and books.

Americans for Progressive Israel (API)
150 Fifth Ave., Suite 911
New York, NY 10011
(212) 255-8760

API was founded in 1948 in support of the Jewish state. A socialist Zionist organization, it strives for socialism in Israel, collectivism, equal opportunity for all. It opposes racism and supports Palestinians who recognize Israel as a state. It publishes the bimonthly journal, *Israel Horizons*.

Anti-Defamation League of B'nai B'rith
823 United Nations Plaza
New York, NY 10017
(212) 490-2525

The organization works to promote understanding among people of different races, creeds, and ethnic backgrounds. Its publications include pamphlets and the *Middle East Notebook*.

Arab American Institute
918 Sixteenth St. NW, Suite 501
Washington, DC 20006
(202) 429-9210

The Arab American Institute national organizing and planning center gives Arab Americans a voice in the nation's political system. It campaigns for civil rights for Arab Americans. It is affiliated with Washington Middle East Associates which publishes books and position papers.

Association of Arab-American University Graduates
556 Trapelo Road
Belmont, MA 02178
(617) 484-5483

The Association of Arab-American University Graduates is an educational and cultural organization dedicated to fostering better Arab-American understanding. To this end, it publishes books and periodicals, organizes conferences and seminars, provides speakers on topics concerning the Arab world and its people, and supports human rights and civil liberties in the Middle East and elsewhere.

Center for Middle Eastern Studies
The University of Texas at Austin
Austin, TX 78712
(512) 471-3881

The Center was designed by the US Department of Education as a national resource center for Middle Eastern studies to promote better understanding of the Middle East. It provides research and instructional materials. The Center publishes two series of books on the Middle East, monographs, and essays.

Foundation for Middle East Peace
1522 K St. NW, #202
Washington, DC 20005
(202) 347-8241

The Foundation assists the peaceful resolution of the Israeli-Palestinian conflict by making grants within the Arab and Jewish communities to promote peace. It publishes books and pamphlets.

The Institute for Palestine Studies
PO Box 25697
Washington, DC 20007
(202) 342-3990

The Institute for Palestine Studies, founded in Lebanon in 1963, is a research, documentation, and publication center specializing in the history and development of the Palestinian problem and the Arab-Israeli conflict. The Institute publishes *The Journal of Palestine Studies*, quarterly.

Jewish Defense Organization (JDO)
134 W. 32nd St., Room 602
New York, NY 10001
(212) 239-0447

JDO is committed to protecting the rights of Jews and fighting anti-Semitism. They offer karate and gun training classes and have a wide variety of publications available.

The Jewish Idea
PO Box 425
Midwood Station
Brooklyn, NY 11230
(718) 646-1552

The Jewish Idea believes that Israel's future is endangered by its Palestinian inhabitants. They believe that Israel must remain Jewish, that Palestinians should not have rights equal to those of Jews, and that intermarriage between Jews and Arabs is wrong. They have several publications available, including *Kahane Magazine* and a newsletter.

Jordan IS Palestine Committee
PO Box 2003
New Hyde Park, NY 11040
(516) 742-7672

The Committee is an independent information project which believes that the Arab-Israeli conflict can be solved if Palestinian Arabs recognize that Jordan is part of the original Palestine Mandate. The Committee contends that the country of Jordan is the Palestinian homeland. It provides film and slide presentations with speakers.

The League of Arab States
747 Third Ave., 35th Floor
New York, NY 10017
(212) 838-8700

The League is a group of independent Arab states working for peace and security in the Arab region and supporting Palestinians' rights to a homeland. It publishes papers and periodicals, including *Arab Perspectives.*

Lebanese Information and Research Center
1926 Eye St. NW
Washington, DC 20006
(202) 347-5810

The purpose of the Center, founded in 1978, is to research the situation in Lebanon and disseminate information. The Center conducts seminars and workshops. It publishes *Lebanon News*, a monthly, as well as issue papers and press releases.

Middle East Outreach Council, Inc. (MEOC)
Center for Near East and North African Studies
144 Lane Hall, University of Michigan
Ann Arbor, MI 48109
(313) 764-0350

MEOC was established in 1981 as a non-political organization that provides factual information about the lands, cultures, and peoples of the Middle East, directed toward secondary education. The Council publishes a resource guide on other organizations and embassies.

Middle East Research & Information Project (MERIP)
PO Box 43445
Columbia Heights Station
Washington, DC 20010
(202) 667-1188

The Project provides information, research, and analysis of US involvement in the Middle East and the Middle East's political and economic development. It publishes the bimonthly magazine, *MERIP Middle East Report*.

National Christian Leadership Conference for Israel (NCLCI)
134 E. 39th St.
New York, NY 10016
(212) 213-8636

NCLCI is a group of church members from diverse theological traditions working to develop positive Christian-Jewish relations and fight anti-Semitism. It acts as a clearinghouse for American Christian organizations working to support Israel through their educational programs. The conference publishes a bimonthly newsletter.

New Jewish Agenda (NJA)
64 Fulton St., Room 1100
New York, NY 10038
(212) 227-5885

NJA was founded in 1981 as a national grass roots organization to promote progressive politics in the Jewish community. It supports a negotiated settlement to the Israeli-Palestinian conflict, including a territorial compromise, mutual recognition, and self determination for all participants. It publishes brochures and a quarterly newspaper, *Agenda*.

November 29th Committee for Palestine
PO Box 27462
San Francisco, CA 94127
(415) 861-1552

The Committee is a national solidarity organization promoting Palestinian rights and is concerned with Israeli policies, the Israeli peace movement and US policy toward the Palestinians. It publishes the bimonthly newspaper, *Palestine Focus*.

Palestine Human Rights Campaign (PHRC)
220 S. State St., Suite 1308
Chicago, IL 60604
(312) 987-1830

The PHRC works for peace and justice for Palestinian refugees. The PHRC monitors human rights violations against Palestinians living under military occupation. It publishes books, reports, and the *Palestine Human Rights Newsletter*.

Palestine Research and Educational Center
2025 Eye St. NW, Suite 415
Washington, DC 20006
(202) 466-3205

The Center is an educational institution specializing in Palestinian affairs. Through research, publication, and education, the Center provides information about the Palestinian people, their history, society, culture, and institutions. It publishes the monthly magazine *Palestine Perspective*, occasional papers, reports, and monographs.

Peace Now
27 W. 20th St., Ninth Floor
New York, NY 10011
(212) 645-6262

Peace Now is an international grass roots movement encouraging a negotiated settlement between the Arabs and Israel which would recognize the national rights of the Palestinian people to self-determination. It publishes a newsletter, *Peace Now*, and pamphlets, including *Everything You Didn't Want To Know About the Settlement on the West Bank*.

Resource Center for Nonviolence
515 Broadway
Santa Cruz, CA 95063
(408) 423-1626

The Center offers the public a broad educational program on the history, theory, and practice of nonviolence as a force for personal and social change. Its Middle East project sends educational and political delegations to the Middle East to promote nonviolent solutions to the region's conflicts. It publishes books, pamphlets, and a quarterly newsletter.

West Bank Data Project (WBDP)
120 E. 56th St.
New York, NY 10022

WBDP is an independent research group established in 1982 to study and analyze demographic, social, legal, economic, and political conditions in the Israeli-occupied territories of West Bank and Gaza, with a continuously updated, computerized data base.

Zionist Archives and Library
515 Park Ave.
New York, NY 10022
(212) 753-2167

The Zionist Archives and Library is a repository for books, pamphlets, newspapers, and periodicals. It has research materials and information on Israel, Zionism, the Middle East, and Jewish life in the Diaspora.

Annotated Book Bibliography

Umar F. Abd-Allah
The Islamic Struggle in Syria. Berkeley, CA: Mizan Press, 1983. An eloquent defense of Islam's revolutionary potential to bring justice to the poor and oppressed in the Middle East.

Ibrahim Abu-Lughod, ed.
Palestinian Rights: Affirmation and Denial. Wilmette, IL: Medina Press, 1982. An excellent, comprehensive collection of essays from a Palestinian perspective.

Haleh Afshar, ed.
Iran: A Revolution in Turmoil. Albany, NY: State University of New York Press, 1985. A scholarly collection of essays, many by exiled Iranians, on factors which led to the fundamentalist revolution.

Naseer H. Aruri
Occupation: Israel Over Palestine. Belmont, MA: Association of Arab-American University Graduates, 1983. A pro-Palestinian anthology criticizing Israel's policies in the occupied territories.

Bernard Avishai
The Tragedy of Zionism. New York: Farrar, Straus, Giroux, 1985. Provides a thorough history of Zionism. Avishai believes Zionism must be a democratic movement that respects the rights of non-Jews living in Israel.

Lynne Reid Banks
Torn Country: An Oral History of the Israeli War of Independence. New York: Franklin Watts, 1982. Includes several interesting interviews with Israelis who had leading roles in the creation of the state of Israel.

Dan Barly and Eliahu Salpeter
Fire in Beirut: Israel's War in Lebanon with the PLO. New York: Stein and Day Publishers, 1984. Defends Israel's involvement in Lebanon as necessary for the security of Israel.

Willard A. Beling, ed.
Middle East Peace Plans. New York: St. Martin's Press, 1986. A comprehensive academic anthology that includes essays by leading American scholars specializing in the Middle East.

Meron Benvenisti
Conflicts and Contradictions. New York: Villard Books, 1986. Benvenisti uses his personal experiences of growing up in Israel and living in an Arab neighborhood to explain why he believes the prospect of solving the Israeli-Palestinian question is bleak.

Cheryl Benard and Zalmay Khalilzad
"The Government of God"—Iran's Islamic Republic. New York: Columbia University Press, 1984. An excellent, closely-argued analysis of Iran's revolution, its foreign policy, and its future.

Wolf Blitzer
Between Washington and Jerusalem. New York: Oxford University Press, 1985. Washington correspondent for *The Jerusalem Post* analyzes and defends the US-Israeli alliance.

Jimmy Carter

The Blood of Abraham. Boston: Houghton Mifflin Company, 1985. Carter believes an active US role is needed to resolve the Arab-Israeli dispute.

Ze'ev Chafets

Double Vision: How the Press Distorts America's View of the Middle East. New York: William Morrow and Company, 1984. A fascinating report of the conditions in which foreign correspondents in the Middle East work. Chafets argues that most Arab governments censor the news in their countries and that this suppression skews American perceptions.

Ze'ev Chafets

Heroes and Hustlers, Hard Hats and Holy Men: Inside the New Israel. New York: William Morrow and Company, 1986. An insightful, entertaining account of the attitudes and politics of Israelis by an American-born Jew who emigrated to Israel in 1967.

Juan R.I. Cole and Nikki R. Keddie, eds.

Shi'ism and Social Protest. New Haven, CT: Yale University Press, 1986. Several well-known scholars have contributed essays to this comprehensive study of Shi'ite protest movements throughout the Middle East.

Abba Eban

Heritage: Civilization and the Jews. New York: Summit Books, 1984. A history of Judaism and its connection to the Holy Land by a leading Jewish scholar.

John L. Esposito

Islam and Politics. Syracuse, NY: Syracuse University Press, 1984. A relatively objective, historical overview of political systems in the Middle East.

Abdallah Frangi

The PLO and Palestine. London: Zed Books, 1983. A PLO official examines Palestinian history, the impact of Jewish immigration to Palestine, and the policies of the Israeli government.

Stephen Green

Taking Sides: America's Secret Relations with a Militant Israel. New York: William Morrow and Company, 1984. Green examines US-Israeli relations since 1948 and concludes it is not in US interests to be closely allied with Israel.

Hassan bin Talal

Search for Peace. New York: St. Martin's Press, 1984. The Crown Prince of Jordan denounces extremism on both the Israeli and Arab sides and argues Palestinian rights are central to Middle East peace.

Mohammed Heikal

Autumn of Fury. New York: Random House, 1983. A leading Egyptian journalist, jailed in Sadat's crackdown on dissenters in 1981, examines causes leading to Sadat's assassination. Contains an excellent chapter on the power of Islamic fundamentalism.

Dilip Hiro

Iran Under the Ayatollahs. London: Routledge & Kegan Paul, 1985. Contends that Iran will win the Iran/Iraq war and that the ayatollahs will continue to be important in Iranian politics after Khomeini dies.

Hatem L. Hussaini and
Fathalla El-Baghdady,
eds.

The Palestinians: Selected Essays. Washington, DC: Arab Information Center, 1976. Five essays by prominent Palestinians explaining the basis of the Palestinian cause. Also has appendices of United Nations' resolutions on the Palestinian issue.

Islamic Revolution's
Guards Corps

A Glance at Two Years of War. Tehran, Iran: Political Office, Islamic Revolution's Guards Corps, 1982. The Iranian government's view of the Iran/Iraq war as a conspiracy against the Islamic revolution by outside forces.

Kahan Commission

The Beirut Massacre. New York: Karz-Cahl Publishing, 1983. The official Israeli investigation of the massacres of Palestinians at the Sabra and Shatila refugee camps in Lebanon.

Meir Kahane

They Must Go. New York: Grosset & Dunlap, 1981. The controversial rabbi explains why he believes Palestinians have no place in a Zionist Israel.

Nikki R. Keddie and
Eric Hooglund, eds.

The Iranian Revolution and the Islamic Republic. Syracuse, NY: Syracuse University Press, 1986. An anthology that includes many Middle Eastern scholars.

Moorhead Kennedy

The Ayatollah in the Cathedral. New York: Hill and Wang, 1986. Exceptional and interesting reflections on the flaws in US foreign policy and attitudes toward Middle Easterners. Written by a former US diplomat held hostage in the American embassy in Tehran from 1979-1981.

Imam Khomeini

Islam and Revolution, trans. by Hamid Algar. Berkeley, CA: Mizan Press, 1981. Khomeini's writings and speeches on the necessity of Islam, most of them written while Khomeini was in exile.

Walt Laqueur and
Barry Rubin, eds.

The Israel-Arab Reader, 11th ed. New York: Facts on File Publications, 1984. A comprehensive collection of primary source documents dating from 1882 to 1983.

Paul Marantz and Janice
Gross Stein, eds.

Peace-Making in the Middle East. Totowa, NJ: Barnes & Noble Books, 1985. Scholarly essays, many of them by Palestinians, on the prospects for Middle East peace.

Dan Nimrod

Peace Now: Blueprint for National Suicide. Dollard des Ormeaux, Quebec: Dawn Publishing Company, 1984. Nimrod argues that the Israeli peace group, Peace Now, would sell out Jewish dreams and that peace is not possible with Palestinians who want to destroy Israel.

Conor Cruise O'Brien

The Siege: The Saga of Israel and Zionism. New York: Simon and Schuster, 1986. A history of Zionism with an eloquent concluding chapter arguing that the popular belief that Israelis should give up the occupied territories in exchange for peace is naive and unworkable.

232

Amos Oz	*In the Land of Israel.* New York: Harcourt Brace Jovanovich, 1983. Interesting interviews with Israelis on their opinions of policies toward Palestinians, conducted by a leading Israeli journalist.
Daniel Pipes	*In the Path of God: Islam and Political Power.* New York: Basic Books, 1983. Argues that Islamic fundamentalism is ultimately doomed because it is incompatible with the modernization that will inevitably continue in the Middle East.
Mansur Rafizadeh	*Witness: From the Shah to the Secret Arms Deal, An Insider's Account of U.S. Involvement in Iran.* New York: William Morrow and Company, 1987. Former chief of the Shah's secret police SAVAK who was also a double agent for the CIA gives a history of US/Iran relations since Kennedy and blames the CIA for US policy mistakes.
R.K. Ramazani	*Revolutionary Iran.* Baltimore: The Johns Hopkins University Press, 1986. A comprehensive study of Iran's effect on the Middle East which suggests that the US come to terms with revolutionary Iran.
Jonathan C. Randal	*Going All the Way: Christian Warlords, Israeli Adventurers, and the War in Lebanon.* New York: The Viking Press, 1983. Gives background information on the war in Lebanon with much of the blame placed on Christian Phalangist forces and the Israelis.
Malise Ruthven	*Islam in the World.* New York: Oxford University Press, 1984. Philosophical study of Islam with interesting discussions of symbolic rituals and a comparison of Christianity and Shi'ism.
Edward W. Said	*After the Last Sky: Palestinian Lives.* New York: Pantheon Books, 1986. Well-known Palestinian scholar explores how exile has affected Palestinian identity. Excellent photographs by Jean Mohr accompany the text.
Edward W. Said	*Covering Islam: How the Media and the Experts Determine How We See the Rest of the World.* New York: Pantheon Books, 1981. Insightful examination of how the media affects American attitudes toward Islam and distorts US policy in the Middle East.
Harold H. Saunders	*The Other Walls: The Politics of the Arab-Israeli Peace Process.* Washington, DC: American Enterprise Institute, 1985. Former US diplomat argues the US can play a major role in achieving Middle East peace.
Ze'ev Schiff and Ehud Ya'air	*Israel's Lebanon War.* New York: Simon and Schuster, 1984. A best-seller in Israel, this book criticizes Israel's involvement in Lebanon and discusses the massacres at Palestinian refugee camps.
Ali Shari'ati	*Marxism and Other Western Fallacies*, trans. by R. Campbell. Berkeley, CA: Mizan Press, 1980. Influential Islamic philosopher explains why Western philosophies are inappropriate for Middle Easterners.

David K. Shipler

Arab and Jew: Wounded Spirits in a Promised Land. New York: Times Books, 1986. *New York Times* correspondent gives a thorough, objective account of the issues in the Arab-Israeli conflict.

Kalim Siddiqui, ed.

Issues in the Islamic Movement. London: The Open Press, 1983. A collection of several editorials reprinted from *Crescent International*, an Islamic fundamentalist newspaper.

Emmanuel Sivan

Radical Islam: Medieval Theology and Modern Politics. New Haven, CT: Yale University Press, 1985. Sivan examines the impact of modernization. He argues that it was the failure of Arab leftists to appeal to the Islamic masses that led to fundamentalism.

Amir Tahéri

The Spirit of Allah: Khomeini and the Islamic Revolution. Bethesda, MD: Adler & Adler, 1986. Biography of Khomeini and a critical examination of the revolutionary government's policies.

Milton Viorst

Sands of Sorrow: Israel's Journey from Independence. New York: Harper & Row, 1987. Prominent American Jewish journalist contends the close US/Israeli alliance promoted the current no peace/no war situation. He suggests steps to take for peace between Israel and its neighbors.

Robin Wright

Sacred Rage: The Wrath of Militant Islam. New York: Simon and Schuster, 1985. Middle East correspondent studies the causes of fundamentalist militancy. Interesting information on Iran's connections to the Lebanese Shi'ite community.

Index

consequences of Iranian victory in, 43, 45-46
destructiveness of, 211-213
Iraqi military superiority in, 45
is a personal feud, 209-210
prolongation of
  by both countries, 208-213
  by Iran, 204-207
  by Iraq, 43, 200-203
  by superpowers, 209
  by UN, 206-207
religious nature of, 40, 48
social consequences of, 64, 74
Iran Liberation, 73
Iraq
  cult of personality in, 209-211
  Iranian air raids on, 205
  peaceful intentions of, 207
    fallacy of, 202-203
  terrorism by, 113
  UN support of, 202
Islam
  and modernization
    requires Westernization, 84-88
      myth of, 76-82, 125
  and Western influence, 77-79, 80-81, 83-89
  beliefs of, 77
  has liberated Iran, 53-60
    myth of, 61-65
  has unified Iran, 66-70
    myth of, 71-75
  reformism in, 86
  revival of, 124
    will not last, 88-89
  goals of, 79, 81-82, 126
  Shiite sect of, 26-29, 39, 45, 62
  Sunni sect of, 26-29, 39
  US must tolerate, 126
Islamic Propagation Organization, 59
Islamic Revolution's Guards Corps, 202
Israel
  and Iran, 38, 41
  and the PLO, 107, 170-171, 173-175
  Arab acceptance of, 105-106
    myth of, 146, 149, 150-151
  in Lebanon, 35-36, 98, 105
  is for Jews only, 162, 163, 167
  land policies of, 140-143, 186-188
  occupation forces of, 139-140
  Palestinian homeland in
    is a right, 136-144, 168-171, 184, 193
    fallacy of, 145-152, 172-175
    options for, 170
  peace movements in, 98, 199
  US alliance with, 17-20, 24

see also Palestinians

Johansen, Robert C., 210
Jordan, 98, 183, 202
  see also Hussein (King of Jordan)

Kafi, Hélène, 71
Kahane, Meir, 161
Kennedy, Moorhead, 52, 118
Khomeini, Ayatollah Ruhollah, 53, 82, 112
  and the cult of personality, 209-211
  domestic policies of, 55-60
  foreign policy of, 103
  moderation of, 211
  US relations with, 122-130
  see also Iran, Iran/Iraq war
Khorassani, Said Rajai, 124
Khouri, Rami, 181
Klibi, Chedli, 206
Koch, Noel, 110
Kristol, Irving, 108

Lebanon
  Arab pressures on, 32-34
  conflict in
    caused by ethnic rivalries, 25-30
    caused by outside intervention, 31-36
  Iranian influence in, 29, 38, 40-41
  Israeli intervention in, 29, 35-36, 98, 105
  national identity of, 29
  Palestinian refugees in, 27-28, 34-35
  political power in, 26-28
  Syrian intervention in, 34-36
  US policy in, 117
Levinger, Moshe, 165, 167

MacNelly, Jeff, 114
McLaurin, R.D., 31
Mahmud, Zaki Najib, 65
Mar'i, Sami, 158-159
Middle East
  Arab nationalism in, 198-199
    myth of, 104, 192-193
  Iran threatens stability of, 37-41
    exaggeration of, 42-47
  peace
    direct negotiations on, 195-199
    international conference on, 191-194
    is possible, 181-184
      myth of, 185-189
    US participation necessary for, 95-101, 195-199
      myth of, 102, 109, 191, 194
    Soviet role in, 21-24, 194, 197

Please remember that this is a library book,
and that it belongs only temporarily to each
person who uses it. Be considerate. Do
not write in this, or any, library book.